A compelling case for backward design, starting with the contemporary and future need for transfer goals that focus on important life skills, such as creative and critical thinking and Habits of Mind. Given a commitment to those goals, the authors contend that the best way to assess student knowledge and ability is through performance tasks and projects.

The contents are a rich itinerary of detailed processes, tools, and strategies that are honed to help educators and students reach the important destination: Self-directed learners ready to contend with the challenges of the 21st century and beyond.

—Bena Kallick, co-director, Institute for Habits of Mind

Recently, we have witnessed to two revolutionary explosions in the realm of assessment practice quite literally around the world: Growth in our understanding of and confidence in performance assessment methodology and a fundamental redefinition of the student's role in the assessment process. This book details practical ways to blend them in the classroom to the immense benefit of our students.

McTighe, Doubet, and Carbaugh show us how to link diverse assessment purposes and complex learning targets into high-quality assessments in ways that do more than merely reflect learning—they can cause learning. These authors show us how student/teacher teams can rely on rich assessments to promote continuous progress and to build student confidence in themselves as lifelong learners.

—Rick Stiggins, retired president, Assessment Training Institute

Designing Authentic Performance Tasks and Projects

JAY McTIGHE • KRISTINA J. DOUBET • ERIC M. CARBAUGH

Designing Authentic Performance Tasks and Projects

Tools for Meaningful Learning and Assessment

Alexandria, Virginia USA

1703 N. Beauregard St. • Alexandria, VA 22311-1714 USA
Phone: 800-933-2723 or 703-578-9600 • Fax: 703-575-5400
Website: www.ascd.org • E-mail: member@ascd.org
Author guidelines: www.ascd.org/write

Ranjit Sidhu, *Executive Director and CEO;* Stefani Roth, *Publisher;* Genny Ostertag, *Director, Content Acquisitions;* Julie Houtz, *Director, Book Editing & Production;* Darcie Russell, *Editor;* Judi Connelly, *Senior Art Director;* Georgia Park, *Senior Graphic Designer;* Valerie Younkin, *Senior Production Designer;* Kelly Marshall, *Interim Manager, Production Services;* Shajuan Martin, *E-Publishing Specialist*

All web links in this book are correct as of the publication date below but may have become inactive or otherwise modified since that time. If you notice a deactivated or changed link, please e-mail books@ascd.org with the words "Link Update" in the subject line. In your message, please specify the web link, the book title, and the page number on which the link appears.

PAPERBACK ISBN: 978-1-4166-2836-1   ASCD product #119021   n2/20

PDF E-BOOK ISBN: 978-1-4166-2887-3; see Books in Print for other formats.

Quantity discounts are available: e-mail programteam@ascd.org or call 800-933-2723, ext. 5773, or 703-575-5773. For desk copies, go to www.ascd.org/deskcopy.

Library of Congress Cataloging-in-Publication Data
Names: McTighe, Jay, author. | Doubet, Kristina, 1969- author. | Carbaugh, Eric M., author.
Title: Designing authentic performance tasks and projects : tools for meaningful learning and assessment / Jay McTighe, Kristina J. Doubet, and Eric M. Carbaugh.
Description: Alexandria, Virginia : ASCD, 2020. | Includes bibliographical references and index. | Summary: "Comprehensive guide to engaging students in active, relevant, and deeper learning as they transfer knowledge, skills, and understandings to the real world"—Provided by publisher.
Identifiers: LCCN 2019033055 (print) | LCCN 2019033056 (ebook) | ISBN 9781416628361 (paperback) | ISBN 9781416628873 (pdf)
Subjects: LCSH: Project method in teaching. | Competency-based education. | Educational tests and measurements.
Classification: LCC LB1027.43 .M37 2020 (print) | LCC LB1027.43 (ebook) | DDC 371.3/6—dc23
LC record available at https://lccn.loc.gov/2019033055
LC ebook record available at https://lccn.loc.gov/2019033056

30 29 28 27 26 25 24 23 22 21   2 3 4 5 6 7 8 9 10 11 12

Designing Authentic Performance Tasks and Projects

Introduction

Once regarded by many K–12 educators as an "extra" in a standards-based world, performance tasks and projects are increasingly being acknowledged as a valuable way to develop and assess deeper learning (Guha, Wagner, Darling-Hammond, Taylor, & Curtis, 2018). By positioning authentic tasks and project-based learning (PBL) at center stage of the educational process, teachers can engage students in transferring their learning to relevant situations. Such tasks and projects emphasize the meaningful application of disciplinary knowledge while also engaging the 21st century skills—critical thinking, creativity, communication, and collaboration—valued in the wider world. When performance tasks and projects are authentic in nature (and known in advance), learners are more likely to see the relevance and purpose of learning the requisite concepts and skills. Teachers often observe that students are motivated and engaged by these real-world projects and tasks. Recognizing the efficacy of performance tasks and PBL, a growing number of teachers, schools, and districts have begun to embrace them as integral components of curriculum design and as alternate means of assessing student learning (e.g., Virginia DOE, 2016).

Although the promise of performance tasks and projects is immense, the challenge lies in the details of design and implementation at the district, school, and classroom levels. This book provides a comprehensive treatment of the topic. We examine the qualities of effective tasks and projects and offer a collection of practical and proven design tools for constructing authentic versions that best suit their curricular, instructional, and assessment purposes. We describe how to design effective evaluation tools and use them in ways that can enhance student performance, not just evaluate it. We highlight connections to other prominent initiatives (e.g., STEM, technology infusion) and explore the instructional implications—how to teach for authentic performance. We explore the concept of equity in performance-based learning and describe a variety of ways for differentiating tasks and projects to address differences in students' readiness needs and interests. We move beyond the classroom level and illustrate how to construct a K–12 curriculum and assessment system that is anchored by authentic tasks and projects. Finally, we tackle the realistic challenges and common pitfalls of implementation that, if not addressed proactively and soundly, can derail well-intentioned efforts to implement worthy performance tasks and project-based learning.

Chapter Summaries and Appendixes

Chapter 1: Implementing Performance Tasks and Projects: What and Why

In the opening chapter we make the case for the importance of engaging today's learners through the use of performance tasks and projects. Our rationale highlights the value of tasks and projects in addressing and assessing academic standards as well as 21st century skills—the capacities needed for success in college and careers. We present and discuss a variety of examples of performance tasks and projects.

Chapter 2: Designing Authentic Performance Tasks

In this chapter we explore the characteristics of a high-quality performance task and present a set of practical and proven design tools for creating them, including Webb's Depth of Knowledge (DOK) Levels 3–4, Wiggins and McTighe's Six Facets of Understanding, and the GRASPS format. We include tips for effective task design and review criteria to use for quality control.

Chapter 3: Crafting Cohesive Project-Based Learning Experiences

In this chapter we examine the characteristics of authentic projects used in project-based learning and reference components from the Gold Standard from PBLWorks (formerly the Buck Institute for Education). We explore the relationship between performance tasks and projects by looking at an array of design variables teachers can control when crafting them. We offer ideas for developing effective projects and provide suggestions for overcoming associated design challenges.

Chapter 4: Constructing and Using Evaluation Tools to Enhance Student Performance

Here we focus on various evaluation tools (criterion lists, holistic rubrics, and analytic rubrics) for assessing student products and performances. We present several practical and proven methods for designing quality rubrics, and we offer review criteria. We describe how to apply the evaluation tools for reliably scoring student work on tasks and projects and how to use them in ways that can enhance student performance and facilitate peer and self-assessment.

Chapter 5: Teaching to Support Student Performance on Tasks and Performances

In Chapter 5 we examine performance-based teaching to prepare students to transfer their learning to authentic situations. Using the analogy of athletic coaching, we provide specific strategies and instructional models that support deeper learning, while highlighting the critical role of formative assessment and feedback in enhancing student performance.

Chapter 6: Tailoring Tasks and Projects for All Students

Chapter 6 explores the issue of equity and presents ways to support student success in task and project implementation through the use of supports, scaffolds, challenge, and student "voice and choice." We present ideas for the strategic use of resources and technology to increase access for all learners.

Chapter 7: Collaborating to Manage Projects and Performances: A Teacher-Student Partnership

In this chapter we provide project-management strategies to help teachers and students navigate the moving parts that support performance-driven classrooms. We address practical concerns, including how to monitor progress, how to encourage and assess collaboration, how to manage differentiated tasks and projects, how to provide needed support, and how to encourage students' self-assessment and reflection.

Chapter 8: Creating a Performance-Based Curriculum

Moving beyond the individual classroom, in this chapter we consider a performance-based curriculum at the district, school, and program levels. We describe the need for a modern education to evolve from a "coverage-based" curriculum to a coherent curriculum and assessment system anchored by a coordinated set of authentic cornerstone tasks and projects. We introduce task frames for multiple content areas and provide a K–12 map of performance tasks and projects for writing.

Appendixes

Here readers will find a storehouse of resources including additional examples of performance tasks, PBL projects, rubrics, technology tools, and a K–12 map of authentic tasks and projects in various subjects. Note that Appendix A is a glossary of key terms referenced throughout the rest of the book, and Appendix B provides a planning tool that references the design elements discussed throughout the book.

Our Hope

We concur with the conclusions of a recent research study on the efficacy of performance tasks:

> If designed and used appropriately... performance assessments could be a key component of K–12 systems and could, along with rigorous curricula and high-quality instruction, drive improvements in teaching and learning. (Guha et al., 2018, p. v)

We hope this book will help educators effectively design and use performance tasks and projects, along with appropriate instruction, to engage students in deeper learning in pursuit of the most important outcomes of a modern education.

1

Implementing Performance Tasks and Projects: What and Why

In a world where information on virtually any topic is instantly accessible on a smartphone or similar device, our relationship to knowledge is changing. Accordingly, the ideas in this book are based upon a two-part claim: (1) a primary goal of a modern education should be to prepare students for transfer, and (2) achievement of this goal requires the systematic use of performance tasks and projects for learning and assessment.

Here's the case for the first part of our claim: Although disciplinary knowledge and skills are certainly relevant, individuals no longer need to be able to remember lists of established facts to be considered educated. Not only is such knowledge just a click away, it is constantly subject to revision and updating. We contend that to remain relevant, education must shift from a coverage orientation, which emphasizes acquisition of factual knowledge and basic skills, to a performance-based curriculum that stresses application—transfer—of learning.

A Focus on Transfer

Transfer refers to the ability to apply learning to a new situation beyond the context in which it was learned. The latest generation of academic standards from multiple disciplines highlights a focus on transfer. For example, the Common Core State Standards (CCSS) in English language arts (ELA) are framed by a set of College and Career Anchor Standards—transfer goals that specify what students should be able to do in reading, writing, listening, and speaking when they leave school:

> Students are able independently to discern a speaker's key points, request clarification, and ask relevant questions. They build on others' ideas,

articulate their own ideas, and confirm they have been understood.... More broadly, they become self-directed learners, effectively seeking out and using resources to assist them, including teachers, peers, print and digital reference materials. (National Governors Association Center for Best Practices, Council of Chief State School Officers, 2010)

The Common Core Mathematics Standards established a set of mathematical practices that must be pursued in a manner similar to the ELA Anchor Standards. These practices call for students to apply mathematical reasoning to real-world problems.

Similarly, the Next Generation Science Standards (NGSS) include scientific practices as a key component of science education, with the following rationale:

The continuing expansion of scientific knowledge makes it impossible to teach all the ideas related to a given discipline in exhaustive detail during the K–12 years. But given the cornucopia of information available today virtually at a touch—people live, after all, in an information age—an important role of science education is not to teach "all the facts" but rather to prepare students with sufficient core knowledge *so that they can later acquire additional information on their own.* (Achieve, 2013, italic emphasis added)

In other words, students should study science in such a way that they are equipped to transfer scientific practices to new and novel situations.

Transfer goals are also prominently featured in the College, Career, and Civic Life (C3) Framework for Social Studies State Standards (National Council for the Social Studies, 2013) through its Inquiry Arc of four dimensions:

- Dimension 1: Developing Questions and Planning Inquiries
- Dimension 2: Applying Disciplinary Concepts and Tools (Civics, Economics, Geography, and History)
- Dimension 3: Evaluating Sources and Using Evidence
- Dimension 4: Communicating Conclusions and Taking Action

Finally, the National Core Arts Standards (NCAS) actually employ the term *Transfer Goals* and reference the importance of using "rich performance tasks" to assess them:

The standards are built this way with the expectation that schools or districts will value the understanding and transfer of knowledge and skills that will come with a standards-based curriculum in the arts and therefore acknowledge that they are important curricular goals. Moreover, NCAS hopes that the inclusion of cornerstone assessments in these standards will focus the great majority of classroom- and district-level assessments around rich performance tasks that demand transfer. This paradigm shift in measuring student learning in the arts will offer relevant and reliable evidence of what students truly understand and know how to do, for it is only when students are able to apply their learning thoughtfully and flexibly to a new situation that true understanding of the content is demonstrated. (National Coalition for Core Arts Standards, n.d., p. 16)

Unlike grade-level standards, these broader process-oriented standards cannot be effectively addressed within a single unit or even in one year. Rather, they must be pursued year after year, with increasing levels of complexity and with decreasing levels of support and scaffolding in order to prepare learners for independent transfer.

Although the standards referenced thus far specify learning goals within academic disciplines, we have also seen a growing demand for the inclusion of transdisciplinary outcomes as new "basics" for today's students. Transdisciplinary outcomes include the 21st century skills of critical thinking, creativity, collaboration, and communication (Partnership for 21st Century Skills, 2009) and dispositional habits of mind such as perseverance and metacognitive self-monitoring (Costa & Kallick, 2009). Such goals are inherently transfer oriented; they reflect the value we place on developing students who are able to (1) think critically about new information and complex issues that they will encounter throughout their lives and (2) persevere when engaged in challenging tasks.

Not surprisingly, the personnel needs of today's employers echo the value of such transfer goals. The National Association of Colleges and Employers (NACE) conducts an annual survey of employers to gather data about their hiring intentions as they relate to new college graduates. Figure 1.1 summarizes the rank ordering of the desired job qualities and skills as reported by employers in its recent survey and report, *Job Outlook* (NACE, 2019).

By citing employability reports, we do not mean to imply that we believe the sole purpose of education is job preparation. On the contrary, we call for a well-rounded education that values the arts and humanities, health and wellness, and responsible citizenship. In other words, we advocate for an education that prepares students to succeed no matter where they "land" following graduation. Not surprisingly, these outcomes are best envisioned as long-term transfer goals that will enable a person to effectively navigate a variety of new challenges and opportunities.

Figure 1.1
NACE Survey Results

Attributes Employers Seek in Job Candidates	
Communication skills (written)	82.0%
Problem-solving skills	80.9%
Ability to work in a team	78.7%
Initiative	74.2%
Analytical/quantitative skills	71.9%
Strong work ethic	70.8%
Communication skills (verbal)	67.4%
Leadership	67.4%
Detail-oriented	59.6%
Technical skills	59.6%
Flexibility/adaptability	58.4%
Computer skills	55.1%
Interpersonal skills (relates well to others)	52.8%
Organizational ability	43.8%
Strategic planning skills	38.2%
Tactfulness	25.8%
Creativity	23.6%
Friendly/outgoing personality	22.5%
Entrepreneurial skills/risk-taker	16.9%
Fluency in a foreign language	11.2%

Source: *Job Outlook 2019* by the National Association of Colleges and Employers, Bethlehem, PA. © NACE. Used with permission.

Characteristics of Transfer Goals

Transfer goals specify particular transfer abilities; they reflect what we want students to be able to do when they confront new information, issues, challenges, and opportunities. Transfer goals have several distinguishing characteristics (McTighe & Curtis, 2019). They

- Are long term in nature (i.e., they develop and deepen over time).
- Are performance based (i.e., they require application rather than simple recall).
- Call for application of learning in new situations, not those previously taught or encountered.
- Require some strategic thinking, not simply plugging in facts or skills acquired in a rote fashion.
- Seek independent performance; upon graduation, learners must be able to apply their learning autonomously, without scaffolding or coaching.
- Typically involve applying habits of mind, such as good judgment, self-regulation, and persistence.

As noted, transfer goals are identified within academic disciplines as well as for transdisciplinary outcomes. Discipline-based transfer goals are often stated in the opening pages of standards documents, where the long-term outcomes of teaching to the standards are explicated. Grade-level standards are usually much more detailed and do not qualify as transfer goals. Figure 1.2 presents examples of disciplinary transfer goals (McTighe & Curtis, 2019). Figure 1.3 presents a few examples of transdisciplinary transfer goals (McTighe & Curtis, 2019), which students in all grade levels can address through a wide variety of content-specific topics.

A Modern Curriculum

Our initial claim contends that a contemporary education should prioritize such long-term transfer goals. This approach calls for planning the curriculum (and associated assessments and learning experiences) backward from these transfer goals. When designing curriculum for the district or school level, we recommend identifying only a small number of transfer goals. Targeting a small number of long-term transfer goals to anchor a curriculum has two virtues.

First, transfer goals become a way of focusing and prioritizing the curriculum. Noted educational researcher Robert Marzano concluded that "a guaranteed and viable curriculum" is the most significant school- [and district-] level factor impacting student learning and achievement (2003, p. 19). His choice of the term *viable* reflects a recognized challenge—standards typically include too much content, and there is not enough time to teach them all well. Trying to "cover" all the listed grade-level standards can result in superficial and disconnected learning. Instead, encouraging a focus on long-term performance goals helps to avoid teachers getting lost in trying to teach and assess hundreds of discrete objectives in isolation.

Figure 1.2
Examples of Disciplinary Transfer Goals

English Language Arts/Writing
- Write to communicate effectively in various genres for a variety of audiences and purposes (e.g., explain, entertain, guide, argue, and challenge).
- Produce effective writing in which the genre, conventions, organization, and style are appropriate for various purposes, audiences, and contexts.

Health and Physical Education
- Make decisions and take actions that support lifelong health and wellness.
- Participate regularly in one or more sports or fitness activities.

Mathematics
- Apply mathematical concepts, reasoning, strategies, and tools to make sense of practical and theoretical problems and persevere in trying to solve them.
- Apply sound mathematical reasoning to construct, justify, and defend viable arguments and respectfully critique the reasoning of others.

Science
- Plan and carry out a systematic investigation to explore phenomena, test a hypothesis, or answer an empirical question.
- Evaluate scientific claims and analyze current issues involving science or technology.

Social Studies/History
- Use knowledge of patterns of history to gain perspective about the present and prepare for the future.
- Actively participate as an informed and responsible citizen.

Visual and Performing Arts
- Develop a personal aesthetic in order to respond to the artistic expression of others.
- Develop competence in [at least one arts discipline] to continue active involvement in creating, performing, and responding to art as an adult.

World Language
- Communicate and interact in [one or more languages], displaying sensitivity to culture and context.
- Adjust one's use of spoken, written, and visual language to communicate effectively and respectfully with various audiences for different purposes.

Source: McTighe & Curtis, 2019. Used with permission.

Figure 1.3
Examples of Transdisciplinary Transfer Goals

Critical Thinking
• Think critically about information and claims encountered at school and beyond by seeking clarity, accuracy, sound evidence, good reasons, and fairness.
• Exercise flexibility in selecting and employing evidence and reasoning for a variety of audiences and purposes.

Collaboration
• Work effectively with others, exchanging ideas and expertise in a variety of situations, both in school and beyond.
• Seek, consider, and incorporate multiple perspectives into group decision making.

Citizenship
• Make informed decisions and take actions for the public good.
• Consider the impact of one's personal decisions and actions on the larger community.

Research
• Formulate a researchable question.
• Locate and critically appraise pertinent information from multiple and varied sources (print, online; primary, secondary).

Habits of Mind—Persistence and Perseverance
• Persist in challenging situations by changing approach, seeking feedback, applying different strategies, and maintaining focus.

Habits of Mind—Open-Mindedness
• Remain open to new ideas and alternate points of view.
• Be willing to change one's mind when convinced by new and valid evidence and sound reasoning.

Source: McTighe and Curtis, 2019. Used with permission.

Second, transfer goals promote cohesion in students' K–12 learning experiences. It is noteworthy that the word *curriculum* is derived from Latin, translating as the "course to be run." This original connotation helpfully suggests that we think of a curriculum as the pathway toward a destination—long-term transfer goals (McTighe & Willis, 2019). Because such goals are conceived as exit outcomes, they provide the end points from which educators can plan a preK–12 curriculum. This approach to backward design leads to greater curriculum coherence because the transfer goals serve as a "north star" to keep teaching and assessing on course. Moreover, vertical alignment within a curriculum is enhanced when all teachers in a subject area focus their teaching and assessments on the same ends.

Designing curriculum that prioritizes a small number of long-term transfer goals does not negate the importance of helping students acquire factual knowledge and basic skills. Indeed, one cannot productively apply learning without knowledge and skills. However, in a world that offers easy access to much of the world's knowledge, we propose that the "basics" should be properly seen as foundational—the floor, not the ceiling.

The ability to transfer also requires deep understanding. If we learn only through rote memorization or repeated practice, we are unlikely to be able to transfer that learning to a new situation; we can only give back what was taught in the way it was taught. Transfer is about intelligently and effectively drawing from a repertoire of knowledge, skills, understandings, and dispositions to navigate new situations independently.

To reiterate our first claim: we contend that a modern curriculum should be framed and developed in terms of worthy outcomes—transfer performances—not simply as a scope and sequence of content inputs to be covered.

Performance-Based Learning and Assessment

We began this chapter by articulating a two-part claim; the first portion highlighted the centrality of transfer goals in the articulation of a sound and viable curriculum. The second part builds upon that premise in the form of an if/then proposition: if we agree that transfer is a primary educational goal for today's learners, then the nature of teaching and assessment should reflect that focus. But how do we teach for and assess students' ability to transfer? We contend that the answer lies in the systematic use of performance tasks and projects for learning and assessment. Let's take a closer look at each.

What is a performance task? In its essence, a *performance task* asks students to "perform" with their learning—to apply their learning in some fashion. More specifically, we define a performance task as any learning activity or assessment that asks students to construct a multifaceted response, create a product, or produce a demonstration—in other words, to perform with their learning.

What is a *project*? A dictionary definition is "an individual or collaborative enterprise that is carefully planned to achieve a particular aim" (https://en .oxforddictionaries.com/definition/project). In education today, projects are often associated with project-based learning (PBL), a pedagogical approach in which learning develops as students pursue answers to complex questions through work on extended learner-directed projects.

Although we have more nuanced descriptions of performance tasks and projects to offer later, take a look at the eight examples of tasks and projects from different grade levels and subject areas shown in Figure 1.4. What characteristics do they share? How do they differ?

These examples illustrate the range and variety of performance tasks and projects being used in schools. Although tasks and projects such as these have been used over the years, we have noticed that educators sometimes find it difficult to differentiate the two. In general, we characterize projects (as conceived under the PBL label) as follows:

- Longer term
- Interdisciplinary
- Open ended
- Focused on genuine issues or problems
- Targeted toward a real audience
- Largely student directed

Performance tasks, on the other hand, are often characterized as follows:

- Shorter in duration
- Generally focused on a single subject (but may be interdisciplinary)
- More structured
- May or may not be set in an authentic context
- May or may not have a real audience other than the teacher (though there may be an imagined audience specified in the task)

In Chapter 3 we will take a closer look at variables to consider in the design of performance tasks and projects. For now, we'll offer a general recommendation. The choice between performance tasks and projects should be based on the nature of the targeted learning outcomes. When the focus is on discipline-specific academic content, a short, subject-specific performance task may be most appropriate. For other outcomes (e.g., 21st century skills), an interdisciplinary, student-directed project may be warranted.

Challenges in Implementation

We conclude this chapter by forecasting potential challenges that teachers and students may encounter—and must overcome—as part of a successful implementation of performance tasks and projects for learning and assessment (we will address them in the chapters that follow):

Figure 1.4
Examples of Performance Tasks and Projects

Example #1—Community Problem Solver (Social Studies, English/Language Arts; Grades K–1)

Students interview family members and neighbors to identify a problem in their community. They decide to focus on the problem of stray animals. They gather information about the nature of the problem (causes and effects) and brainstorm ways to address the problem. Each student contributes to creating a display board to use in an oral presentation to share findings and recommendations with members of the community.

Source: Adapted from Katherine Smith Elementary School, San Jose, California. https://video.search.yahoo.com/yhs /search?fr=yhs-domaindev-st_emea&hsimp=yhs-st_emea&hspart=domaindev&p=kindergarten+pbl+on+stray+animals +youtube#id=1&vid=d0f87333ffc0f9423d78e44c3bfa78e3&action=click

Example #2—Mail-Order Friend (English/Language Arts; Grades 1–2)

Note: This task is associated with a literary unit that includes reading and discussing stories involving the theme of friendship.

Imagine that you have an opportunity to "order" a true friend by telephone from a mail-order catalog. Remember the stories we read and the songs we learned about friends. Think about the characteristics of a friend that we listed on our friendship web. Now, think about the qualities that you want in a friend. Before you "order" your friend over the telephone, practice asking for three characteristics that you want in a true friend and giving an example of each characteristic. Remember to speak clearly and loudly enough so that the salesperson will know exactly what kind of friend to send.

Source: McTighe & Wiggins (2004), p. 168.

Example #3—Tour Director (Social Studies, Math; Grades 4–5)

The State/Provincial Department of Tourism has asked for your help in planning a four-day tour of (your state or province) for a group of foreign visitors (who speak your language). Plan the tour to help the visitors understand the history, geography, and key economic assets of (your state or province). You should prepare a written itinerary, including an explanation of why each site was included on the tour. Include a budget for the four-day tour.

Source: Adapted from McTighe & Wiggins (2004), p. 168.

Example #4—Scientific Investigator (Science; Grades 5–6)

The Pooper Scooper Kitty Litter Company claims that their litter is 40% more absorbent than other brands. You are a consumer-advocate researcher who has been asked to evaluate their claim. Develop a plan for conducting the investigation to determine the accuracy of the company's claim. Your plan should be specific enough so that the lab investigators could follow it to evaluate the claim. You should also prepare a presentation or report that will clearly communicate your findings to potential consumers.

Source: Adapted from McTighe (2013), p. 42.

Example #5—The Global Challenge (Multidisciplinary; Grade 8)

At the end of the school year, students work in teams on a week-long project based on the United Nations' 17 Sustainable Development Goals (SDGs). Each student chooses a global development challenge of interest (e.g., malnutrition, education, gender equality, the environment) and then joins four other students to research the challenge, define problems, and propose solutions. They then develop a proposal for funding to present to a panel of adults in a simulated *Shark Tank* setting. Students are assessed on developed rubrics on Problem Solving, Communication, Collaboration, and Result (i.e., did the panelists approve their funding request?)

Source: Adapted from Wise & McTighe, 2017, pp. 12–18. See also http://markwise8.wixsite.com/globalchallenge

Example #6—See My World (Visual Art; Middle School)

You have recently analyzed the narrative work of Faith Ringgold to identify ways she communicated ideas about her world. Think about your own world—your family, friends, hobbies and interests, daily experiences, and the things that are important to you. Select a drawing or painting medium, or use mixed media, to create your own narrative work that visually communicates your personal ideas about your world.

Source: Adapted from Daisy McTighe, Baltimore County Public Schools; McTighe (2013), p. 51.

Example #7—Tiny House Project (Multidisciplinary; High School)

Students work in teams over the course of a semester to research, design, and construct a "tiny house" (350 square feet) that is both energy self-sufficient and livable. Teams create videos and a website to document their process. The project culminates with a public showing of the house in a park in San Diego, California.

Source: Adapted from Maria Alcoke, High Tech High School, San Diego, California. https://sites.google.com/site/hthtinyhouse/our-company

Example #8—Active Citizen (Social Studies/Government; High School)

After investigating a current political issue, prepare a position paper or presentation for a public policymaker (e.g., a U.S. representative) or group (e.g., school board, legislative committee). Assume that the policymaker or group is opposed to your position. Your position statement should provide an analysis of the issue, consider options, present your position, rebut opposing positions, and attempt to persuade the public policymaker or group to vote accordingly. Cite relevant evidence to support your argument. Your position can be communicated via a written report, a blog, or a presentation.

Source: Adapted from Littleton High School, Colorado.

- *Too much content.* Teachers may believe that they do not have enough time for students to work on performance tasks and projects because there are so many grade-level standards to cover.
- *Standardized tests.* Administrators and teachers may question why they should use performance tasks and projects when they are being held accountable for scores on multiple-choice accountability tests.
- *Reliable evaluation.* Judgment-based evaluation of performance tasks and projects may be seen as overly subjective. Parents and students might challenge the grades they receive.

- *Schedule.* The school schedule (especially in high schools) may mitigate opportunities to plan for, teach toward, and implement multidisciplinary projects.
- *Students' skills.* Teachers may worry that some students will not have the skills or maturity to direct themselves during long-term projects.
- *Cooperation challenge.* When students work in groups on performance tasks and projects, some group members can shirk while others shoulder the load.
- *Grading and reporting.* Although performance tasks and projects are well suited to developing and assessing transdisciplinary outcomes (e.g., 21st century skills and habits of mind), these outcomes do not appear on most report cards.
- *Students' expectations.* Some students have come to excel at the "school game"; they are compliant and will do what the teacher directs, as long as it "counts." Some may rebel if they have to think too hard on performance tasks and projects.
- *Parents' expectations.* Some parents expect students to sit in rows, listen to the teacher's lectures, do homework from a textbook, memorize information, and take tests of recall. They may not understand—and may object to—performance-based learning and assessment because these are likely very different from their own school experiences.

Conclusion

A modern education extends beyond knowledge acquisition; it calls for students to be able to *transfer* their learning to real-world situations. Accordingly, performance tasks and projects can serve as an effective means by which teachers can foster the development of students' capacities to apply their learning in meaningful ways. Performance tasks and projects have multiple benefits: (1) Set in authentic contexts, students are more likely to see the relevance of what they are learning; (2) work toward authentic performance helps students to synthesize discrete knowledge and skills into a more coherent whole; and (3) performance on tasks and projects by students provide the assessment evidence of their understanding and ability to apply their learning. Moreover, authentic tasks and projects are ideal vehicles for integrating 21st century skills (critical thinking, creativity, collaboration, communication, technology, and other transdisciplinary outcomes) with academic content. For performance tasks and projects to deliver on their promise, they must be carefully crafted. In the next two chapters we will propose sets of criteria for judging high-quality performance tasks and projects. We'll present practical and proven practices for designing authentic tasks and projects that meet these criteria and address challenges of design and implementation.

2

Designing Authentic Performance Tasks

In this chapter we will focus on the design of authentic performance tasks that teachers can use as rich learning activities as well as for assessment. As advocates of *backward design*, we will begin with the end in mind by identifying the characteristics of high-quality tasks. These characteristics serve two functions: (1) as targets to guide the design work and (2) as criteria to use in evaluating the resulting draft tasks. We'll outline a general task design process and present three proven task design frameworks (Depth of Knowledge, Facets of Understanding, and GRASPS) to use in developing performance tasks that align with targeted learning outcomes. Finally, we'll address key challenges designers may face when developing performance tasks.

Performance Task Criteria and Design Process

Whether used as rich learning activities or as assessments, the most effective performance tasks reflect important characteristics. We have identified these qualities as a set of criteria for successful task design (see Figure 2.1). This set includes eight essential and three optional (but recommended) characteristics that can guide the development of new tasks as well as the evaluation of existing tasks.

The criteria shown in Figure 2.1 reflect the goal—or destination—for effective performance task design; they do not, however, explain *how* to arrive at that destination. In Figure 2.2 we outline a general design process for creating a first draft of an authentic task. Although the figure suggests a linear, step-by-step sequence, task design is actually iterative, much like writing itself. In fact, it is common for task developers to revise task directions or modify the evaluative criteria as they work on task directions. Additionally, feedback from self-assessment, peer review, and classroom implementation will likely suggest further refinements to the task and the rubric.

Figure 2.1
Essential Criteria for Performance Task Design

Key: 3 = The characteristic is strongly reflected in this performance task. 2 = The characteristic is reflected to some extent in this performance task. 1 = The characteristic is not yet reflected in this performance task.			
		Score	
Primary Criteria	**3**	**2**	**1**
1. The performance task aligns with targeted standard(s)/learning outcome(s).			
2. The task calls for **application** and requires extended thinking, not simply recall or a formulaic response.			
3. The task establishes an authentic context; i.e., includes a realistic purpose, a target audience, and genuine constraints.			
4. The task requires explanation or support, not just an answer.			
5. The task includes criteria/rubric(s) for judging performance based on the targeted standard(s); i.e., criteria do not simply focus on the surface features of a product or performance.			
6. The task directions for students are clear.			
7. The task is feasible to implement in classrooms.			
8. The task does not contain biased language or stereotypes, or tackle overly sensitive or offensive topics inappropriate to the age of students or community norms.			
Optional (but Recommended) Criteria			
9. The task allows students to demonstrate their understanding of or proficiency with some appropriate choice/variety (e.g., of products or performances).			
10. The task effectively integrates two or more subject areas.			
11. The task incorporates appropriate use of technology.			

Source: © 2017b by Jay McTighe. Used with permission.

Figure 2.2
A Process for Designing Performance Tasks

1. Identify learning goals.	*What learning goals do we seek to develop or assess through this task?* Goals can include the following: • Standards—Discipline-based subject-matter goals identified in national, state, or district documents • Outcomes related to state, district, or school missions (e.g., Portrait of a Graduate, 21st century skills, habits of mind)
2. Consider key traits implied by the goals.	*What important qualities must students demonstrate to show attainment of standards and other identified goals?* These will serve as the success criteria by which student performance is judged.
3. Consider one or both of these frameworks.	*How will the task involve higher-order thinking?* Consider the following: • Depth of Knowledge (DOK) • Facets of Understanding
4. Generate initial task ideas.	*How will learners demonstrate their understanding and proficiency?* Outline the basic task to use in developing and deepening students' understanding and proficiency and for providing assessment evidence.
5. Check for validity and alignment.	*To what extent will this task provide acceptable evidence of the targeted goals?* Consider this question: Could students perform this task and meet the evaluative criteria without demonstrating evidence of the targeted goals?
6. Establish an authentic context for performance.	*How will the task establish an authentic context for student performance?* When establishing the context, consider real-world application of learning along with students' interests and experiences. The GRASPS elements will help establish an authentic performance situation.
7. Develop scoring rubric(s).	*How will student performance be evaluated? How good is good enough?* Use the key qualities (traits) identified in #2 to flesh out a more detailed rubric.
8. Differentiate the task as needed.	*In what ways might the task be differentiated?* You may need to modify the task for special populations (e.g., ELL, SPED, G/T). This can be done by adjusting the context, audience, product options, time frame, and degree of support.
9. Assess the entire draft task and rubric using review criteria.	*Is this task ready to use?* Self-assess the task against the review criteria (see Figure 2.1). If possible, get feedback from colleagues as well as experts in the content. Then, revise as needed based on feedback.
10. Develop detailed directions for students.	*What exactly are students being asked to do?* Once the draft task has met the review criteria, develop detailed directions for students. Include guidelines, accompanying resources, and response forms as appropriate.

Task Design Frameworks

With clear criteria and a general design process in mind, let's now examine three useful frameworks for beginning the design of authentic tasks: Depth of Knowledge (DOK), Facets of Understanding, and GRASPS.

Design Framework #1—Depth of Knowledge

Norman Webb (2002) developed the Depth of Knowledge (DOK) framework to distinguish four levels of rigor and cognitive complexity in assignments, performance tasks, and projects. Figure 2.3 summarizes the cognitive demands of the four levels with examples of how they apply to the design of tasks involving mathematics and reading.

Depth of Knowledge has proven to be a valuable framework to ensure a proper level of rigor, worthy of the time and effort required by performance tasks. We recommend that tasks reflect the cognitive complexity described in DOK Level 3, while more complex tasks and authentic, longer-term projects can target DOK Level 4. Here are three examples of performance tasks operating at DOK 3 and two that engage students at DOK 4:

3rd Grade ELA Task—DOK Level 3

You've discovered how to recognize bias and faulty reasoning from our study of "The Three Little Pigs" and the book *The True Story of the Three Little Pigs*. Now it's time to use your skills to catch another narrator in the act of stretching the truth. We will read the stories "Cinderella" and "Jack and the Beanstalk" and the books *Seriously, Cinderella Is So Annoying* and *Jack's Beanstalk Stinks*. You will choose one book to read more closely to find examples of when the narrator demonstrates bias and uses poor reasoning. Record a video for next year's 3rd graders warning them about the book's tricky narrator. Explain key examples of biased language and poor reasoning in the text. Be sure to explain how you were able to spot each example.

8th Grade ELA Task—DOK Level 3

We have read several texts written from the perspective of an "outsider." You will examine each of these texts—as well as two additional texts of your choice—to determine what causes someone to become an outsider in his or her school or community. Write a blog post that draws from all texts to explain the factors that may lead to a person becoming distanced from or mistreated by others. Be sure to use examples from the texts to explain your thinking. End by stating your opinion about this phenomenon and what you feel should be done about it.

Figure 2.3
Depth of Knowledge Framework with Examples

DOK Level	Description	Reading Tasks Require	Mathematics Tasks Require
1	• Requires students to recite or recall information including facts, formulas, or simple procedures. • May require students to demonstrate a rote response, use a well-known formula, follow a set procedure (like a recipe), or perform a clearly defined series of steps. • Typically focuses on a "correct" answer.	• Recalling literal information from a text. • Paraphrasing basic details from the text. • Using a dictionary to find the meanings of words.	• Recalling information (e.g., a math fact or definition). • Using a one-step, well-defined procedure (e.g., a formula). • Plugging numbers into a given algorithm. • Using a set procedure with a clearly defined series of steps.
2	• Focuses on application of basic skills and concepts. • Involves some reasoning beyond recall. • Requires students to perform two or more steps and make some decisions on how to approach the task or problem.	• Summarizing main idea(s). • Predicting an outcome based on text information. • Using context cues to identify the meaning of unfamiliar words.	• Applying some mathematical reasoning to - multistep, yet routine, problems. - one-step, simple word problems. • Collecting, classifying, organizing, and comparing simple data. • Organizing and displaying simple data in tables, graphs, and charts. • Interpreting noncomplex numerical information.
3	• Requires strategic thinking and reasoning applied to situations that generally do not have a single "right" answer. • Requires students to go beyond the information given to generalize, connect ideas, evaluate, and problem solve. • Expects students to support their interpretations and conclusions with evidence and to explain their thinking.	• Comprehending and interpreting abstract ideas (e.g., metaphor, analogy). • Going beyond the literal text by summarizing, generalizing, and connecting ideas from multiple sources. • Supporting interpretation(s) with textual evidence and reasoning.	• Applying sound mathematical reasoning to multistep, nonroutine problems. • Analyzing problem situations (e.g., determining what information is needed). • Explaining one's thinking and reasoning. • Interpreting complex numerical or statistical information. • Making and supporting mathematical conjectures.

DOK Level	Description	Reading Tasks Require	Mathematics Tasks Require
3 **(cont.)**		• Analyzing literary elements (e.g., author's style in literature; character traits). • Applying critical thinking (e.g., distinguishing fact and opinion; recognizing bias or flawed reasoning).	• Showing some perseverance.
4	• Requires extended thinking and complex reasoning over an extended period of time. • Expects students to transfer their learning to novel, complex, and "messy" situations. • Requires students to devise an approach among many alternatives for how to approach the task or problem. • May require students to develop a hypothesis and perform complex analysis.	• Applying information/ideas from a given text to a new task. • Developing hypotheses and performing complex analyses across texts. • Analyzing and synthesizing information from multiple sources. • Evaluating alternative perspectives across multiple sources. • Extracting common ideas/themes across texts from different times and cultures.	• Applying sound mathematical reasoning to confront complex, ill-structured problem situations. • Analytical and creative thinking. • Transferring mathematical concepts and processes to new contexts (e.g., in science). • Interpreting complex numerical or statistical information from multiple sources.

11th Grade Math Task—DOK Level 3

Using what we've studied in class, analyze and both determine and defend a conclusion for the following situation: "One plan for a state income tax requires those persons with income of $10,000 or less to pay no tax and those persons with income greater than $10,000 to pay a tax of 6 percent only on the part of their income that exceeds $10,000. A person's effective tax rate is defined as the percent of total income that is paid in tax. Based on this definition, could any person's effective tax rate be 5 percent? Could it be 6 percent? Explain your answer. Include examples to justify your conclusions. (Webb, 2006)

Middle School Science Task—DOK Level 4

We have studied the _____ ecosystem and examined the interdependent relationships between the system's organisms and abiotic components. We also discussed the case of the Northern Snakehead fish, an invasive species in

Maryland, its effects on the Potomac River ecosystem (and beyond), and the efforts that are being made to reduce its impact. In an effort to avoid future negative effects on our ecosystem as a result of the introduction of a competitive or predatory organism, you are charged with the following task: Select one outside organism, hypothesize how it might be introduced to our ecosystem, and predict the patterns of competitive or predatory interactions that might occur between it and other organisms and abiotic components. Then, design a containment protocol to limit its destructive influence and explain how your plan will limit ecosystem damage or disruption.

High School Government—DOK Level 4

We have examined several local issues that have dominated discussion and debate in our community over the past two years. Choose one of these issues that you believe may have an impact beyond our community (at the national or global level). Articulate how you believe this issue could affect others in our nation or the world, using research to support your hypothesis. Then conduct research to determine how other communities—both national and international—have grappled with similar issues and what action they have taken. Finally, offer possible solutions to your chosen issue, supported by the experiences of multiple communities as well as by your own ideas and reasoning.

Although we have seen performance tasks that focus on DOK Level 2, we discourage them, except for very young children. Level 1 tasks and projects? Forget about it!

Design Framework #2—Facets of Understanding

Performance tasks and projects are meant to engage students in inquiry and authentic application as a way to develop and deepen understanding. As assessments, they serve to check for understanding and transfer ability. Wiggins and McTighe (2011) have described six Facets of Understanding that serve as indicators of understanding. These are summarized in Figure 2.4. It is important to note that unlike the Depth of Knowledge framework, the facets are not meant to be hierarchical. Rather, the intention is to use the facet or facets that will be most helpful in developing and assessing certain learning outcomes. For example, a social studies unit might emphasize *perspective* and *explanation*, asking students to consider different points of view on historical or political conflicts and explain the various perspectives. A mathematics unit might involve students in the *application* of mathematical concepts and skills to a

Figure 2.4
The Six Facets of Understanding

The Facets of Understanding provide *indicators* of understanding and thus can be used to select or develop performance assessments as well as engaging learning activities.

If we really understand something, we can...

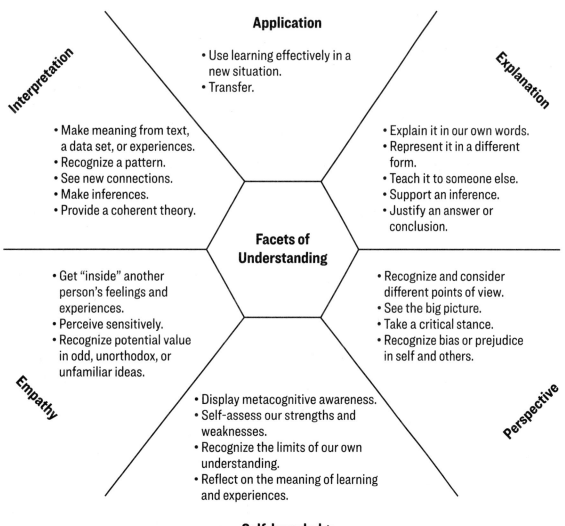

Application
- Use learning effectively in a new situation.
- Transfer.

Interpretation
- Make meaning from text, a data set, or experiences.
- Recognize a pattern.
- See new connections.
- Make inferences.
- Provide a coherent theory.

Explanation
- Explain it in our own words.
- Represent it in a different form.
- Teach it to someone else.
- Support an inference.
- Justify an answer or conclusion.

Facets of Understanding

Empathy
- Get "inside" another person's feelings and experiences.
- Perceive sensitively.
- Recognize potential value in odd, unorthodox, or unfamiliar ideas.

Perspective
- Recognize and consider different points of view.
- See the big picture.
- Take a critical stance.
- Recognize bias or prejudice in self and others.

Self-knowledge
- Display metacognitive awareness.
- Self-assess our strengths and weaknesses.
- Recognize the limits of our own understanding.
- Reflect on the meaning of learning and experiences.

Source: G. Wiggins & J. McTighe, 2011 [supplemental materials]. Used with permission.

complex problem and an *explanation* of their reasoning. A literature unit might ask learners for an *interpretation* of the text and the development of *empathy* for literary characters. Figure 2.5 presents a sample for a unit on nutrition to illustrate how the different facets can reveal different aspects of understanding.

One practical way to employ the Facets of Understanding is to use performance verbs associated with each facet (see Figure 2.6, p. 28). The verbs can be used to frame learning objectives, assignments, and assessment tasks.

Here are four examples of performance tasks showing different combinations of performance verbs and Facets of Understanding:

Personal Trainer (Health and Physical Education)

As a fitness trainer, your task is to *design* a personalized plan to help a client meet her fitness goals. (Client goals and characteristics are provided.) You should *explain* how your recommended exercises will improve the client's aerobic and anaerobic conditioning and improve her flexibility.
Facets: *Application, Perspective, and Explanation*

Editorial (Social Studies, English Language Arts)

Should schools be allowed to filter internet sites that students can access? Review academic articles on this issue and decide on your position. *Explain* and *support* your position using reasons and evidence. Be sure to acknowledge opposing positions and *rebut* competing views.
Facets: *Perspective and Explanation*

Spot Remover (Science)

Chris wants to decide which of two spot removers is best. First, he tried Spot Remover A on a T-shirt that had fruit stains and chocolate stains. Next he tried Spot Remover B on jeans that had grass stains and rust stains. Then he compared the results. *Troubleshoot* Chris's approach and *explain* why it will be hard for him to decide which spot remover works best. Then help him *redesign* his test to answer the question.
Facets: *Application and Explanation*

Tell a Story (Social Studies, English/Language Arts)

Imagine that you are an elderly tribal member who has witnessed the settlement of the plains by the "pioneers." *Tell a story* to your granddaughters to show the impact of the settlers on your life.
Facets: *Interpretation, Empathy, Perspective, and Explanation*

Figure 2.5
The Facets of Understanding Applied to a Unit on Nutrition

The Facets of Understanding provide *indicators* of understanding and thus can be used to select or develop performance assessments as well as engaging learning activities.

If we really understand something, we can...

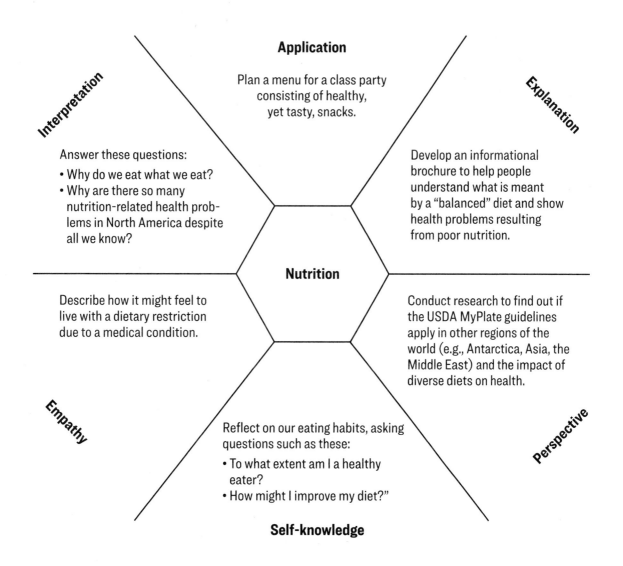

Application

Plan a menu for a class party consisting of healthy, yet tasty, snacks.

Interpretation

Answer these questions:
- Why do we eat what we eat?
- Why are there so many nutrition-related health problems in North America despite all we know?

Explanation

Develop an informational brochure to help people understand what is meant by a "balanced" diet and show health problems resulting from poor nutrition.

Nutrition

Describe how it might feel to live with a dietary restriction due to a medical condition.

Conduct research to find out if the USDA MyPlate guidelines apply in other regions of the world (e.g., Antarctica, Asia, the Middle East) and the impact of diverse diets on health.

Empathy

Perspective

Reflect on our eating habits, asking questions such as these:
- To what extent am I a healthy eater?
- How might I improve my diet?"

Self-knowledge

Source: G. Wiggins & J. McTighe, 2011 [supplemental materials]. Used with permission.

Figure 2.6
Performance Verbs Associated with the Six Facets of Understanding

Application	Interpretation	Explanation	Perspective	Empathy	Self-knowledge
adapt build create debug decide design exhibit invent perform produce propose solve test troubleshoot use	create analogies critique document evaluate illustrate judge make meaning of make sense of provide metaphors read between the lines represent tell a story of translate	demonstrate derive describe design exhibit express induce instruct justify model predict prove show synthesize teach	analyze argue compare consider contrast criticize infer	be like be open to believe consider imagine relate role-play	be aware of realize recognize reflect self-assess

Source: From *The Understanding by Design Guide to Creating High-Quality Units* (p. 100), by G. Wiggins and J. McTighe, 2011, Alexandria, VA: ASCD. Copyright 2011 by G. Wiggins and J. McTighe. Used with permission.

The Facets of Understanding have proven to provide a practical framework for ensuring that a task provides evidence of understanding, not just recall of information. However, it is important to note that the goal is *not* to try to use all of the facets in a performance task! On the contrary, teachers should choose only the facet or facets that are appropriate for the targeted learning outcomes.

Design Framework #3—GRASPS

As discussed in Chapter 1, one of the long-term aims of a modern education is to prepare students for transfer—that is, to be able to apply their learning to new situations they will face in school and beyond. Accordingly, we recommend that teachers provide multiple opportunities for learners to confront realistic and messy issues, problems, and design challenges. As assessments, such authentic tasks and projects provide evidence of students' understanding and transfer ability. As rich learning activities, they tend to be more meaningful and engaging to students.

We suggest that the concept of authenticity can be considered in terms of two dimensions:

- *The world beyond the school.* In this sense, authentic tasks and projects reflect how people apply learning to address realistic goals and genuine issues and problems.
- *The experiences and interests of learners.* A situation may be authentic to the real world but beyond the realm of young people, or they could see it as irrelevant or boring.

We'll discuss the notion of authenticity in further detail in the next chapter. Ideally, performance tasks and projects are authentic on both counts. The acronym GRASPS provides a practical tool for designing the elements of authentic tasks (Wiggins & McTighe, 2012). It encompasses the following elements:

- G—a real-world *goal*
- R—a meaningful *role* for the student
- A—a target *audience*
- S—a contextualized *situation* that involves real-world application
- P—student-generated culminating *product(s)* and *performance(s)*
- S—criteria for judging *success*

Here is an example of a performance task that was created using the GRASPS elements:

> You are an aspiring screenwriter (*R*). You know that many movies and plays originated from published novels or short stories. Identify a novel or short story that you think would make an entertaining or thought-provoking film or play (*S*). Then, write a proposal (*P*) to a movie or theater producer (*A*) to persuade him to hire you to develop the screenplay (*G*). Explain why you think this would be a successful film/play, suggest the actors to play the key roles, and include a sample scene to display your writing talent (*S*). Be sure to carefully proofread your proposal, as any grammatical or spelling errors (*S*) will not impress the producer with your writing ability!

Figure 2.7 presents a set of prompts that can help to frame an authentic context for a performance task. Along with the prompts in Figure 2.7, here are some additional considerations for using GRASPS:

Goals. Note that the *G* in *GRASPS* refers to the goal *for the students* in the task rather than the learning goal or assessment target of the teacher. However, the two should have an overall linkage. Sometimes the goal for the student is directly aligned with a transfer goal; for example, for Argumentation, "Your goal is to… convince readers of the community newspaper to vote on the proposed ballot measure" (as a result of the argument you make in your editorial). In other cases, the learning goal should be evident through the overall task; for example, "Your goal is to… explain the scientific concept of buoyancy to kindergarten students."

Figure 2.7
GRASPS Prompts

Goal:
Your task/goal is _____
The problem/challenge/obstacle is _____

Role:
You are/Your job is _____
You have been asked to _____

Audience:
The target audience is _____
Your client(s) is (are) _____

Situation:
The context/situation is _____

Product/Performance and Purpose:
You will create _____ in order to _____
You need to develop _____ so that _____

Success Criteria:
Your work will be judged by _____
Your product/performance must meet the following standards _____

Source: From *The Understanding by Design Guide to Advanced Concepts in Creating and Reviewing Units* (p. 80), by G. Wiggins and J. McTighe, 2012, Alexandria, VA: ASCD. Copyright 2012 by G. Wiggins and J. McTighe. Used with permission.

Roles and Audiences. In a performance task, it is important for students to consider the voice they should assume, which is determined by the task's intended role and audience. Figure 2.8 offers a variety of possible roles or audiences for the *R* and *A* in *GRASPS*. This list was derived from a storehouse of teacher-developed tasks in a variety of subjects and grade levels. By simply

Figure 2.8
Sample Roles and Audiences

actor	family member	playwright
advertiser	farmer	poet
artist/illustrator	filmmaker	police officer
author	firefighter	pollster
biographer	forest ranger	radio listener
board member	friend	reader
boss	geologist	reporter
boy/girl scout	government official	researcher
businessperson	historian	reviewer
candidate	historical figure	sailor
carpenter	illustrator	school official
cartoon character	intern	scientist
cartoonist	interviewer	ship's captain
caterer	inventor	social scientist
celebrity	judge	social worker
CEO	jury	statistician
chairperson	lawyer	storyteller
chef/cook	library patron	student
choreographer	literary critic	taxi driver
clients/customer	lobbyist	teacher
coach	meteorologist	tour guide
community members	museum director/curator	trainer
composer	museum goer	travel agent
construction worker	neighbor	traveler
dancer	newscaster	tutor
designer	novelist	TV/movie character
detective	nutritionist	TV viewer
editor	panelist	viewer
elected official	parent	visitor
embassy staff	park ranger	website designer
engineer	pen pal	zoo keeper
expert (in __)	photographer	
eyewitness	pilot	

Source: From *Understanding by Design Professional Development Workbook* (p. 173), by J. McTighe & G. Wiggins. (2004). Alexandria, VA: ASCD.

scanning this list, teachers can often come up with ideas for new tasks. For example, by considering the role of a museum director, a team of 4th grade teachers decided to have their classes prepare museum displays to illustrate science concepts that were taught. Natural audiences for the displays were other classes and parents who were invited to the "museum." It is also important to remember that—at times—the students' role can be "themselves." For example, recall that Example 8 in Chapter 1 (see Figure 1.4, p. 15) asks each student to advocate for a governmental policy that is of personal importance. In this task, then, the role is "self."

Products and Performances. The *P* in *GRASPS* refers to the products and performances that students will produce to demonstrate their understanding and proficiency in conjunction with targeted learning goals. Figure 2.9 presents a range of possibilities, framed in terms of performance genre. Although alignment is a general characteristic, it is especially important that the resulting products and performances provide appropriate *evidence* of the targeted standards or outcomes when using a task as an assessment.

In sum, the GRASPS format offers a practical framework if and when you need to establish a more authentic context for a performance task. Of course, GRASPS tasks are not needed for everything you teach. They are most appropriately used in conjunction with the most important ideas and processes that you want students to understand and ultimately be able to transfer. Practically speaking, we encourage teachers to include at least one authentic task when planning a major unit of study. See Appendixes E, G, J, and M for additional and extended examples of tasks designed using the GRASPS format.

Challenges in the Design of Performance Tasks

The task design frameworks we offer will help you design a more authentic, rigorous, and engaging performance task. However, the task development process is not always easy, and designers face predictable challenges. We end this chapter by highlighting four common challenges—alignment, time, bias and stereotyping, and fairness—and offering suggestions for overcoming them. We address additional challenges related to the design and use of tasks and projects in subsequent chapters.

Alignment

Recall that the first criterion for quality performance tasks (see Figure 2.1, p. 19) had to do with alignment between the task and the targeted standards and

Figure 2.9
Sample Products and Performances

Written Products	Oral Performances	Visual Products
advertisement	audiotape	advertisement
biography	conversation	animation
blog	debate	banner
book report/review	discussion	book/CD cover
brochure	dramatic reading	cartoon
crossword puzzle	dramatization	collage
editorial	infomercial	computer graphic
essay	interview	data display
field guide	newscast	design
historical fiction	oral presentation	diagram
journal	oral report	display
lab report	podcast	drawing
letter	poetry reading	exhibit
log	puppet show	flowchart
magazine article	radio script	flyer
manual	rap	game
memo	skit	graph
newscast	song/recital	map
newspaper article	speech	model
play	TED Talk	movie
poem	teaching a lesson	painting
policy brief		photograph(s)
position paper	Other:	poster
proposal		presentation software
questionnaire		scrapbook
research report		sculpture
screenplay		social networking page
script		storyboard
story		vodcast
test		website
tweet		
		Other:
Other:		

learning outcomes. We have observed that sometimes the task can "get away" from designers; in other words, it is easy to lose sight of your original intent as you engage in the creative work of task design. Here is an efficient way to check the alignment between your task and the intended outcome: show your task and associated rubric to another teacher and ask her to tell you by only viewing the task and rubrics what she thinks the standards/learning outcomes are. This simple process provides valuable feedback on the degree of alignment.

Another dimension of alignment has to do with the connection between your designated product or performance and the role, audience, and situation you've established. For example, if you ask students to assume the role of a scientist and examine dinosaurs' body structures to determine how the creatures may have moved and what they may have eaten, a diorama is not a logical product. Rather, as scientists, students may address other scientists in the form of a conference presentation (poster board or electronic display). Alternatively, if their audience is the public, they may share their findings via an illustrated article or a YouTube video. Thinking about the alignment of role, audience, situation, and product/performance is important to realizing a coherent and authentic task.

Time

With performance tasks and projects, the time and energy needed to design, implement, and score them must be worth the effort. They must promote meaningful and lasting learning around important outcomes that matter.

We once heard of a teacher in Colorado who had her 4th graders spend a week working on a performance task associated with their study of state geography. Students worked in teams baking and decorating sheet cakes to represent Colorado. The snow-capped Rocky Mountains came alive with whipped cream, and blue food coloring highlighted the major rivers. Although we imagine that students were engaged, we doubt that this task would pass the "worth the effort" test, unless it was used in a Family and Consumer Sciences unit on baking or an art unit on three-dimensional design. Indeed, examples of this sort can give performance tasks a bad name, leading some teachers and administrators to view them as fluffy time wasters.

Accordingly, as you are designing a task, we recommend that you regularly check to make sure that the task activities and associated products or performances will be manageable. Often designers recognize the need to scale back an ambitious task to ensure that it will be an effective and efficient use of time.

Bias and Stereotyping

Because rich projects and performance tasks are contextualized, we must be careful to establish situations or scenarios that do not inadvertently stereotype or discriminate against certain groups. For example, insensitivity to diverse religious beliefs (e.g., choosing reading passages involving only Christian holidays), gender roles or racial images (e.g., depicting all doctors as white males), or socioeconomic status (e.g., assuming that all kids have access to the internet or a smartphone) may negatively influence students' attitudes toward—and performances on—classroom tasks and projects.

Given the potential for unconscious biases to creep into performance tasks and projects, we encourage designers (including students) to consider the questions in Figure 2.10 when developing or reviewing tasks and projects (and associated materials) as a way of checking for overt and subtle cases of racial/ethnic, religious, cultural, political, or gender bias. The state of Washington offers a helpful set of criteria for reviewing educational materials for bias (see http://www.k12.wa.us/Equity/pubdocs/WashingtonModelsfortheEvaluationofBias .pdf).

Fairness

A concern about fairness can arise if some learners receive assistance during a summative assessment task. In other words, is it fair to evaluate all students against the same rubric if certain students have been given extra help? One way to handle such cases is to use a companion evaluation tool to provide qualifying information, such as the degree of support offered or the degree of independence by the learner. See Figure 2.11 for an example of a tool that can allow teachers to honestly communicate the extent to which students received assistance in completing the task.

A related aspect of fairness arises when students are expected to do a significant amount of work on tasks and projects outside school—especially if the task is being used as a summative assessment. In such cases, some students may receive significant help from parents and siblings, whereas others will be working on their own. A simple solution to this challenge is to provide time for the bulk of the work to be done at school.

We will provide further thoughts about issues of fairness and equity in subsequent chapters.

Figure 2.10
Review Questions for Bias and Stereotyping

Language Bias

Do the task or project activities and materials contain

+ Language that has the same basic semantic content for all persons regardless of race, gender, ethnicity, age, sexual orientation, or physical or mental condition?

+ Names that connote a broad balance of national origins and gender in both traditional and nontraditional roles?

- Emotionally loaded language that reinforces biases?

- Potentially negative or pejorative labeling of individuals or groups?

Stereotyping

Do the task or project activities and materials

+ Represent men and women; younger and older persons; religious, ethnic, and racial minorities; and persons with disabilities in many different environments and occupations, and in roles of diverse status and power?

+ Depict people with disabilities as productive members of society?

+ Show people with disabilities interacting positively in a variety of interpersonal relationships—that is, not always being helped by others?

- State or imply that a population group has a genetic deficit or surplus in some area of intellect, talent, or ability?

- Suggest that a population group is deserving of a particular fate?

- Make a causal link between membership in a particular population group and poverty, crime, intelligence, physical talents, or work ethic?

Figure 2.11
Companion Tool for Degree of Independence

How much support was received?	Student Comments	Teacher Comments
• The student performed the task completely independently. • The student performed the task with only minor assistance. • The student could only perform the task with some assistance. • The student could only perform the task with considerable assistance.		

Conclusion

Not all performance tasks are created equal. The fact that students may be "performing" does not ensure that the tasks are worthwhile. We have seen cases where "performance-based" activities lack rigor, authenticity, and alignment to any worthy goals. Indeed, we have met some teachers (especially at the secondary level) who regard performance tasks as simply fluffy activities that take time away from more substantive learning. To combat this potential problem, we recommend that any potential performance tasks meet the quality criteria that we have presented. Moreover, by using the design tools described in this chapter (e.g., Facets of Understanding, Depth of Knowledge, and GRASPS), it is more likely that you will design performance tasks that will support deep and meaningful learning while providing evidence on outcomes that matter. In Chapter 3 we will follow a similar structure to explore the process of developing robust projects for project-based learning.

3

Crafting Cohesive Project-Based Learning Experiences

The previous chapter detailed various methods and tools for developing rich performance tasks. This chapter addresses a related topic: the design of high-quality projects for use in project-based learning (PBL) and as authentic assessments. We begin by examining the characteristics of authentic projects used in PBL. Then we'll explore the relationship between performance tasks and projects by looking at an array of variables teachers can control when designing them. Finally, we'll offer ideas for developing effective projects and suggestions for overcoming associated challenges.

Elements of Effective Projects

Whether used as rich learning activities, in project-based learning, or for assessment purposes, the most effective projects have particular characteristics. In identifying these, we embrace the qualities identified by PBLWorks (formerly the Buck Institute for Education), a world leader in project-based learning. PBLWorks has identified a set of essential design elements for a Gold Standard PBL (Larmer, Mergendoller, & Boss, 2015). We have developed criteria for high-quality projects based on these elements (see Figure 3.1). We'll describe them in more detail later in this chapter. The project design elements serve several purposes: they can (1) guide the development of new projects, (2) assist in the refinement and implementation of existing projects, and (3) serve as criteria to use in evaluating project quality.

Variables in Task and Project Design

With these project criteria in mind, teachers and curriculum teams can better conceptualize the design of authentic projects. However, before examining design tips based on these criteria, let's explore a set of variables to consider in the development of either performance tasks or projects. Indeed, performance tasks and projects have many common features, and the lines between them can be blurry. Thus, we don't believe it is necessary to view them as dichotomous, either-or choices. Instead, think of differences in tasks and projects in terms of

Figure 3.1
Criteria for High-Quality Project Design

Key: 3 = The characteristic is strongly reflected in this performance task. 2 = The characteristic is reflected to some extent in this performance task. 1 = The characteristic is not yet reflected in this performance task.			
Criteria	**Score**		
	3	**2**	**1**
1. The project aligns with student learning goals that include academic content standards and 21st century skills.			
2. The project is based on a challenging problem or question.			
3. The project will require sustained inquiry by learners.			
4. The project reflects authenticity in one or more of these ways: a. Presents a real-world challenge. b. Uses real-world processes, tasks, tools (including technology), and performance standards. c. Has an impact on others. d. Addresses the personal interests and experiences of students.			
5. Students have voice and choice within the project in one or more of the following ways: a. Identifying the topic focus and generating the driving question. b. Specifying task(s) and role(s). c. Determining and accessing needed resources. d. Deciding on the culminating product(s).			
6. The project results in a public project for a genuine audience.			
7. The project includes opportunities for feedback and revision.			
8. The project allows for students' reflection.			

a series of dimensions, with each dimension operating like a sliding control on a sound or lighting board. Designers can then "dial" in the variables according to the *targeted outcomes* (e.g., disciplinary or transdisciplinary), the *purpose* of the task or project (e.g., will it primarily serve as a rich learning experience or as a summative assessment?), the available *resources* (including time, materials, equipment), the *nature and needs of the students*, and the *feasibility* of implementation. In this way, teachers can approach any task or project design in a flexible and fluid manner. Figure 3.2 (pp. 42–43) presents a set of design variables to consider when crafting tasks and projects. Each of them presents designers with the opportunity to structure tasks or projects so that they are a good fit for curricular goals, instructional time, and learner needs. Please note that the sliders are placed arbitrarily in Figure 3.2, and that one end of the spectrum is not inherently better than the other. Let's examine each variable in more detail.

1. Time Frame

How long will students be involved in this task or project (including time for presentations and evaluations)?

The time frame of a performance task can range from one or two class periods to a week, whereas projects tend to take longer—two to three weeks, or up to several months. Jay's daughter taught at High Tech High School in San Diego, a public charter school established to develop 21st century skills and student-directed learners in which the entire curriculum was designed around authentic, long-term projects. One of her student-directed projects involved the research, design, and construction of an energy-efficient "tiny home," erected for public display at a regional fair (see Example 7 in Figure 1.4, p. 15; see also https://sites.google.com/site/hthtinyhouse/our-company for an overview of this project). This project, which took a full semester to complete, lies on the far end of the time dimension. Whereas specialized PBL schools can engage in such long-term projects, teachers working in traditional schools may be responsible for covering a large number of standards in various disciplines and will thus find it challenging to devote long blocks of time to a single task or project.

When considering the time frame, teachers should determine the targeted outcomes (e.g., standards in content areas, 21st century skills), the purpose of the task (e.g., is it primarily a learning experience or an assessment?), the needs and skill sets of students, and the opportunity costs of implementation (e.g., is it worth the time?). If the task or project engages students, exercises important skills, and results in deeper learning, we can usually say that it *is* worth the time. For example, a performance task or project may be designed to serve as an assessment, but students' preparatory work can be just as valuable as the end product. Said differently, tasks and projects, although often assessed and graded, also serve as learning experiences through which students can acquire valuable knowledge and skills and have opportunities to apply—to transfer— that learning. In fact, a 2016–2017 study found that elementary school students engaged in a well-designed social studies PBL curriculum showed improved achievement on social studies and reading tests versus students who were taught through more traditional instruction (Barshay, 2018). We'll take a closer look at teaching for performance in Chapter 5.

2. Integration of Subjects

To what extent is the task/project interdisciplinary?

We see a strong connection between variables 4 and 5. In general, we have found that the more authentic a task or project, the more likely it will involve more than a single discipline. This conclusion should not be a surprise, as most issues and problems in the world beyond the classroom are not contained within a single, subject-specific silo; they naturally involve the application of knowledge and skills from more than one discipline and often include the application of transdisciplinary, 21st century skills such as critical and creative thinking, collaboration, and communication. Having noted this, we certainly recognize the value of rich tasks and projects that are focused on standards within a particular discipline.

3. Cognitive Demand/Rigor

Where does the task/project fall on the Depth of Knowledge (DOK) scale?

In general, we recommend that performance tasks be nested in Level 3 of Depth of Knowledge, and more complex, longer-term projects in DOK 4. An exception may be made for the primary grades (preK to grade 1), where teachers may begin the school year with simpler, DOK 2 tasks. However, even for young children, we recommend that the complexity of the tasks increase to DOK 3 over the course of the year.

4. Level of Inquiry

Are students engaged in the process of answering a question, exploring an issue, or solving a problem?

Figure 3.2
Design Variables for Performance Tasks and Projects

---

1. Time Frame: How long will students be involved in this task or project (including time for presentations and evaluations)?

1–4 Class Periods   5–10 Class Periods   More Than 2 Weeks

2. Integration of Subjects: To what extent is the task/project interdisciplinary?

Single Discipline   Two Disciplines   Multidisciplinary

3. Cognitive Demand/Rigor: Where does the task/project fall on the Depth of Knowledge (DOK) scale?

DOK Level 2   DOK Level 3   DOK Level 4

4. Level of Inquiry: Are students engaged in the process of answering a question, exploring an issue, or solving a problem?

Limited/No Inquiry   Structured/Guided Inquiry   Open Inquiry

5. Degree of Authenticity: To what extent is the task/project authentic—that is, featuring a real challenge, problem, or issue; a genuine product/performance; an authentic audience; and real-world constraints?

Decontextualized   Simulates an Authentic Context   Fully Authentic

6. Audience for Student Product(s) and Performance(s): To whom will students present their products and performances?

Classroom Teacher   Other Students/School Staff   Authentic Audience Beyond the School

7. Performance Mode: How will students work on the task/project?

Individually   Some Group and Some Individual Work   All Work Done in Groups

8. Direction: Who will direct the task/project?

Teacher Directed   Teacher with Some Student Self-Direction   Student Directed

9. Student Choice: To what extent will students have choices regarding any of the following: (a) task/project topic, question, problem, issue; (b) product(s)/performance(s); (c) audience(s)?

No Choice   Some Choices   Many Choices

10. Access to Resources: To what extent will the resources needed (e.g., information, supplies, equipment) be provided?

All Resources Provided   Some Resources Provided   Students Locate
All Needed Resources

11. Degree of Scaffolding: To what degree will students be provided with instructional support and scaffolding as they work on the task?

Considerable Support   Some Support   No Support

12. Evaluation of Student Product(s)/Performance(s): Who will be involved in evaluating student products and performances?

Classroom Teacher   Team of Teachers   External Evaluators/Experts

Designers can effectively frame both performance tasks and projects around inquiry. Accordingly, such tasks and projects are especially well suited to developing and assessing the skills of research, critical thinking, and problem solving. For example, as described in the "Community Problem Solver" paragraph in Figure 1.4 (p. 14), a kindergarten class at Katherine Smith Elementary School in California worked on a project to address the problem of stray animals in their community. They researched the problem by interviewing family members, neighbors, police, an animal control officer, and staff members from an animal adoption center. They then proposed a number of possible solutions and presented these to adults. You can view their presentations at https://www.youtube.com/watch?v=cPuQ5_Tr7qo.

This project required students to conduct primary-source research through interviews, which also presented them with the opportunity to exercise effective speaking and listening skills, all of which informed their process of real-world problem solving. Clearly, this project registers high on the inquiry scale. Keep in mind that although inquiry is a design element for projects, an inquiry orientation is not a requirement for a performance task to be considered worthwhile. Effective tasks can simply require learners to apply their knowledge and skills to a new or unfamiliar situation. For example, a world language teacher might design a task that engages students in a simulated dialogue with a new exchange student (in the target language) to introduce the newcomer to school routines. As with other design variables, the learning outcomes should dictate the extent to which the task or project is inquiry oriented.

5. Degree of Authenticity

To what extent is the task/project authentic—that is, featuring a real challenge, problem, issue; a genuine product/performance; authentic audience; and real-world constraints?

Authentic work is work that has value outside the classroom. Weaving authenticity into school tasks can increase students' motivation and help them to see value in what they are learning.

Authenticity can be established in four ways: (1) setting the task in a real-world *context*; (2) using real-world *processes, tools (including the use of technology), or standards*; (3) examining the *impact* on others; and (4) cultivating *personal authenticity* (Larmer et al., 2015). We discuss this approach to establishing authenticity in greater detail later in this chapter. As discussed in Chapter 2, authentic tasks don't necessarily require that students assume a real-world role. For example, a science teacher might give students a design challenge to solve in 15 minutes or less. In this instance, students perform as themselves while simulating the conditions that NASA engineers faced on the Apollo 13 mission—a real-world *context*. Involving students in authentic work has been shown to increase motivation and investment in learning (Gambrell, Hughes, Calvert, Malloy, & Igo, 2011; Wentzel & Brophy, 2014). Doing so is particularly important when asking students to engage in longer-term project-based experiences.

6. Audience for Student Product(s) and Performance(s)

To whom will students present their products and performances?

One of the opportunities that authentic tasks and projects offer is the possibility of involving real audiences beyond the teacher. Here are some possible audiences:

- Peers (in class)
- Other school staff
- Students from other classes or schools
- Parents
- Members of the community
- Outside mentors or content experts
- Virtual audiences (e.g., through a blog, website, Skype call, or webcast)

As with authenticity, students will often engage more deeply, be motivated to apply greater effort, and strive for higher quality when they know that their work will be viewed by an audience other than just their teacher.

7. Performance Mode

How will students work on the task/project?

In the wider world beyond the classroom, many jobs require teamwork. Rich performance tasks and projects can offer opportunities for students to exercise the skills of collaboration. If a task or project is being employed as a formative learning experience, it makes sense to allow students to work with a partner or a team (for at least some aspects of the task). However, when it is intended as a summative assessment, then a teacher must consider if, and to what degree, teamwork on the task is appropriate. For example, if a group of four students collaborate to produce a single product (e.g., video, website, policy brief, mural), how will the teacher know what each individual contributed unless she watches and takes notes as they work? In other words, carefully considering how and when to assess individual mastery of content in the context of group work can be tricky. Later in this chapter we present some important issues and ideas regarding assessment when student collaboration is involved or expected, and in Chapter 7 we will delve deeper into important issues related to evaluating team-oriented tasks and projects.

8. Direction

Who will direct the task/project?

Performance tasks and projects can be directed by the teacher, by the student, or by a combination of the two. In teacher-directed tasks, the teacher establishes the learning destination *and the route* by designing the task, assigning roles and requisite steps, and determining the schedule. In a student-directed project, students have a say in both the destination and the pathway, making decisions about product, process, resources, and timeline. Appendixes E and G feature tasks that are more teacher directed. Appendixes F, H, and L provide examples of more student-directed projects. Regardless of who directs the task or project, students should be afforded a certain degree of ownership, although student-directed tasks also ask students to operate more autonomously. As such, another way to conceptualize who serves as the "director" of the task or project is considering the degree of *student choice* involved; this is design variable number 7.

9. Student Choice

To what extent will students have choices regarding any of the following: (a) task/project topic, question, problem, issue; (b) product(s)/performance(s); (c) audience(s)?

As noted, variables 6 and 7 are closely linked. Generally in project-based learning, students are expected to exercise some control over their work. Thus we might expect that they will have more choices and greater responsibility for directing their tasks and projects. Teachers can give students a number of possible choices. Here are a few, with examples:

- *Task Topic and Guiding Question.* If the learning outcome involves research, then students might be allowed to pick the topic or guiding question for their investigation.
- *Product/Performance.* If a performance task focuses on a concept in science or social studies, learners may be given some options regarding how they demonstrate their thinking and learning, such as a poster, a blog, or

an oral presentation. However, if the standard involves expository writing, then the students will need to write but might still have some choices regarding the particular form and audience.

- *Audience.* For some tasks and projects, it may be appropriate to allow the students to select an audience (e.g., younger students, readers of a community newspaper, viewers of a website) for their product or performance.

Once again, the purpose of the task, along with the targeted skill sets and students' developmental levels and learning needs, will determine whether students should be given choices and, if so, which are the appropriate options. We will explore additional ways that teachers can differentiate tasks and projects in Chapter 6.

10. Access to Resources

To what extent will the resources needed (e.g., information, supplies, equipment) be provided?

In many cases, the task or project directions will provide all of the necessary information and resources. However, if one purpose of the task or project is to assess whether the students can determine what information is needed and how to access needed resources, then the task or project would be more open and less structured. In such cases, the evaluation tool (detailed in the next chapter) would need to include criteria for evaluating students' effectiveness in locating and accessing appropriate information or resources.

11. Degree of Scaffolding

To what degree will students be provided with instructional support and scaffolding as they work on the task?

Determining the amount of support to provide is based on the purpose of the task or project and the needs of the students. When using a task or project primarily as a learning activity or a formative assessment, it is appropriate to provide scaffolding as well as feedback and guidance along the way. However, if the task is being used as a summative assessment, it's important to determine what students can do on their own. Here are the basic options:

1. Present the task/project and provide no extra support (i.e., the students must perform the task autonomously without teacher guidance or peer support).

2. Present the task and offer some support (e.g., partner work time, graphic organizers, step-by-step process guides, checklist of needed elements).

3. Present the task and provide extensive support as needed (e.g., tips, ongoing feedback, opportunities to practice or redo).

We will explore this variable in greater detail when we address differentiation in Chapter 6.

12. Evaluation of Student Product(s) and Performance(s)

Who will be involved in evaluating student products and performances?

In most cases, teachers evaluate their students using an established set of criteria or a scoring rubric (a topic we address in detail in Chapter 4). However, for some tasks and projects, it is worth enlisting others to view and evaluate student performances. Of course, this is a common practice for science fairs, art exhibits, and music competitions. Possible evaluators can include other staff members, expert judges, peers, parents, and community members.

At High Tech High (the school where Jay's daughter, Maria, taught), students regularly conduct POLs—presentations of learning—in which their projects are reviewed by panels of experts (e.g., an editor, a community planner, an engineer) from fields associated with the projects (in addition to the teachers). Maria and her colleagues observe that students are generally very attentive to the quality of their work when they know that external audiences or expert judges will be involved in rating their performance (similar to when public audiences are involved). She noted that her students take these external reviews very seriously, strive to perform at their best, and often dress up on presentation day! (Go to http://www.hightechhigh.org/student-work/student-projects/ to see samples of projects and portfolios of student work from High Tech High.)

Given the motivational influence, we encourage teachers to be on the lookout for ways to expand the audience for worthwhile tasks and projects. Simply inviting another class, school staff, parents, or community members can have a positive influence on student motivation and performance.

Regardless of who evaluates a task or a project performance, we recommend that students be regularly involved in self-assessment of their work, using established criteria as communicated in rubrics. The capacity for honest self-appraisal is a lifelong skill and the hallmark of an effective performer in all fields of endeavor. Schools can cultivate this important capability by making self-assessment an expectation in all subjects and for all grades.

In sum, designers of performance tasks and projects can navigate the "slider" across each of these 12 dimensions. Figures 3.3 and 3.4 (pp. 50–51) present examples to illustrate how the variables work together within a performance task and within a project.

Using these variables as a guide, educators can better adapt designs based on required learning goals, individual experience, available resources, and other factors. We suggest that teachers just getting started with performance tasks or projects consider starting with shorter, more structured tasks for students. Doing so can allow for targeted refinement and troubleshooting before embarking on more sophisticated, longer-term projects.

Developing Coherent, High-Quality Project-Based Learning

The term *project* can mean a variety of things to different people. Eric remembers an inquiry-based project his 6th graders completed over the course of four weeks. They acted as historians, posing rich and interesting historical questions and researching answers to these questions. For example, one student investigated whether the influenza pandemic of 1918 could have been avoided. Another was interested in the origins of the electoral college (coming off the 2001 presidential election) and whether our current circumstances still require the use of this system to elect a president. They had "coaches" throughout the building (such as other 6th grade teachers, guidance counselors, administrators) with whom they would meet regularly to receive feedback, encouragement, and assistance with time management and research. Once students formulated answers to their questions based on sound source analysis, they wrote research papers outlining their findings. They submitted several drafts until the papers "met expectations" as outlined in the evaluation tools. They also created detailed displays that visually represented their written work and shared the displays with parents and the community during a "museum night." Extensive thought and planning went into this project, as Eric and the other 6th grade teachers spent an entire school day developing all of the tools, resources, instructions, rubrics, and other elements necessary for successful completion of the project. As a result of this upfront investment of time and effort, the team of teachers had established favorable conditions for high-quality student work.

Sadly, not all of Eric's projects met such a high standard. He also remembers the "Great Poster Debacle" of 2003. At that point, he was teaching world history to 9th graders and was looking for an engaging way to help his students learn

Figure 3.3
A Performance Task Illustrating Design Variables

This performance task is designed for middle school English/language arts.

Goal: Students will create a storyboard that depicts the elements of plot and theme.

Role: You are a screenwriter who needs to create a storyboard for a short movie.

Audience: Your target audience is the director of your movie.

Situation: You have pitched a movie idea to a director, and he or she has accepted the idea. You have already given the director the script and now you need to supply a simple storyboard of how you would like events to play out. The director would like your storyboard to focus on the movie's plot, and it must include at least one theme.

Performance/Product: Generate an idea for a movie. Then, create a storyboard depicting the plot and theme to present to the director. Finally, write a reflection describing your thinking process and the story you have created.

Design Variables:
1. Time Frame: Two classes/blocks
2. Cognitive Demand/Rigor: DOK Level 3
3. Level of Inquiry: Limited inquiry
4. Degree of Authenticity: Simulates an authentic context
5. Integration of Subjects: Single discipline
6. Direction: Teacher directed
7. Student Choice: Choice of movie ideas for storyboard, based on student's preferred genre
8. Performance Mode: Individual
9. Access to Resources: Necessary resources provided by the teacher
10. Audience for Student Product: Classroom teacher
11. Degree of Scaffolding: Miniworkshops on creating storyboards, as well as generating plot and theme, provided as needed
12. Evaluation of Student Performance: Classroom teacher

Source: Ashley Sullivan, Wilbur Pence Middle School, Rockingham County Schools, Virginia.

about the lasting impact of the fall of communism. He had enjoyed creating posters for projects when he was in high school and thought that using the same approach would similarly engage his students. The day students presented their posters was a clear indication that something had gone wrong with the planning of the project. The problem wasn't the topic or the use of posters as a product, but that students ended up creating products without doing much thinking. Eric had hoped students would be able to locate present-day images that they felt reflected the impact of the fall of communism and then be able to describe their rationale for including them on the posters. Instead of hoping, however,

Figure 3.4
A Project Illustrating Design Variables

The Global Challenge is an 8th grade multidisciplinary project introduced in Chapter 1 (see Figure 1.4, pp. 14–15).

Summary

At the end of the school year, 8th grade students work in teams on a week-long project based on the United Nations' 17 Sustainable Development Goals (SDGs). Each student chooses a global development challenge of interest (e.g., malnutrition, education, gender equality, the environment) and then joins four other students to research the challenge, define problems, and propose solutions. They then develop a funding proposal to present to a panel of adults in a simulated *Shark Tank* setting. Students are assessed on developed rubrics on Problem Solving, Communication, Collaboration, and Result (i.e., did the panelists approve their funding request?). See http://markwise8.wixsite.com/globalchallenge.

Design Variables

1. Time Frame: One week at the end of the school year
2. Cognitive Demand/Rigor: DOK Level 4
3. Level of Inquiry: Significant inquiry/research
4. Degree of Authenticity: A truly authentic challenge
5. Integration of Subjects: Involves multiple disciplines *and* 21st century skills
6. Direction: Student directed
7. Student Choice: Student choices of (a) the Global Challenge on which they work, (b) how they work, (c) research sources examined, (d) solution options, and (e) ways to present to the adult panels
8. Performance Mode: Group work
9. Access to Resources: Some resources provided; students find others
10. Audience for Student Product: Adults, including experts in challenge areas
11. Degree of Scaffolding: Teachers work to develop students' needed skills throughout the school year; however, the students are expected to work independently on the project without teacher support or guidance
12. Evaluation of Student Product: Evaluation by panels of adults using established rubrics; also, peer and self-assessment of work on the project

---

he should have spent more time planning. One crystalizing moment occurred when a student explained, "I put an image of McDonald's because it represents the opposite of communism." As evidenced by this comment, student thinking was, for the most part, shallow. Students failed to make meaningful connections as to how historical events often have ripple effects into the future. But this outcome was the result of the project not being designed or communicated in a manner that would facilitate deeper learning. Although the project was, for some, fun and engaging, it lacked sophistication, detail, and structured opportunities for students to think critically about history. As a result, they displayed only surface-level processing through their posters and discussions.

The Gold Standard PBL Model

The "debacle" just described illustrates why a structured approach to project design is so essential. Models such as the Gold Standard PBL from PBLWorks offer guidance for effective project design and implementation.

PBLWorks describes its Gold Standard PBL model in terms of three parts: (1) key knowledge, understandings, and success skills; (2) essential project design elements; and (3) project-based teaching practices (Larmer, 2015). In this chapter we address the first two parts of the model; we discuss the third part (project-based teaching practices) in Chapters 5 and 6.

Knowledge, Understandings, and Success Skills

The best designs begin with the end in mind. Accordingly, working backward from a clear and coherent set of learning goals is at the center of the Gold Standard PBL model (as indicated in the first element in Figure 3.1, p. 39). Project designers should start by first identifying the conceptual understandings, knowledge, and skills (including success skills) that students should master—or demonstrate mastery of—through PBL. In Chapter 1 we advocated that districts and schools identify a small number of transfer goals to frame curriculum design. We also acknowledged the importance of acquiring specific knowledge and skills, as the application, or transfer, of learning requires the use of these more discrete learning outcomes. It is worth noting that the conceptual understanding referenced in the Gold Standard PBL model, as well as the Understanding by Design framework (Wiggins & McTighe, 2005), is a different aim than simply "knowing" or "comprehending" content. Students cannot transfer their learning if they are only familiar with the content. As a result, developing deep understanding involves "more sophisticated instruction and assessment than teaching and testing for knowledge and skill alone" (Wiggins & McTighe, 2011, p. 6).

"Success skills" are also essential learning goals for project-based learning. These include the skills of critical thinking/problem solving, collaboration, and self-management (Larmer et al., 2015). The first type of success skill—critical thinking/problem solving—aligns with our discussion of "transfer goals" in Chapter 1. As such, the transfer goals in the examples that follow serve as learning goals that encourage deeper levels of rigor. The remaining two types of success skills (collaboration and self-management) could be considered "process skills" that are important aspects of the learning process (versus content knowledge and skills that relate more directly to what students are learning).

The following are several examples of learning goals that could represent the desired outcomes for PBL across various grade levels and content areas:

Elementary School Math: Addition and Subtraction

Transfer Goal: Students will develop viable arguments to communicate mathematical reasoning.

Understanding: Students will understand that effective argumentation can be used to support mathematical reasoning.

Knowledge: Students will know the different types of addition and subtraction problems; key mathematic vocabulary such as *addition, subtraction, equals,* and so on.

Skills: Students will be able to write an equation for a given word problem; they will be able to use mathematical vocabulary to explain a solution.

Success Skill: Students will be able to respectfully listen and respond to the ideas of others.

Middle School Social Studies: Industrial Revolution

Transfer Goal: Students will formulate investigations on the impact of change on society.

Understanding: Students will understand that changing industries have social, economic, and political impacts.

Knowledge: Students will know the major inventions of the industrial revolution; what life was like on American farms during the rise of industry; the working conditions in factories.

Skills: Students will be able to compare and contrast life before and after industrialization.

Success Skill: Students will be able to contribute to the success of a team through thoughtful discussion.

Source: Kaleigh Smith, James Madison University, Harrisonburg, VA.

High School Biology: Classification of Organisms

Transfer Goal: Students will design an experiment to investigate and classify organisms based on their unique characteristics.

Understanding: Students will understand that a logical and scientific classification system is based on the structure and function of organisms.

Knowledge: Students will know key structures and functions of various organisms.

Skills: Students will be able to compare and contrast the four kingdoms of Eukarya.

Success Skills: Students will be able to set and meet deadlines for first and second drafts and to describe improvements made between drafts.

Source: Augustus Snyder, James Madison University, Harrisonburg, VA.

These learning goals are a necessary condition for any high-quality curricular or assessment design. What follows are additional design elements that reflect the Gold Standard of PBL (Larmer et al., 2015).

Essential Project Design Elements

The Gold Standard PBL model incorporates the following design elements: (1) driving questions, (2) sustained inquiry, (3) authenticity, (4) student voice and choice, (5) feedback, reflection, and revision; and (6) public product. Let's examine each of these in turn.

Driving Questions

McTighe and Wiggins (2013a) have written extensively about developing and using "essential questions" to frame curricular units of study. These questions are open-ended and thought provoking, raise additional questions, spark inquiry, require support and justification (not just an answer), and are worthy of debate or discussion. The primary intent of essential questions is to frame units of study and engage students in meaning making that builds toward deeper levels of understanding. As such, essential questions may extend to students' work on performance tasks/GRASPS. In high-quality PBL, similar questions—called "driving questions"—are used to provide purpose for the project.

Driving questions have three primary criteria: they should be (1) engaging for students, (2) open-ended, and (3) aligned with learning objectives. In high-quality PBL, driving questions provide a focus for the project and are designed to promote student investment by sparking interest and a feeling of achievable challenge (Miller, 2015). Achievable challenge is established as a result of these questions having a "low floor"—they are accessible to all learners regardless of background knowledge; and a "high ceiling"—they do not limit the depth and breadth of thought or investigation that students might engage in (Willis, 2010). Consider the question "Why are rules important?" Students with little background knowledge can still explore the role of rules in their own lives. Students ready to think more abstractly about rules can engage at deeper cognitive levels (e.g., consider how a 1st grader might relate to this question versus a teenager). Ultimately, the goal of project-based learning using the Gold

Standard PBL model is for students to formulate one or more answers to a driving question through the completion of their project, keeping in mind that these questions have a variety of possible answers.

The type of project should dictate the type of driving question. Projects can be classified in five categories: (1) solve a real-world problem, (2) meet a design challenge, (3) explore an abstract question, (4) conduct an investigation, or (5) take a position on an issue (Larmer et al., 2015). Here are a few examples of driving questions for the five types:

Solve a Real-World Problem
• How can we turn our beliefs into political action?
• How can we increase recycling in our neighborhood?

Meet a Design Challenge
• How can we create an accurate scale model of our school to help visitors navigate the building?
• How can we restructure the electoral college system to better represent the popular vote?

Explore an Abstract Question
• How do biases impact our actions?
• What is the best way to display data? Why?

Conduct an Investigation
• How has U.S. foreign policy over the last 20 years both harmed and helped citizens from the U.S. and abroad?
• How can we determine the impact of pesticides on our health?

Take a Position on an Issue
• Should museums profit by selling artwork to private collectors?
• Has technological innovation helped or hurt humanity?

Additional examples of each type of driving question are included in Appendix D, which serves as a template for honing a project's purpose and crafting an associated driving question.

Readers familiar with essential questions will notice that although the primary purpose of driving questions is different, those that are designed to "explore an abstract question" meet the same criteria as essential questions. As such, all essential questions can serve as driving questions, but not all driving questions qualify as "essential."

Generating driving questions from transfer goals

Driving questions form the heart of the project, and so their development and use require careful consideration. One option is to craft driving questions that reflect, or flow from, transfer goals. As discussed in Chapter 1, transfer goals signal student application of learning to new or unique situations and contexts. To better ensure alignment of the project to these worthy outcomes, designers might consider working backward from transfer goals, rephrasing them in the form of a driving question. Figure 3.5 presents both content-specific and interdisciplinary transfer goals from Chapter 1 (see Figure 1.2, p. 10) along with driving questions derived from them. Notice that each question is phrased using student-friendly language and, through the use of the words *we* and *our*, signals that collaboration will be a key component of each investigation. After each question, we have indicated in parentheses which type of driving question gives purpose to the project.

Generating driving questions from students

One way to boost relevance and invite students to engage in PBL is to have them generate their own driving questions based on a project topic. For example, teachers could present students with a project on "Shapes in the Real World." Some student-created driving questions might be "How can we use our knowledge of shapes to stage a bedroom with kid-friendly furniture?" or an abstract question such as "How do shapes affect our lives?" This approach, although not reserved only for older students, is likely to be more successful when students have a larger knowledge or skill base regarding the project topic; otherwise questions might lack the sophistication or purpose necessary for successful PBL. If teachers plan on using this approach, they should also explicitly teach students the characteristics of good driving questions as well as the different types. They should also be cautious and check to make sure the students' questions align with the purpose of the project and will facilitate transfer of learning.

An alternative to student-generated driving questions—without sacrificing relevance—is to have learners identify their own guiding questions that relate to and help answer a driving question. For example, a teacher-identified driving question for a project on geography and culture might be "How does where we live affect how we live?" Once presented with this driving question, students could be given time to generate the guiding questions they would like to explore. One student might be curious as to why no nearby apartment buildings go above

Figure 3.5
Examples of Transfer Goals Converted to Driving Questions

Discipline	Transfer Goal	Driving Question (with Type of Project)
ELA	Write to communicate effectively in various genres for a variety of audiences and purposes (e.g., explain, entertain, guide, argue, and challenge).	How does purpose influence how we write? (Explore an Abstract Question)
Math	Apply sound mathematical reasoning to construct, justify, and defend viable arguments and respectfully critique the reasoning of others.	How can we use mathematics to support an argument for our cause? (Solve a Real-World Problem)
Science	Evaluate scientific claims and analyze current issues involving science or technology.	How can we develop a website that uses scientific findings to affect public policy? (Meet a Design Challenge)
Social Studies	Actively participate as an informed and responsible citizen.	How can we turn our beliefs into political action? (Solve a Real-World Problem)
Health and PE	Participate regularly in one or more sports or fitness activities.	What methods can we employ to determine how lifestyle changes both positively and negatively affect our overall health? (Conduct an Investigation)
Visual/ Performing Arts	Develop competence in at least one arts discipline to continue active involvement in creating, performing, and responding to art as an adult.	How can we use our performance to elicit emotion from an audience? (Solve a Real-World Problem)
World Language	Communicate and interact in one or more languages, displaying sensitivity to culture and context.	In what ways does culture influence our societal norms, including language? (Conduct an Investigation)
Interdisciplinary	Think critically about information and claims encountered at school and beyond by seeking clarity, accuracy, sound evidence, good reasons, and fairness. Consider the effects of personal decisions on the larger community.	How can we develop a protocol to help others determine what media are trustworthy? (Meet a Design Challenge) How can we most effectively educate members of the city council on ways they can positively affect their community? (Solve a Real-World Problem)

two floors whereas others across town have as many as four floors. Another student may have always wondered about the origin and purpose of the windmills in the Netherlands. The open-ended nature of driving questions gives students the opportunity to personalize specific aspects of PBL and to spark the process of inquiry.

Refining and extending driving questions

No matter how they are generated, it is important to test the strength of a driving question before using it to frame a project. One way to do this is to pose the question to students to see how they respond. As students discuss the question in small groups, the teacher can circulate and make notes. Later the teacher can examine student responses and consider if the question seems to elicit the type of thinking that could sustain inquiry in a genuine fashion. Are any revisions necessary? Could the question be improved? If so, it is better to discover and address these issues before launching the project.

It's also important to carefully consider and craft follow-up prompts and questions to probe student thinking during the inquiry process. Such prompts and questions can help students organize and process their ideas. For example, consider the driving question "How can we best determine the usability of water in our community?" The following questions or prompts could be used to stimulate investigation of the driving question:

- Can you think of any similar questions you've seen or discussed previously?
- Does this question relate to any current events? If so, what can you learn from them?
- Analyze the question. Does breaking it down into parts help to stimulate additional ideas?
- How might you explain this question in your own words?
- What tools do experts use to solve problems like this one?

Follow-up questions can promote deeper thought and processing while avoiding the trap of ushering students down a prescribed thinking path.

Sustained Inquiry

As discussed earlier in this chapter, performance tasks are typically designed to occur over shorter durations of instructional time than are long-term projects. Sophisticated PBL often engages students in sustained inquiry—a process that involves asking additional questions, finding resources, and then asking even deeper questions (Larmer, 2015). Consider the following example for an interdisciplinary PBL project (English language arts and science) for kindergarteners, in which students investigate the habitats of a wolf spider to answer the question "What can we learn about an arachnid based on where it lives?" Over the course of the semester, the class takes weekly trips around the school to explore various known habitats of the wolf spider (shrubs, woodlands, gardens). After each excursion, the class gathers data about the habitats and any specimens they might come across on their nature walks. They also brainstorm additional questions that might be worth investigating. Toward the end of the semester, the teacher asks students to draw pictures and write words (from the class word wall) that illustrate how the various habitats of the wolf spider help it survive. Last, the teacher helps the class prepare a report and presentation on how the community can take steps to support the survival of these spiders if they are ever endangered. Students' understanding deepens during the process of inquiry as they investigate content-based knowledge and skills while developing the success skills of critical thinking/problem solving and collaboration over the course of the semester.

Authenticity

Recall that we described *authenticity* as referring to work that has value outside the classroom and reflects students' experiences and interests. It can be established in PBL in four ways: (1) *context* (e.g., "How can we determine the maximum weight capacity of a bridge?"); (2) the use of real-world *processes, tasks, tools, and quality standards* (e.g., "What level of precision is necessary when designing a scientific experiment?"); (3) *impact* on others (e.g., "How might these findings help our community?"); and (4) *personal* authenticity (e.g., "How do the media affect how my family perceives important issues?") (Larmer et al., 2015). Often a task or project is authentic in several of these ways. For example, in the kindergarten example, authenticity is established through real-world processes (examining the world through a scientific eye) and context (investigating a native arachnid). It is important to remember that this conception of authenticity refers to what is authentic for *students*, which might be different from what adults view as authentic. A 2nd grader's beliefs about planning a weekly budget are (likely) very different than those of someone nearing retirement age. Teachers would be wise to think empathetically when considering authenticity. Figure 3.6 provides examples of driving questions and associated tasks that promote authentic student work.

Figure 3.6
Authenticity Four Ways

---

1. Authentic context

Driving Question: Were historical events inevitable?

Task: Students investigate whether U.S. involvement in World War II could have been avoided, and if so, how?

2. The use of real-world processes, tasks, tools, and quality standards

Driving Question: How can we determine the quality of art?

Task: Students select a well-known artist and research that artist's "breakthrough" piece. What is different about the individual's work from that point forward?

3. Impact on others

Driving Question: How can our words and deeds affect those in our community?

Task: Students survey patients at a local children's hospital to determine their favorite types of stories. They then write stories of interest for the children at the hospital. Students also research existing stories that align with patients' interests and raise funds to provide them with copies of these stories.

4. Personal authenticity

Driving Question: How can I design or improve a product or process?

Task: Students pick an area of interest and propose a way of improving a related product or process. They present their design idea to a *Shark Tank* panel to convince panelists to invest in their idea.

Student Voice and Choice

Giving students a say over what and how they learn leads to greater willingness to engage with a task, retain information while working on a task, and persist in completing the task (Sousa & Tomlinson, 2018). Students might take ownership over the content—what they are learning; the process—how they will come to learn it; the product—how they will show evidence of learning; or the environment—how the classroom feels and works (Tomlinson, 2017). In the wolf spider example, the teacher could provide students with several possible options for which animal/insect/arachnid they would like to follow over the course of the semester (choice and voice of *content*). Additionally, inviting student-generated driving questions, or follow-up guiding questions about teacher-generated ones, can help fuel student voice and choice in PBL by adding personal relevance (e.g., "Is shade important to wolf spiders when it's hot?"). In

Chapter 6 we will delve deeper into the notion of differentiated performances or projects.

Feedback, Reflection, and Revision

The best projects are iterative or cyclical in nature rather than linear. Instead of progressing blindly through a project with the hope of success at the end, students should be provided with feedback as well as with opportunities for reflection and revision along the way. Although the PBLWorks Gold Standard model includes reflection as a separate design element from feedback and revision, we see these processes as interrelated and as such address them together here.

Effective feedback, reflection, and revision require two important conditions. First, students should be made aware of the learning goals toward which they are working. Communicating clear goals from the onset of any task or project helps students focus on the work ahead (Sousa & Tomlinson, 2018). Second, teachers should also share with students the expectations for quality work using rubrics, other evaluation criteria, and exemplary products or performances. Once the goals and criteria have been established (ideally, early on), targeted feedback and critiques (from teachers, other students, other teachers, outside experts, etc.) can be provided to students throughout the course of the project, helping them revise their work—establishing a *cycle* of learning. Teachers should consider building in specific formal and informal checkpoints along the way for students to reflect upon the process of learning as well as their progress toward the goals and criteria. Structured time for reflection can help improve student work on the current project, as well as students' approach to and management of future projects (Larmer, 2015). As such, reflection can and should occur both *during* and *after* completion of the project, signaling to students that learning is a continuous process.

Note: In Chapter 4 we provide additional ideas regarding the use of rubrics to promote feedback, revision, and reflection. Chapter 6 discusses the role of ongoing assessment and adjustment in successful completion of a product or performance.

PBLWorks has created several resources for teachers looking to implement high-quality PBL with various sample projects. These resources can be found at these websites: http://ootg.pblworks.org/ootg/#projects and https://my.pblworks.org/projects. See also Appendixes F, H, and L for examples of PBL implemented across a range of content areas and grade levels.

Public Product

In high-quality PBL, students have opportunities to share or display their work in public settings. These displays might take the form of school- or district-based exhibitions, presentations to community members, or the online publication of videos, podcasts, and other products. Extending PBL beyond a teacher-student event adds a social dimension to learning that can have a positive impact on the school culture and classroom community by involving others in determining what should be learned and what quality evidence of learning looks like (Larmer, 2015). Making student work public also communicates why rich tasks and projects are valuable instructional and assessment models. It helps the community understand that learning in the modern world is less about rote memorization and practice, and more about how students can apply their learning to unique situations and contexts.

Upgrading Performance Tasks and Projects with Technology

Authentic performance tasks and projects offer many opportunities for involving students in the purposeful and productive use of technology for finding and processing information, interacting with others, and communicating. With so many students having grown up with technology, it makes sense to let them play in the digital sandbox—in fact, technology tools can infuse authenticity into a project (e.g., creating a digital flyer using Canva to market a student's design). Moreover, an increasing number of schools provide personal devices or allow students to BYOT (bring your own technology device) to enhance learning. We believe that the incorporation of digital tools can transform a mundane task and engage more learners. However, we caution that teachers should avoid making technology the focal point of the task or project and instead use it as a tool to support students as they explore, create, solve, develop, and otherwise tackle the work at hand. Said differently, it is important to maintain a focus on the learning (transfer goal, big idea understanding, or knowledge and skills) rather than on the product or tool used during the project or performance (see the following chapter on evaluation tools for further discussion on ensuring that learning is the primary aim of these tasks and projects).

Here is an example of a performance task upgrade using technology:

Traditional Task: Write a book report on *A Sick Day for Amos McGee* following the given format.

Upgraded Task: Submit a review of *A Sick Day for Amos McGee* to the GoodReads website (www.goodreads.com). Kids visit this website to find out about books that they might like to read. Your review should summarize the basic plot, discuss the strengths and weaknesses of the writing, and make a recommendation. Before you begin, review the website and make a list of what you believe to be essential characteristics of an effective review.

See Appendix C for a collection of free or inexpensive technology tools to use in upgrading performance tasks and projects. This list includes both websites and apps that reflect a variety of purposes, content areas, and grade levels.

Sensitive Topics—A Challenge to Project or Task Design

The more authentic the task or project, the more likely it may touch on—or directly tackle—highly sensitive or offensive topics inappropriate to the age of students or to community norms. This is a common challenge in project-based learning that gives students opportunities to select the project issue or problem. Here are some examples of sensitive or potentially disturbing topics:

• Abortion	• Birth control/condoms
• Child abuse/child neglect	• Death
• Divorce	• Drugs/alcohol
• Family problems	• Genocide
• Ghosts/spirits	• Guns/gun laws
• Homelessness	• Incest
• Murder	• Pregnancy
• Racism	• Religion
• Religious holidays	• Same-sex marriage
• Sex/sexuality	• Sexual assault
• Sexually transmitted disease	• Suicide

Teachers should use their judgment to determine if student-generated topics are appropriate. When in doubt, it makes sense to seek opinions of colleagues, administrators, and even parents. We have seen cases where teachers and schools have become the targets of parental protests and condemnation by boards of education when a well-intentioned task or project was seen as inappropriate for students. At the same time, we have seen instances of teachers collaborating with administrators, parents, and the community to explore controversial issues in a safe and productive fashion. Here is a link to several related stories illustrating how Nashville schools have chosen to integrate social-emotional learning into their curriculum, including confronting issues related to race and conflict: https://www.edutopia.org/package/how-district -integrates-sel-academics. The bottom line is that we must know and operate within our context when considering topics that can be seen as traditionally controversial or contentious.

Conclusion

The design variables introduced in this chapter present teachers with many decisions to consider as they construct tasks and projects. It is important to note that one "side" of the scale is not better than the other. Rather, the variables should be adjusted with the goal of determining how to (1) best meet student needs, (2) leverage teacher strengths and comfort-levels, and (3) capitalize on available resources (including time). The Task and Project Planning Tool featured in Appendix B can help guide decisions regarding the design variables. The "Planning Task/Project Elements" section of that tool provides prompts to help designers get started. In succeeding chapters, we will explore more tools to guide the design process. Specifically, in the next chapter, we will explore effective design and use of evaluation tools to help ensure fairness and reliability in appraising and grading performance tasks and projects.

4

Constructing and Using Evaluation Tools to Enhance Student Performance

In Chapters 2 and 3 we outlined various methods for creating high-quality, rich performance tasks and projects. One of the challenges associated with their design and implementation is how to evaluate the student products and performances that emerge from these open-ended and often complex assignments. Compared with scoring test items that have a single correct answer, evaluating student projects or performances requires teachers to exercise judgment when providing feedback or assigning grades. By using a set of carefully considered and established criteria aligned with the learning goals for a particular task or project, it is possible to make a judgment-based evaluation process fair, consistent, and defensible. In this chapter, we'll explore different types of criteria and criterion-based tools, practical processes for designing effective rubrics, and principles for effective use of criteria and rubrics in the classroom.

Evaluative Criteria

Criteria are guidelines, rules, or principles for judging student responses, products, or performances. In essence, they describe what is most important in student work. Criteria serve as the foundation for the development of a more detailed rubric, a tool for evaluating student performance. (We'll say more about rubrics shortly.)

How do we decide which criteria to use for evaluating student performance on a task? The answer may surprise you. In a standards-based system, criteria come primarily from the targeted standards or outcomes being assessed rather than from the specific assessment task. For example, if a teacher is focusing on an ELA standard for expository writing, then the criteria for any associated performance task will likely require students to be *accurate* (the information presented is correct), *complete* (all relevant aspects of the topic are addressed), *clear* (the reader can easily understand the information presented; appropriate descriptive vocabulary is used), *organized* (the information is logically framed and sequenced), and *conventional* (proper punctuation, capitalization, spelling, and sentence formation/transitions are used so that the reader can follow the writing effortlessly).

This point may seem counterintuitive. How can you determine the criteria until you know the task or the product that students will produce? What if one version of a science task required students to produce a visual product, such as a poster or a graphic organizer, and another version of the same task asked students to give a verbal explanation? Aren't different criteria involved in evaluating such different products and performances?

Certainly there may be different *secondary* criteria related to the features of a particular product or performance. For example, if students were to create a visual product to show their understanding of a concept in science, then we might expect the visual to be neat and graphically appealing. But the *primary* criteria would focus on the content linked to the associated science standards and learning outcomes instead of only the surface qualities of the product (in this case, a visual display).

This point can be lost on students who fixate on the features of whatever performance or product they are to develop at the expense of the content being assessed. (Think of the science fair projects in which the backboard display is an impressive work of art, but the depth of the science content or the conclusions are superficial.) Eric once worked with a social studies teacher who had his students present their own "Class Bill of Rights." His hope was for students to evaluate the importance for our current society of the U.S. Bill of Rights and to better understand the effects of history on our lives. Instead of providing them with evaluative criteria that reflected these content outcomes, he gave them a checklist with items such as "length of presentation" and "number of rights to be included." Some student presentations showed evidence of strong connections to the purpose of the Bill of Rights and how it might be applied to their classroom. Others, however, heard "presentation" and lost focus on what content was relevant, instead emphasizing their timing and delivery. As a result, the teacher had one student who decided to "dance" his Bill of Rights (interpretively, of course!) and another who used a comedy show to share her ideas. Although both were gifted performers, a simple follow-up question or two revealed only a surface-level understanding of afforded rights.

This story reminds us not to assume that students can get into our heads and know what we expect. The following year (having learned from the experience), the teacher distributed a rubric for the task that appropriately highlighted the core knowledge and skills expected. Although he encouraged creative presentations, he also made it clear that the main emphasis for the task was a deeper understanding of how the Constitution and the Bill of Rights affect today's society.

Such experiences make it incumbent upon teachers to clearly explain the goal of a performance task or project and present the evaluative criteria or rubric in advance, so that students understand the relative importance of the various elements. Even with shorter, less complex tasks, teachers will find they elicit higher-quality student work when they make evaluative criteria explicit. Otherwise, students might spend an inordinate amount of time and energy on the secondary criteria at the expense of the content being assessed. Of course, if the content happens to be in the visual or performing arts, then the primary criteria *will* properly focus on features such as artistic composition, craftsmanship, and creativity.

Types of Criteria

A complex performance or project generally involves several important elements or traits that are primarily derived from key learning goals. For example, in a project involving the analysis of a complex issue, the designer might identify conceptual understanding, problem-solving methods, organization, and persuasiveness as evaluative criteria. However, a finer-grained view shows that these specific criteria can be organized under a broader frame of criteria types. Grant Wiggins and Jay McTighe (2012) have identified four general categories—content, process, quality, and impact—described as follows:

- *Content criteria* are used to evaluate the degree of a student's knowledge and understanding of facts, concepts, and principles specified in a content standard. Examples of descriptive terms for this category include *accurate, clearly explained, complete, expert, knowledgeable.*
- *Process criteria* are used to evaluate the effectiveness of the methods and procedures used in a task, as well as the proficiency level of a skill performance specified in process standards. Examples of descriptive terms for this category include *collaborative, coordinated, efficient, methodical, precise.*

- *Quality criteria* are used to evaluate the overall quality and craftsmanship of a product or performance. Examples of descriptive terms for this category include *creative, organized, polished, properly designed, well crafted.*
- *Impact criteria* are used to evaluate the overall results given the purpose and audience. Examples of descriptive terms for this category include *entertaining, informative, persuasive, satisfying, successful.*

When we conduct workshops on rubric design, we find it helpful to illustrate the use of these categories with a familiar example—evaluating a restaurant. We often hear participants discuss various evaluative criteria such as atmosphere, service, cleanliness, menu options, recommendations to friends, and others. Here is an example of how someone could use the four criteria types to evaluate a restaurant dining experience:

- *Content*—The server accurately describes the appetizers, main courses, side items, desserts, drinks, and specials; once received, all meals and drinks are as described and as ordered; the menu offers a variety of available options that appeal to various tastes and dietary needs.
- *Process*—The kitchen staff collaborates well and coordinates with the server; the server checks on diners regularly and attends to their needs; dishes are served and cleared promptly; lights are dimmed and the music volume lowered (or raised!) when necessary.
- *Quality*—All dishes optimize flavor, freshness, temperature, and texture; portion sizes are satisfying; food pairings enhance each dish; dishes are presented in an aesthetically pleasing manner.
- *Impact*—The meal is tasty and satisfying to all guests; the atmosphere facilitates a relaxed and enjoyable dining experience; patrons would recommend the restaurant to their closest friends.

It is important to note that in this example the four criteria are relatively independent of one another. For example, the server may accurately describe the menu items (content), but the food may arrive late (process) or be overcooked (quality). When different traits or criteria are important in a performance, they should be evaluated individually. This approach allows more specific feedback to be provided to the learner (as well as used by the teacher) than does an overall rating. It also helps the scorer reliably report student performance on distinct criteria. Alternatively, if key learning goals are spread across several different criteria, reporting mastery of those goals becomes much more difficult.

Consider another example using content, process, quality, and impact criteria for a kindergarten "Zoo Review" task (see Figure 4.1). The goal of this task is for students to convince the zoo owners to add a new animal and construct an appropriate habitat for it. They will prepare a report with words and pictures to explain their choice of animal and describe and illustrate the environment that the animal will need to survive. They should also include any special qualities the animal has that will help it survive in that environment.

Figure 4.1
Zoo Review Rubric

Criteria	Expert	Needs Improvement
Description of Animal and Habitat (Content)	• Your words and pictures tell and show us what makes this animal different from other animals like it and unlike it. • Your words and pictures tell and show us how to meet all your animal's basic needs (air, water, food, shelter) and the special needs of your animal.	• You have not yet explained how your animal differs from others like it and unlike it. • Your words and pictures don't tell us how to meet all the animal's basic needs (air, water, food, shelter) and the special needs of your animal.
Research (Process)	• At least 3 appropriate resources are used to locate words and pictures to describe your animal and its habitat. • Your report clearly reflects the information from your research.	• Fewer than 3 resources are used to research your animal, or the resources chosen are not appropriate. • Your report only partially reflects your research, or it shows no evidence of research at all.
Professionalism (Quality)	• You are ready to present this to the zoo: - You used punctuation, capitalization, and spaces correctly. - You correctly spelled words taken from research or the word wall. - Your pictures are accurate (based on images in resources). They help people recognize your animal.	• You need to fix these things before presenting it to the zoo: - Punctuation, capitalization, and spaces. - Spelling of words taken from research or the word wall. - The accuracy of your picture.
Impact	• Your words and pictures provide enough information for the zoo owners to prepare for the new animal. • The animal would have its needs met in its new habitat.	• Your words or your pictures need additional information to help the zoo owners make their decision. • The animal would not have all of its needs met in its new habitat.

This example illustrates the importance of including impact criteria in authentic tasks and projects. The more each task or project is set in an authentic context (which is increasingly likely with project-based learning), the more important it is to consider the overall impact of the resulting performance. Indeed, we want students to move beyond "compliance thinking"—for example, *How many words does it have to be? Is this what you want? How many points is this worth?*—to consider the overall effectiveness of their work given the intended purpose and target audience (reinforcing the importance of identifying this audience for students). Impact criteria suggest different questions that students should ask themselves, such as these:

- Did my story entertain my readers?
- Could the visitors find their way using my map?
- Did my design achieve its purpose?
- Did I find answers to my research questions?
- Was my argument persuasive?
- Was my diagram informative?
- Was the problem satisfactorily solved?

By highlighting impact, teachers can help their students develop real-world habits.

Note that although these four categories reflect possible types of criteria, we do *not* mean to suggest that you must use all four for every performance task. Rather, you should select only those that are appropriate for the goals being assessed and for which you want to provide feedback to learners. Once you determine which types to apply, you can use the design tool in Figure 4.2 to develop descriptors for the different types of rubric criteria.

Criterion-Based Evaluation Tools

Once teachers have identified the key criteria for a given performance (based primarily on the targeted learning goals), they can use them to develop more specific evaluation tools. These evaluation tools can be generic (e.g., a writing rubric that can be used numerous times throughout the year, with criteria such as sentence structure and grammar) or task-specific (e.g., a rubric used for a complex math performance task that involves modeling data trends using equations). Both types could include any combination of content, process, quality, and impact criteria.

Figure 4.2
Design Tools for Different Types of Criteria

Content	Process	Quality	Impact
Refers to the appropriateness and relative sophistication of the understanding, knowledge, and skill employed	Refers to the quality and appropriateness of the procedures, methods, and approaches used, prior to and during performance	Refers to the overall quality, craftsmanship, and rigor of the work	Refers to the result, success, or effectiveness of performance, given the purpose(s) and audience
Questions designers can consider: • Was the work accurate? • Did the product reveal deep understanding? • Were the answers appropriately supported? • Was the work thorough? • Were the arguments of the essay cogent? • Was the hypothesis plausible and on target?	**Questions designers can consider:** • Was the performer methodical? • Was proper procedure followed? • Was the planning efficient and effective? • Did the reader/problem solver employ apt strategies? • Did the group work collaboratively and effectively?	**Questions designers can consider:** • Was the speech organized? • Was the paper mechanically sound? • Was the chart clear and easy to follow? • Did the story build and flow smoothly? • Was the dance graceful? • Were the graphics original?	**Questions designers can consider:** • Was the desired result achieved? • Was the problem solved? • Was the client satisfied? • Was the audience engaged and informed? • Was the dispute resolved? • Did the speech persuade? • Did the paper open minds to new possibilities?
In sum: Was the content appropriate to the task, accurate, and supported?	*In sum:* Was the approach sound?	*In sum:* Was the performance or product of high quality?	*In sum:* Was the work effective?
Descriptive terms: • accurate • appropriate • authentic • complete • correct • credible • explained • important	**Descriptive terms:** • careful • clever • coherent • collaborative • concise • coordinated • effective • efficient	**Descriptive terms:** • attractive • competent • creative • detailed • extensive • focused • graceful • masterful	**Descriptive terms:** • beneficial • conclusive • convincing • decisive • effective • engaging • entertaining • informative

(continued)

Figure 4.2
Continued

Content	Process	Quality	Impact
Descriptive terms: • in-depth • insightful • justified • logical • makes connections • precise • relevant • sophisticated • supported • thorough • valid	**Descriptive terms:** • flawless • followed process • logical/reasoned • mechanically correct • methodical • meticulous • organized • planned • purposeful • rehearsed • sequential • skilled	**Descriptive terms:** • neat • novel • organized • polished • precise • proficient • rigorous • skilled • smooth • stylish • unique • well-crafted	**Descriptive terms:** • inspiring • meets standards • memorable • moving • persuasive • proven • responsive • satisfactory • satisfying • significant • understood • useful

Let's now examine three types of criterion-based evaluation tools for use with performance tasks and projects—criterion performance lists, holistic rubrics, and analytic rubrics.

Criterion Performance Lists

A basic and practical tool for evaluating student performance is simply a list of key criteria, sometimes referred to as a criterion performance list (Hibbard et al., 1996). A criterion performance list consists of a set of criteria or key traits/elements, space for feedback and reflection, and, in some instances, a rating scale that allows teachers to rate the various rubric elements by assigning points to each of the respective criteria. This format enables a flexible "weighting" of certain elements over others based on the relative importance given the content (e.g., instructional time devoted to specific targets during an instructional unit). The lists may be configured for easy conversion to conventional letter grades, if need be. For example, a teacher could assign point values and weights that add up to 25, 50, or 100 points, enabling a straightforward conversion to a district or school grading scale (e.g., A = 90–100; B = 80–89; and so on). When shared with students in advance, the lists provide a clear performance target, signaling to them what elements should be present in their work and their relative importance. Figure 4.3 is an example of a performance list for composing a fairy tale.

Figure 4.3
Criterion Performance List for a Fairy Tale

Elements	Points Possible	Self/Peer	Teacher
1. Plot: The plot has a clear beginning, middle, and end and is carried throughout the tale.			
2. Setting: The setting is described with details and shown through the events in the story.			
3. Characterization: The characters are interesting and fit the story.			
4. Details: The story contains descriptive details that help explain the plot, setting, and characters.			
5. Fairy Tale Elements: The story contains the elements of a fairy tale (e.g., appropriate characters, settings in the past, events that can't really happen).			
6. Pictures: Detailed pictures are effectively used to help tell the story.			
7. Mechanics: The fairy tale contains correct spelling, capitalization, and punctuation. There are no errors in mechanics.			
Totals:			

A criterion performance list may also include columns for peer and self-assessment (as shown in the fairy tale example) as well as feedback and goal setting. In fact, many teachers who use this format have their students complete a self-assessment and turn it in with their work. Then teachers can see if students are capable of honest self-appraisal based on the criterion elements. Figure 4.4, page 74, presents an example of a form with space for feedback and goal setting. By regularly engaging students in such self-assessment and reflection, teachers are contributing to the development of critical habits and a growth mindset.

Because of their simplicity, criterion performance lists are ideal for use with students in the primary grades. Figure 4.5, page 75, presents an example for writing a fictional story. Note the use of kid-friendly language for the story

Figure 4.4
Performance List for Participation in Student Self-Assessment and Goal Setting

Evidence of Meeting or Exceeding Standards	Expected Participation Behaviors	Areas for Growth
	1. **Prepares for and engages in class learning: The student** a. Consistently prepares to collaborate with classmates with the goal of supporting individual and peer learning. b. Actively engages during instruction and in all collaborative activities. c. Respectfully interacts with others, including peers and the teacher. d. Regularly takes initiative to share ideas in a whole-class setting, via oral and written formats.	
	2. **Maintains a focus on growth: The student...** a. Demonstrates a desire and willingness to learn and improve. b. Responds favorably and appropriately to suggestions and constructive criticism; welcomes feedback as an opportunity for growth. c. Responds to feedback in a timely fashion to maximize the learning impact. d. Completes tasks without multiple reminders, pleading, or threats. Takes ownership of and responsibility for own learning.	
	3. **Uses technology appropriately: The student...** a. Keeps phone off the table when not in use for class purposes. b. Uses laptops and tablets *only* for educational purposes during class time (break excluded). c. Avoids social media, text messaging, e-mailing, registering for classes, checking a fantasy team, shopping, and streaming videos. (Student is aware that if he wonders if the use of technology is appropriate, it probably isn't.)	

elements, written as questions to encourage students to self-assess as they work on their story and examine their drafts. Notice also that the emoji faces in the three-point scale do not include a frowning face; the lowest level is flat or neutral, suggesting that the goal is to get better. We do not want young students thinking that the teacher is frowning on their performance or that they are not

Figure 4.5
Criterion Performance List for Writing a Story (Primary Grade Level)

	Terrific	Almost There	Needs Work
1. I have an interesting setting and characters for my story.			
2. The problem in my story will be clear to my readers.			
3. My story events are in order.			
4. The solution will be clear to my readers.			
5. I used many describing words to tell what is happening.			
6. My words "paint a picture."			
7. I have a title that goes with my story.			
What will you try to do better the next time you write a story?			

liked. Rather, the spirit is "Let's look at how your story is developing and think about how you can make it better."

Well-developed criterion performance lists identify the key elements that define success on a performance task. When they are provided in advance (a recommended practice), the lists clearly communicate task expectations and parameters for quality work. They also encourage self-assessment and refinement by students as they work.

Despite these benefits, criterion performance lists have limits. Most notably, they do not provide detailed descriptions of performance levels. In other words, there are no qualitative descriptions of the difference between a rating of 15 and a rating of 9 for a given element (or a full smile versus a partial smile on the emojis). Thus, students may not understand what they need to do to improve simply by seeing the ratings presented to them (or by their self-assessment of the criteria). Similarly, despite identified criteria, different teachers using the same performance list may rate the same student's work quite differently, which detracts from the list's reliability. To illustrate this second point, let's consider an extremely high-stakes competition where consistency is crucial—Olympic diving. Divers are scored from 0 to 10 based on five different criteria: approach, take-off, elevation, execution, and entry. Quality descriptors explicate what each of these elements would look like at a 10, 9, 8, and so on. If judges had access only to descriptors of what a 10 was, providing consistent scores for less successful dives would be extremely difficult. What qualifies as a 9 or a 7? For a more consistent evaluation, it is important that judges have access to descriptors for all degrees of quality (in the case of diving, 1 to 10). So, if reliability, or consistency, of scoring is important—as it usually is in higher-stakes tasks that are cumulative in nature—a criterion performance list may not be the best tool, as it makes assigning specific *degrees* of quality much more subjective than does an analytic or a holistic rubric (see the next section). Criterion performance lists are best suited for low-stakes assignments, where the feedback is valued more than the provision of a reliable score for evaluating student performance.

Note: We sometimes hear educators refer to a criterion performance list as a "single-point rubric" because this type of scoring tool yields a single score. However, a performance list is *not* a rubric because it does not include graduated levels of performance. Let's take a closer look at different types of rubrics and how to create them.

Rubrics

Like criterion performance lists, rubrics are based on a set of criteria; but unlike lists, they include descriptions of the levels of performance according to a fixed scale (e.g., four points). Figure 4.6 illustrates how a rubric differs from a criterion performance list by including a scale with designated levels of quality (in this case, 1 through 4). Let's take a closer look at two widely used types of rubrics—holistic and analytic.

Holistic rubrics

A holistic rubric provides an overall impression of a student's performance, yielding a single rating or score. Holistic rubrics are well suited to judging simple products or performances, as well as gauging the overall impact of a student's work (e.g., *To what extent was the essay persuasive? Did the concert entertain the audience?*). Figure 4.7 is an example of a holistic rubric for a performance task in which students created a public service message on a billboard, poster, or website.

Figure 4.6
Rubric Components: Criteria, Levels of Performance, and Descriptors

Criteria	Levels of Performance			
	4	**3**	**2**	**1**
Conceptual understanding				
Problem-solving methods				
Organization of presentation				
Persuasive argument				

Note: Rubrics can be oriented with the levels placed in columns and the criteria in rows, as shown here, or vice versa, depending on designer preference or agreed-upon formatting decisions.

Because they offer an overall rating, holistic rubrics are well suited to assigning a summative grade. However, they typically do not provide a detailed analysis of the strengths and weaknesses of a student's work according to specific elements. (Note that there are no criteria specified in the rubric in Figure 4.7.) Thus, they are less effective at providing feedback to learners about what they have done well and the particular areas needing improvement.

A holistic rubric can also present a challenge for teachers when they are evaluating a complex performance with multiple dimensions. For example, consider two students who have completed a graphic design project. One student uses visual symbols to clearly communicate an abstract idea. However, her design involves clip art images that are sloppily pasted onto the graphic. A second student creates a beautiful and technically sophisticated design, yet his main idea is trivial. How would those respective pieces be scored using a holistic rubric? Often the compromise involves averaging, whereby both students might receive the same score or grade, yet for substantially different reasons. Without more detailed feedback than a score or a rating, it is difficult for the student to know exactly what the grade means or what refinements are needed in the future. This potential problem is evident in Figure 4.8, an example of a

Figure 4.7
Holistic Rubric for a Public Service Message

Levels	Descriptors
Expert **4**	The billboard, poster, or website conveys a clear and compelling message that calls for public action to address a need. The overall graphic design is well coordinated, with words and visuals working together to enhance the message and the call to action.
Proficient **3**	The billboard, poster, or website conveys a message for the public but does not call for specific action. The overall graphic design is generally coordinated. The words and visuals work together in support of the message but do not communicate needed actions by the public.
Emergent **2**	The billboard, poster, or website suggests a message, but it is unclear exactly what the viewers should take from it. The visuals do not clearly support the words of the message or communicate needed public action.
Novice **1**	No clear message is evident. The visuals seem random and do not convey any message. The overall graphic design is sloppy and unappealing.

Figure 4.8
Holistic Rubric for a Scientific Investigation

Levels	Descriptors
Excellent **4**	The student's investigation includes a stated hypothesis, follows a logical and detailed procedure, collects relevant and sufficient data, thoroughly analyzes the results, and reaches a conclusion that is fully supported by the data. The investigative process and conclusion are clearly and accurately communicated in writing so that others could replicate the investigation.
Good **3**	The student's investigation includes a hypothesis, follows a step-by-step procedure, collects data, analyzes the results, and reaches a conclusion that is generally supported by the data. The process and findings are communicated in writing with some omissions or minor inaccuracies. Others could most likely replicate the investigation.
Fair **2**	The student's stated hypothesis is unclear. The procedure is somewhat random and sloppy. Some relevant data are collected but not accurately recorded. The analysis of results is superficial and incomplete, and the conclusion is not fully supported. The findings are communicated so poorly that it would be difficult for others to replicate the investigation.
Give it another try **1**	The student's investigation lacks a stated hypothesis and does not follow a logical procedure. The data collected are insufficient or irrelevant. Results are not analyzed, and the conclusion is missing or vague and not supported by data. The communication is weak or nonexistent.

holistic rubric for a scientific investigation. Given the multiple dimensions of a scientific investigation, it is unlikely that a student's performance would fall exclusively within one of the four score categories. For example, a student may conduct a sound investigation (Level 3) but communicate the results poorly and in such a way that the process could not be replicated (Level 1). This problem can be minimized through the use of an analytic rubric.

Analytic rubrics

An analytic rubric divides a product or performance into distinct criteria and judges each criterion independently. Analytic rubrics are well suited to evaluating complex projects and performances (e.g., multifaceted problem solving or a research project with a write-up and an oral presentation) involving several significant dimensions. As evaluation tools, they provide more specific information (feedback) to students, parents, and teachers about the strengths and weaknesses of a performance. Figure 4.9 presents an example of an analytic rubric for mathematical problem solving (McTighe, 2013). Analytic rubrics such as this one help students understand the nature of quality work because these evaluation tools identify the important dimensions of a product or performance and various degrees of quality. Moreover, teachers can use the information provided to target instruction to particular areas of need (e.g., the students are generally accurate in their computations but less effective at describing their mathematical reasoning).

Evaluating student work using an analytic rubric may take a bit more time because the teacher must consider several traits. However, we believe the more specific feedback that results is well worth the effort, especially given the ultimate goal of improving learning and performance, not just judging and grading.

Consider the difference between these two types of rubrics—holistic and analytic—using the following scenario: Imagine that you have just seen a movie with plenty of Oscar "buzz" on its opening weekend, and, given your love of movies, your neighbor asks you how you liked it. If you answered, "Pretty good—I'd give it three out of four tubs of popcorn," you would be offering a holistic rating. Alternatively, if you gave your neighbor an analytic evaluation, it would sound a bit different: "The acting was terrific, and the cinematography was exquisite. But the plot was difficult to follow in parts, and the soundtrack didn't always complement the storyline. Overall, I'd give it three out of four tubs of popcorn." In this case, your evaluation judges the various dimensions of the film even though your general rating of three tubs of popcorn stayed the same.

Figure 4.9
Analytic Rubric for Mathematical Problem Solving

Level	Traits and Descriptors			
	Reasoning	**Computation**	**Representation**	**Communication**
4	An efficient and effective strategy is used and progress toward a solution is evaluated. Adjustments in strategy, if needed, are made, or alternative strategies are considered. There is sound mathematical reasoning throughout.	All computations are performed accurately and completely. There is evidence that computations are checked. A correct answer is obtained.	Abstract or symbolic mathematical representations are constructed and refined to analyze relationships, clarify or interpret the problem elements, and guide solutions.	Communication is clear, complete, and appropriate to the audience and purpose. Precise mathematical terminology and symbolic notation are used to communicate ideas and mathematical reasoning.
3	An effective strategy is used, and mathematical reasoning is sound.	Computations are generally accurate. Minor errors do not detract from the overall approach. A correct answer is obtained once minor errors are corrected.	Appropriate and accurate mathematical representations are used to interpret and solve problems.	Communication is generally clear. A sense of audience and purpose is evident. Some mathematical terminology is used to communicate ideas and mathematical reasoning.
2	A partially correct strategy is used, or a correct strategy for solving only part of the task is applied. There is some attempt at mathematical reasoning, but flaws in reasoning are evident.	Some errors in computation prevent a correct answer from being obtained.	An attempt is made to construct mathematical representations, but some are incomplete or inappropriate.	Communication is uneven. There is only a vague sense of audience or purpose. Everyday language is used, *or* mathematical terminology is not always used correctly.
1	No strategy is used, or a flawed strategy is tried that will not lead to a correct solution. There is little or no evidence of sound mathematical reasoning.	Multiple errors in computation are evident. A correct solution is not obtained.	No attempt is made to construct mathematical representations, *or* the representations are seriously flawed.	Communication is unclear and incomplete. There is no awareness of audience or purpose. The language is imprecise and does not use mathematical terminology.

Source: From *Core Learning: Assessing What Matters Most* (p. 91), by J. McTighe, 2013, Midvale, UT: School Improvement Network. Copyright 2013 by J. McTighe. Used with permission.

The analytic evaluation provides more specific information to help your movie-going neighbor decide whether or not to view the film.

Choosing the Best Evaluation Tool

So, what's the best type of evaluation tool? The answer depends upon the *purpose* of the task or project and the rubric. In other words, teachers must choose the tool that best fits the job. We wouldn't expect a carpenter to nail something with a screwdriver, just as we wouldn't expect an Olympic judge to assign scores without a consistent understanding of degrees of success criteria. If a teacher is looking for a tool that communicates clear expectations for low-stakes tasks when reliability isn't a concern, criterion performance lists are suitable.

For evaluation of student performances and products where reliable scoring is important, well-developed analytic rubrics are needed. Figure 4.10 summarizes the advantages and disadvantages of each type of tool for evaluating student performance.

Considering these advantages and disadvantages along with the following questions will help focus your choice of evaluation tool:

- What is the purpose of the performance task—formative assessment, summative assessment, or simply a learning activity?
- What evaluation tool is most appropriate given the purpose and context of use?
  - criterion performance list
  - holistic rubric
  - analytic rubric
- Will the rubric be generic (e.g., an expository writing rubric that can be used again and again) or task-specific (customized for a particular performance task)?
- What is an appropriate range for the scoring scale (e.g., three, four, or six points) to accommodate the likely variation in performance levels?
- Who will use the rubric for evaluative purposes (teachers, external scorers, students, others)? Will the rubric be used to provide feedback or simply a score?
- Will students be expected to apply the feedback to refine their work?
- Will students be expected to use the rubric for self-assessment? Peer assessment? If students are expected to use it, then the rubric should be written in language appropriate for the grade level.

The answers to these questions will inform the design of a rubric.

Figure 4.10
Advantages and Disadvantages of Evaluation Tools

Evaluation Tool	Advantages	Disadvantages
Criterion Performance List	• Is easiest to develop. • Is useful for low-stakes assessments and assignments. • Allows for open-ended feedback in response to articulated criteria.	• Lacks the ability to reliably differentiate among degrees of quality when evaluating products and performances. • Students might not understand what they need to do to improve.
Holistic Rubric	• Is easy to develop and score. • Is easier for students to read and understand (i.e., less overwhelming). • Provides degrees of quality for identified criteria. • Is more useful for products and performances with fewer criteria.	• Conflates areas of strength and weakness. • Allows the same score to be given for vastly different reasons.
Analytic Rubric	• Is more detailed, with specific criteria broken down by degrees of quality. • Provides a more reliable measure of degrees of quality regarding student products and performances. • Allows for the weighting of different criteria based on aligned learning outcomes. • Is ideal for more complex performances and products.	• Takes longer to develop and to use as a scoring tool. • Without proper teacher guidance, some students may become overwhelmed by the amount of text.

Designing Effective Rubrics

In this section we present two complementary processes for constructing and refining a sound rubric. The first process is for the development of new rubrics, and the second is for the refinement of existing rubrics using student work.

Rubric Design Process #1

As we discussed earlier, rubrics are essentially a list of criteria that describe understanding, proficiency, or quality across a scale. One practical process for designing a rubric is to begin by identifying the key qualities associated with the targeted standard/outcome and fleshing out the descriptions along the performance scale. Revisiting our earlier restaurant rubric discussion, we illustrate this process by using the following step-by-step procedure to develop a four-point analytic rubric for a server in a restaurant:

Step 1: Begin at the top end of the rubric scale and think about the qualities of a performance that demonstrates the highest levels of understanding, proficiency, and quality. Consider questions such as these:

- What distinguishes an expert performer?
- What are the indicators of an in-depth understanding?
- What are the characteristics of a highly effective performance or product?
- What would we see if someone met or exceeded the standard?

Make a list of these quality indicators. Here is an example:

A highly effective server—
    – Knows the menu well and explains it clearly.
    – Takes orders carefully and delivers the correct drinks and food items.
    – Is attentive to the customers.
    – Is friendly and flexible (e.g., allows substitutions).
    – Is well dressed and groomed.

Step 2: Next, set up a three-column table. In the left-hand column, identify important performance traits (categories). In the center column, describe the "high" performance level for each identified trait. In the right-hand column, describe a "low" performance level for each trait. Consider questions such as these:

- What distinguishes an expert performer from a beginner?
- What are the indicators of someone having an in-depth understanding versus someone who harbors misconceptions?
- What are the characteristics of a highly effective performance or product, compared to one that is not effective?

In essence, we are beginning to construct the rubric by starting at the two ends—high and low. (See the example in Figure 4.11.)

Step 3: Flesh out the descriptions for the two middle levels of the rubric. To do this, we recommend using parallel sets of descriptive terms to differentiate the four performance levels. Figure 4.12 shows a generic set of parallel descriptive terms that can be used to describe differences in degree.

Figure 4.11
High-End and Low-End Characteristics for a Restaurant Server

Key Traits	High End	Low End
Knowledge	Server knows the menu well and can clearly describe the various items, daily specials, food preparation, and the drinks. Server makes knowledgeable recommendations when asked.	Server does not know the menu well and cannot correctly describe various items, daily specials, food preparation, and drinks. Server is unable to make knowledgeable recommendations if asked.
Accuracy	Server brings the correct meals and drinks to the diners. The bill is totaled accurately.	Server makes errors in fulfilling orders or makes errors in totaling the bill. Numerous errors by server affect the satisfaction of the dining experience.
Attitude/ Flexibility	Server is polite and well-mannered around customers; strives to provide good service. Server is friendly and open to accommodating customers' requests (e.g., allows substitutions in accordance with restaurant policy; provides separate checks if asked).	Server is curt or rude to customers (e.g., makes sarcastic remarks or complains about other employees or customers). Makes no effort to accommodate customers' requests. Seems disinterested in offering good service. Server is rigid and inflexible.
Attentiveness	Server is attentive to customers' needs (e.g., checks in to ensure satisfaction) but is not intrusive.	Server is inattentive to customers' needs (e.g., does not check in) and disappears for long periods. Or, server is hovering and overly intrusive.
Appearance	Server is appropriately dressed for the restaurant and well-groomed. Clothing is stylish, clean, and neat.	Server is dressed inappropriately for the restaurant or is dressed sloppily (e.g., shirt hanging out, food stains on clothing).

Source: From *Core Learning: Assessing What Matters Most* (p. 95), by J. McTighe, 2013, Midvale, UT: School Improvement Network. Copyright 2013 by J. McTighe. Used with permission.

Here are a few additional notes about this process. First, using sets of parallel descriptive terms keeps the level descriptions similar across the scale. As the example for the restaurant server illustrates, you can use different descriptive

Figure 4.12
Descriptive Terms for Differences in Performance Levels

	Knowledge or Understanding	Proficiency	Quality
4	Thoughtful/Complete	Highly Skilled	Excellent
3	Substantial	Generally Skilled	Good
2	Partial/Incomplete	Minimally Skilled	Fair
1	Misunderstanding	Unskilled	Poor
	Effectiveness	**Frequency**	**Autonomy**
4	Highly Effective	Always; Consistently	Completely Independent
3	Generally Effective	Mostly; Generally	Mostly Independent; Needs a Little Help
2	Only Somewhat or Partially Effective	Occasionally; Intermittently	Requires Considerable Assistance
1	Ineffective	Never; Rarely	Completely Dependent

Source: From *Core Learning: Assessing What Matters Most* (p. 87), by J. McTighe, 2013, Midvale, UT: School Improvement Network. Copyright 2013 by J. McTighe. Used with permission.

terms for different traits (e.g., "Knowledge" descriptors for degrees of knowledge; "Frequency" for degrees of attentiveness), but the terms should be parallel within a trait category. Second, this process helps people construct a solid, *first-draft* rubric, but the work is not yet done! The rubric will become more precise when it is used to evaluate student work. By applying the rubric to judge actual products and performances, teachers will be able to determine if they have identified all of the key traits. Also, they will be able to use the characteristics of student work to sharpen the language of the indicators and the level descriptors.

Rubric Design Process #2

Rubric Design Process #2 explains how to refine a draft rubric using student work samples. Process #1 identifies four levels of quality, and process #2 generally focuses on three (strong, mid-range, and weak). Here are the steps in this process.

Step 1: Gather samples of student performance that illustrate the desired understanding or proficiency. Choose as large and diverse a set of samples as possible, ideally from different classrooms where students have worked on the same performance task.

Step 2: Review student work and place the samples into three piles (e.g., strong, mid-range, and weak). While sorting, write down reasons for placing pieces in the various stacks. For example, if a selected work is placed in the "strong" pile, describe its distinguishing features. What qualities distinguish this from works of lesser quality? What makes this work stand out? What specific feedback might you offer a student as you return this work? The qualities that you identify reveal criteria. Keep sorting until you are not adding anything new to your list.

Step 3: This initial sorting process is holistic because the student products are sorted according to an overall rating (high, mid-range, and low). However, some examples will not fall neatly into one of the piles because the work may be strong on one trait but weak on another. This situation raises the need for an analytical rubric reflecting two or more traits. When this occurs, make a list of the key traits or dimensions.

Step 4: Write a definition of each trait. These definitions should be "value neutral"—that is, they describe what the trait is about, not what good performance looks like. Describe the performance levels along the three-level scale.

Step 5: Find samples of student performance that illustrate the various score points. Ideally, you can identify samples of student work that provide good examples of strong, weak, and mid-range performance on each trait. These samples, sometimes called "anchors," provide concrete illustrations of the traits and of the various performance levels.

Step 6: Criteria and rubrics evolve with use. Try them out and be open to making continuous adjustments and refinements as needed. You are likely to find that some parts of the rubric work fine, but there are also rough spots. Revise traits if necessary. Add or modify the level descriptions so that they communicate more precisely. Choose more illustrative anchors for each trait. And don't forget to get feedback from students!

Regardless of whether you develop a holistic or an analytic rubric, the best rubrics meet the criteria presented in Figure 4.13. You can use these criteria to self-assess rubrics that you design and use, as well as to gauge the quality of rubrics from other sources (e.g., online or in textbooks).

Figure 4.13
Criteria for Reviewing a Rubric

Key: 3 = Extensively   2 = To some degree   1 = Not yet

Review Criteria	Score		
1. The rubric contains criteria derived from the targeted standard(s)/ outcome(s).	3	2	1
2. The rubric includes all relevant traits associated with successful performance (not just those that are easiest to observe, count, or score).	3	2	1
3. The scale of the rubric is sufficient to accommodate a full range of levels of proficiency or degrees of understanding.	3	2	1
4. The language of the rubric is specific enough to provide useful feedback as well as to guide reliable scoring.	3	2	1
5. The descriptive terms used to distinguish performance levels are parallel across the scale.	3	2	1
6. The rubric is written in student-friendly language to enable student self-assessment.	3	2	1

Source: From *Core Learning: Assessing What Matters Most* (p. 98), by J. McTighe, 2013, Midvale, UT: School Improvement Network. Copyright 2013 by J. McTighe. Adapted with permission.

Additional Thoughts on Rubric Design and Use

To this point we have provided you with the nuts and bolts of rubric design. Before concluding this chapter, we want to provide a few additional suggestions for rubric design and use.

Determining the Number of Levels in a Rubric

It is important to consider the number of quality levels that will be provided for each criterion. Much like selecting a rubric type, this decision depends greatly on the product, the purpose of the task (e.g., for summative purposes versus for the development of transfer skills during a unit of study), the grade level, and the discretion of the task designer. For example, a 1st grade science task that asks students to select and describe an appropriate habitat for a new animal being brought to the zoo might need only two levels of descriptors (e.g., Acceptable, Try again), but a high school science task that includes complex data collection and analysis could require more levels. Generally, we suggest anywhere from two to five levels.

Involving Students in Peer and Self-Assessment

We recommend that teachers involve their students in reviewing their own work as well as that of their peers. For this strategy to be effective, it is important to first model helpful feedback as well as to provide clear expectations for student roles and behaviors. One potential strategy we have found to be successful is to take students through a product/performance analysis activity to promote more autonomous student reflection and revision. If you have previous examples of student work, then you would select (1) an example with common errors or mistakes that students make and (2) an exemplar that illustrates high-quality student work. If you are implementing a performance task or project for the first time, then you can develop an anticipatory list of student errors and create your own "high quality" and "in need of work" versions of student products to use during this activity.

The next step in this process is to review the rubric descriptors with students to ensure they understand the evaluation criteria. Once students are clear about expectations for the task, they can individually review the products using the rubric and provide feedback for various evaluative criteria (Figure 4.14 shows a sample graphic organizer for helping students organize their ideas). To add a collaborative component to this activity, students could then pair up or form small groups to share their feedback, starting first with positive feedback before moving on to suggestions for growth. A whole-class discussion and individual reflection about personal areas for growth or improvement could conclude this activity. By engaging students in deeper processing regarding the rubric components, they will likely have a better understanding of the evaluation criteria and consequently be more prepared to gauge the quality of their own work.

Translating Rubric Levels into Point Values and Grades

One of the questions teachers often have is how they can translate the levels of quality they've identified in their rubrics to actual point values and grades.

Clearly, there is linkage because both a letter grade (*A*) and a rubric score (4) are symbols for specifying a performance level. For a holistic rubric, some teachers and schools simply equate the levels by using a five-point rubric scale to allow a direct conversion (e.g., 5 = *A*, 4 = *B*). This approach is fine as long as a five-point scale is appropriate for the performance being evaluated. However, in some cases, a five-point spread may be unnecessarily broad.

Figure 4.14
Sample Graphic Organizer for Student Review of Products Using Rubric Criteria

Rubric Criteria	What are some specific examples of how this product illustrates high-quality work?	What are some specific examples of common errors that should be avoided?
Content		
Process		
Quality		
Impact		

Alternately, a straightforward mathematical conversion may be sufficient. That is, simply derive a percentage based on the total number of points possible against a student's rubric score. However, we urge caution here because such a calculation may yield a percentage that does not seem to be a fair grade for the performance. For example, a holistic rubric score of 3 on a four-point scale would mathematically convert to a score of 75 percent—a *C* in many school districts. But a 3 on a four-point rubric is generally seen as "good," not "fair." Similarly, imagine that a teacher is using a four-trait analytic rubric with a four-point scale so that the total number of possible points would be 16. Students receiving a rating of 11 out of 16 on this rubric would get a score of 68.75 percent according to common conversion practices, equating to a *D* by most grading standards. Would a *D* be an appropriate grade for a "fair to good" performance?

Regardless of how rubric criteria are translated into point values or how grades are assigned in any particular classroom, designers should be careful to ensure that the grade reflects the degree of student mastery regarding key learning goals measured by the task.

Aligning Rubrics

As described earlier in our discussion of primary versus secondary evaluative criteria, a common issue when designing rubrics involves a general lack of alignment between learning goals and rubric criteria. Creating a simple alignment guide to compare rubric criteria and descriptors to learning goals can help determine how appropriate the rubric is for evaluating articulated outcomes. This guide can be created with a two-column table that has key learning goals listed on the left side and rubric criteria and descriptors on the right side. Ideally, using an alignment guide can help teachers implement two quality checks: (1) Does the rubric align with the assessment's learning goals? and (2) Does the rubric avoid overemphasizing nonessential, secondary criteria?

If these quality checks reveal unnecessary or superficial rubric criteria, or learning goals that aren't assessed by the rubric, then the designer should revise the rubric to improve alignment. For example, a rubric for a social studies poster that heavily weights the creativity and visual appeal at the expense of accuracy and completeness of conveying scientific concepts would need revision! Figure 4.15 shows an example of a high school geometry task. Figure 4.16 shows the performance-task rubric, and Figure 4.17 is the alignment guide that articulates where in the rubric the key learning goals are assessed.

Concerns About Subjectivity

We often hear concerns about subjectivity in conjunction with performance-based evaluation, whether during an Olympic diving event, at a juried art exhibit, or when teachers grade student essays. Arguably, all performance evaluation can be considered subjective in that it requires human judgment. However, that does not mean that such judgments are destined to be biased or arbitrary. Indeed, student performance can be reliably judged, as has been demonstrated by years of experience in statewide writing assessments, music adjudications, and reviews of advanced placement art portfolios. Rubrics, properly designed using the information in this chapter, can help teachers more objectively assess open-ended, subjective tasks.

Figure 4.15
High School Geometry Performance Task

Right-Triangles Performance Task

Goal: Use your knowledge of right triangles to assess a business's needs and to offer potential solutions to make the business more inclusive.

Role: You are a government architect/engineer hired to determine if a local business complies with the Americans with Disabilities Act (ADA). You will inspect a local business for ADA compliance and produce models that could be solutions.

Audience: Your client is a local business owner of your choice.

Situation: The government has given you a new assignment related to the ADA, so you'll first need to view the video on the ADA to understand the law. Part of the ADA ensures that local businesses don't have physical barriers that prevent people with disabilities from using their services; therefore, businesses often construct ramps for those who need mobility accommodations. You will choose a local business that you believe either needs to add a ramp to their building or needs to improve a ramp they already have. You will design two potential ramps that meet ADA specifications and could be implemented by the business.

Product/Performance and Purpose: You will need to create clearly and accurately labeled blueprints or models for two ramps (and their landings) that could be used by potential builders to implement your design based on the specifications given by the business. You will write a letter to the local business that explains the key features of the ADA and how the business could better meet ADA specifications. Your letter will include scale drawings of the two ramps (and landings) along with details of where you believe the chosen ramp should be placed (this will depend on how many runs it has). Explain why the ramp is safe to implement, why it is better than what the business currently uses, and how you performed your calculations (to increase your credibility).

Success Criteria: See the rubric for the detailed expectations. The clients will want to see precise and accurate numbers and features labeled in your product. They also want to see multiple methods for solving the problem (including the best method) and all mathematical work involved (to increase their confidence in using your ideas).

Source: Jenna Guenther, James Madison University, 2019. Used with permission.

Note that some people argue that high-stakes tests should only be *objective* to ensure that the assessments are fair and impartial. By *objective*, they generally mean that the test items should require selected responses and have a correct answer that cannot be debated. However, there is no such thing as a purely objective test because human judgments factor into its construction! Indeed, someone or some group has to decide: *What content will be*

Figure 4.16
High School Geometry Performance Task Rubric Alignment Guide

Right-Triangles Performance Task Rubric

	Ready for implementation!	Almost ready for implementation!	Implementation postponed for further review
Accuracy (Content) __/15	15 pts • All side lengths, angle measures, and any other relevant values to your scenario are calculated, labeled appropriately with numerical value and vocabulary term (e.g., *opposite, adjacent, hypotenuse*), and accurate • Explanations and justifications are focused, thorough, and complete, using appropriate vocabulary terms related to triangles with no errors in logic	10 pts • Most side lengths, angle measures, and any other relevant values are calculated, labeled appropriately with numerical value and vocabulary term, and accurate • Explanations and justifications are substantial but may lack focus, used appropriate vocabulary terms related to triangles with few errors in logic	5 pts • Few to no side lengths, angle measures, or other relevant values are calculated, labeled appropriately with numerical value or vocabulary term; few to none accurate • Explanations and justifications are only partial or incomplete, lack focus, lack vocabulary terms related to triangles, and have multiple errors in logic
Methods Used (Process) __/15	15 pts • Visibly showed all mathematical work/steps for more than one method for solving right triangles in scale drawings and written explanations • Methodically explained logical steps in written product for each method used • Included the *most* efficient method to solve the problem and justification for using this method is logical and included in written product	10 pts • Visibly showed all mathematical work/steps for only one method **or** superficially showed some work for more than one method for solving right triangles • Generally explained logical steps in written product for the method(s) used • Included an efficient method to solve the problem in the letter; the justification for using this method is reasonable, but not the most logical	5 pts • Showed little to no mathematical work/steps for solving right triangles in scale drawings and written explanations • Partially explained logical steps in written product for any method used • Included only an inefficient or irrelevant method to solve the problem with little to no justification for using the method in the letter

	10 pts	7 pts	4 pts
Communication and Realism (Impact) __/10	• Ideas and products are thoroughly informative, easy for the audience to follow, and satisfactorily demonstrate the significance of your work • Explanations and justifications are significantly convincing, practical, and effective in communicating solutions to designated audience • Calculations and explanations are so clear that they could be successfully implemented without alterations	• Ideas and products are generally informative, fairly easy for the audience to follow, and adequately demonstrate the significance of your work • Explanations and justifications are generally convincing, practical, and effective in communicating solutions, but could be improved with more detail and/or clearer language • Calculations and explanations are generally clear; they could be successfully implemented, but with a few alterations	• Ideas and products are partially informative and difficult for the audience to follow or distracting, and ineffectively demonstrate the significance of your work due to lack of details and clarity • Explanations and justifications are unconvincing, impractical, and ineffective. They require significantly more details and much clearer language • Calculations and expectations are unclear and could not be successfully implemented without major alterations

	5 pts	3 pts	1 pt
Overall Presentation (Quality) __/5	• Diagrams are careful and well-crafted with all measurements (including units!) and key features identified • Final product is polished, detailed, and organized, and demonstrates exceptionally careful attention to details and clear explanations • All components of final product are included, clearly distinct from one another, and extremely well organized	• Diagrams are neat and clear with most measurements (including units!) and key features identified • Final product is neat, substantial, and mostly organized, but cursory attention to detail and explanations occasionally detracts from the overall presentation • All components are included, somewhat distinct from one another, and fairly well organized	• Diagrams are disorderly and poorly crafted with few labels and key features identified • Final product is partial or incomplete and unorganized; lack of attention to detail and explanations often detracts from the overall presentation • Components of final product are missing, components are not distinct from one another, and are poorly organized

TOTAL ___ **/45**

Source: Jenna Guenther, James Madison University, 2019. Used with permission.

Figure 4.17

High School Geometry Performance Task and Rubric Alignment Guide

Rubric Alignment Guide	
Key Learning Goals (Aligned to Math Standards)	**Aligned Rubric Criteria**
Solve for missing side lengths of a right triangle using the Pythagorean Theorem, special right triangle relationships, and trigonometric ratios	**Accuracy (Content)**: All side lengths, angle measures, and any other relevant values to your scenario are calculated, labeled appropriately with numerical value and vocabulary term (e.g., *opposite, adjacent, hypotenuse*), and accurate.
Distinguish which trigonometric functions and strategies can be used and justify which is best to use to solve for missing pieces of a right triangle	**Methods Used (Process)**: Showed all mathematical work/steps for more than one method for solving right triangles in scale drawings and written explanations. Included the *most* efficient method to solve the problem and justification for using this method is logical and included in written product.
Communicate precisely to others using clear definitions in their own reasoning and a degree of precision appropriate for the problem context.	**Communication and Realism (Impact)**: Explanations and justifications are significantly convincing, practical, and effective in communicating solutions to the designated audience.

Source: Jenna Guenther, James Madison University, 2019. Used with permission.

tested? *What specific questions or prompts will be used? What distractors will be included?* So the idea that selected-response questions are more "objective" than constructed-response questions is a questionable assertion.

Benefits of Using Quality Rubrics

Rubrics have numerous benefits for both teachers and students. They can be used as a tool to promote consistency of grading, a basis for communication, a means of focusing instruction, and a method for providing effective feedback on student work. Let's consider the benefits in more detail.

Benefits for Teachers

Scoring reliability. We've referred earlier to the notion of reliability as the degree to which scoring of student work is consistent. A rubric constructed around clearly defined performance criteria helps teachers to reduce subjective judgments when they evaluate student work. The resulting performance evaluations, including grades, are thus more defensible to students and parents. When a common rubric is used throughout a department or grade-level team, school, or district (with accompanying anchor examples), the consistency of judgments (i.e., scoring reliability) by teachers across classrooms and schools increases.

Focused instruction. Clearly developed rubrics provide more than just evaluation tools for grading. They help clarify the meaning of standards and learning objectives, and they serve as targets for teaching. Indeed, teachers often observe that the process of both developing rubrics and evaluating student work against established criteria helps them crystalize the qualities that distinguish successful performance and makes them more attentive to addressing those qualities in their teaching.

Benefits for Students

Clear targets (Where am I going?). When well-developed rubrics are presented to students early on, they are not left to guess about what is most important or how their work will be judged. By knowing the evaluative criteria in advance, they have clear targets for their work. In other words, the "mystery" is taken out of the assessment and grading process.

Feedback (How am I doing? How can I close the gap between where I am now and where I want to be?). Educational research conclusively shows that formative assessment and feedback can significantly enhance student achievement (Black & Wiliam, 1998; Hattie, 2012). Clear performance criteria embedded in performance lists and analytic rubrics enable teachers to provide the detailed feedback that learners need to improve their performance. Such feedback must be goal referenced, timely, actionable, and user friendly if it is to be most helpful to students (Wiggins, 2012).

Guides for self-assessment. When teachers share performance criteria and rubrics with students, they also share (1) ownership of the task and (2) responsibility for the success of the performance, because students are expected to use these tools for self-assessment. By modeling self-assessment and goal setting (and expecting it from their students), teachers help learners become more effective at honest self-appraisal and constructive self-improvement.

Conclusion

Evaluation tool development is not an "afterthought;" rather, effective designers strategically select success criteria *as* they craft their tasks and projects. The planning tool in Appendix B reflects this principle by featuring the articulation of success criteria as part of the initial planning phase. By thoughtfully selecting evaluative criteria, carefully crafting—and recrafting—descriptions of quality, and persistently using evaluation tools to communicate, teachers can support student success in tasks and projects. Further, a strong evaluation tool can help facilitate effective *teaching*. In Chapter 5, we move into the instructional realm to explore how to teach for transfer and authentic performance.

5

Teaching to Support
Student Performance on
Tasks and Projects

In Chapters 2 and 3 we focused on design principles and processes for constructing rich, authentic tasks and projects. In Chapter 4 we explored the hallmarks of effective evaluation tools and strategies for facilitating communication and student success. In this chapter, we extend those same principles to the design and implementation of *instruction* that supports performance assessment and project-based learning.

The quality of a performance task or project will quickly erode if the unit's instruction does not prepare students to be successful. In other words, we can't design a task or project that calls for critical thinking, creativity, and collaboration and then spend three weeks lecturing and assigning worksheets. The task or project will fail because students will not be equipped to handle it. High-quality assessment demands high-quality instruction. If a complex task or project is the learning destination, then the instructional route to that end should be punctuated with multiple opportunities for practice, feedback, and scrimmage-like performances.

Teaching for Transfer = Thinking Like a Coach

Authentic performance tasks and projects call for students to transfer their learning to new situations. Accordingly, preparation must help learners to be able to apply their understanding, knowledge, and skills to the new contexts posed by the tasks and projects. Said differently, teaching for transfer is the model for instruction when the end goal is competent performance on a complex task or project. We must teach so that students have regular opportunities for practice, feedback, and refinement of skills (core, disciplinary, and 21st century). Thus, in many ways, teaching for transfer reflects the principles of effective coaching (Larmer et al., 2015; McTighe, 2013; Sizer, 1984).

It is not surprising that backward design is the norm in performance-based courses (e.g., visual and performing arts, career and technology education), as well as in extracurricular activities (e.g., athletics, yearbook, debate). This overlap likely springs from the fact that these areas are directed toward an authentic performance, such as the game in athletics, the concert in band, the public display in visual art, the production of the yearbook. Teaching, learning, and practice are thus orchestrated to prepare learners for performance. The football coach doesn't simply cover the playbook page by page. Instead, the coach uses the playbook strategically as a resource to help the team prepare for the game.

But… isn't that teaching to the test? Yes! The backward design approach *does* teach to the test, but that's not a bad thing if the test (the performance task or project) reflects what matters most: authentic performance reflecting core standards and 21st century skills. Just as coaches do not apologize for coaching for the next game or theater directors do feel guilty asking their actors to rehearse for the play, teachers need not apologize for teaching for authentic performance on worthy tasks.

How should teaching for transfer shape instruction throughout the unit? When considering the best coaches and how they use assessments, we can recognize that they (1) assess players in the beginning, (2) set the tone for success, (3) rehearse the skills of the game, (4) monitor progress, (5) provide targeted feedback to individuals and groups, and (6) incorporate opportunities for scrimmage.

1. Assess students in the beginning. Effective coaches will not begin practice until they have assessed the members of their teams to find out their skill level, knowledge of the game, conditioning level, and ability to work (play) collaboratively with teammates. The information they obtain is essential to help them shape their practices to yield maximum effect. Likewise, effective teachers use pre-assessment to check the understanding, knowledge, and skill levels students bring to a unit of study. The recognition that students may bring misconceptions (or preconceptions) into the classroom has direct implication for learning; if teachers don't identify potential misconceptions, these erroneous ideas are likely to persist even in the face of good teaching. Therefore, the use of targeted pre-assessments at the unit's outset is vital.

2. Set the tone for success. Strategic coaches recognize that winning seasons are launched during the opening moments of the team's first meeting.

In these moments, the coach sets the tone for the season by sharing expectations and casting a vision for the team's success. In a performance-based unit of study, the *launch* serves the same purpose. Teachers use it to introduce the task or project, foster student investment and motivation, and create a sense of purpose for completing the task.

3. Rehearse the skills of the game. As the season begins, the coach runs plays, conducts drills, and engages players in strength- and endurance-building activities. So it is in a performance-based classroom: students build expertise by learning to apply key skills *in the context* of a variety of settings, with the goal of transferring them to game-time performances. Moreover, learners are more likely to work on developing the necessary skills when they see purpose and relevance in what they are being asked to learn, just as athletes work harder in practice because they are training for authentic performance in upcoming games.

4. Monitor progress. No winning coach waits until the big game to see how the team is doing. Indeed, the essence of coaching is monitoring the progress of individual players—as well as the team as a whole—with the goal of using that information to direct the next steps in coaching. By using ongoing, formative assessments in performance-based classrooms, teachers remain aware of student progress. They monitor each individual student's grasp of the learning goals as well as the progress that individuals and groups have made in completing tasks and projects.

5. Provide targeted feedback to individuals and groups. As legendary football coach Vince Lombardi reportedly said, "Feedback is the breakfast of champions." Using what they learn from progress monitoring, coaches give continuous feedback to athletes to help them refine their skills and strategies during practices. Effective coaches recognize that taking time to help players acknowledge, analyze, and learn from their mistakes is key to improving individual and team performance. The same approach pays dividends in the classroom. As research has conclusively confirmed, feedback given throughout the unit—by both teachers and peers—paves the route to improved performance on a task or project (Black & Wiliam, 1998; Hattie & Clarke, 2019).

6. Incorporate opportunities for scrimmage. A scrimmage is a practice game. It gives players experience using their knowledge (e.g., of plays) and skills in a game-like setting. Coaches also use scrimmages to gather further information about team and player progress and to expose athletes to situations that don't arise during more isolated practice drills. Likewise, teachers in performance-based classrooms engage learners with minitasks—simplified versions of the summative task—to monitor their readiness to transfer knowledge and skills; to provide additional, more nuanced feedback on their performances; and to direct the future flow of practice and revision (based on the feedback).

So what does performance-based teaching look like? How do the practices just described play out in the classroom? Let's explore each through the use of specific examples.

Pre-assessment: Assessing Students

A pre-assessment need not cover *everything* teachers plan to teach; that would be exhausting for both the teacher and the students! Rather, a pre-assessment should give the teacher a preview of students' grasp of *key* knowledge, skills, and understandings, along with areas of interest that might be pertinent to the investigation (Tomlinson & Moon, 2013). In addition, it should pique students' interests and serve as an "invitation" to the unit of study (Hockett & Doubet, 2013/2014). Finally, in the case of project-based learning, pre-assessment should help the teacher gather information that can inform the strategic formation of collaborative groups. Before beginning a project-based learning experience or a performance task, therefore, teachers should choose pre-assessment prompts. For example, the questions in Figure 5.1 could serve as a pre-assessment for the task of designing a local memorial to honor veterans of the Iraq war and the U.S. war in Afghanistan. So, why these five questions? Let's examine the rationale for choosing each.

Question 1. A teacher preparing to launch this project would need to know students' background knowledge about the U.S. wars in Iraq and Afghanistan, and their answers to the first part of the question would reveal this, along with potential misconceptions about the war that the teacher may need to correct. If it became clear that the class included a few resident experts, the teacher may want to distribute them among the various collaborative groups. Answers to the second part—where the student got the information—provides the teacher with not only a deeper understanding of the source (and therefore the validity) of students' knowledge of the wars, but also a heads-up about potential resources for interviews later in the investigation.

Question 2. This item (along with drawings students may produce in Question 4) will help the teacher (1) get to know students better and (2) identify students with an artistic or architectural inclination so that they can be distributed among collaborative groups.

Figure 5.1
Sample Pre-assessment for Memorial Design Challenge

---

1. What do you know about the U.S. wars in Iraq and Afghanistan? Where did you get this information from (another class, a relative, a trip, a movie)?

2. On a scale of 1 to 10, how interested are you in creating visual designs (e.g., architecture, interior/exterior home design, illustrations for stories or texts, murals)? 1 = don't know or care; 10 = super-interested! Explain your rating.

3. If you had the chance to interview a war veteran (from any war), what question would you ask that person? Why would you have asked that particular question?

4. What would you choose as a symbol for either yourself or your family? You can use an existing symbol or create your own. Draw or describe it. Explain the significance of your symbol.

5. Please read the passage bookmarked on your device. Then share what you think is the main idea and the two most important details (and why).

Question 3. Conducting interviews will emerge as a key component of this historical investigation. This item helps the teacher ascertain what—and how much—instruction is needed to prepare students for this portion of the project. All students may need guidance and practice, some students may be ready to roll, whereas others may need more guidance and experience. Thus, this question can also help the teacher determine the need for differentiated instruction once the unit gets started (for more on this, see Chapter 6).

Question 4. Like Question 3, this item previews students' readiness to employ symbolism and to communicate meaning. Students' answers can inform both whole-group and small-group instruction. In addition, the answers can shed new light on what makes each student tick and provide insights not yet revealed by other community-building activities.

Question 5. This is a skill-based question that allows the teacher to check students' agility in gleaning meaning from text. Because students will be doing much of their own research, the teacher needs to be vigilant about supporting those students who need additional scaffolds in that process.

As this set of questions illustrates, a good pre-assessment will provide teachers with actionable information while providing insight on how to best tailor their instruction to fit students in terms of readiness, interests, and learning preferences. A good pre-assessment will help determine important first steps in teaching for transfer. But student needs may change as they encounter new material and wrestle with additional skills. Therefore, frequent monitoring during the course of instruction is necessary to make sure students continue to progress (see the section "Formative Assessment: Monitoring Progress" beginning on p. 105).

The Launch: Setting the Tone for Success

From the opening moments of a performance-based unit of study, instructional methods should support critical thinking. Posing an overarching essential question can set the stage for sustained thinking on multiple levels. Beginning a history class by asking students to explore the essential question "Is conflict productive or destructive?" in terms of their *personal* experiences allows students to dig into the conceptual underpinnings of the course in a content-free manner. Students can discuss the implications of the question on their personal lives, drawing from rich and diverse backgrounds to explore those implications in terms of relationships, sports, the arts, and other matters. Such an experience will help students more readily connect with the content as it launches them into the exploration of the same question applied to various conflicts across time periods and parts of the world.

In project-based learning, the "driving question" serves a similar purpose (see Chapter 3). The kind of driving question a teacher chooses will determine how she launches the unit. For example, inquiry that is driven by *Exploring an Abstract Question* invites project launches similar to those for essential questions (as illustrated in the "conflict" example). Other types of driving questions—*Solving a Real-World Problem, Meeting a Design Challenge, Conducting an Investigation,* and *Taking a Position on an Issue*—invite more concrete launch experiences that both preview the project and foster investment in its outcome:

> **The project is launched** when the teacher conducts an entry event that lets students know this is not just another assignment. The event engages their interest in the project and sparks questions about the topic and the process. After the teacher presents the driving question (or creates one with students), a list of student questions is generated, which will guide the inquiry process.

In other words, all launches should, in some way, connect students in a meaningful fashion to what they are about to study. Figure 5.2 presents specific ideas for launching units. Approaches vary according to the different types of driving questions chosen as the task's focus.

Figure 5.2
Using Driving Questions for Unit Launches

Type of Question	Examples	Potential Launch Ideas
Exploring an Abstract Question	How can art exert influence?	Students identify works of art (e.g., visual, musical, poetic) that have had the power to influence some aspect of their personal lives (e.g., mood, perspective, motivation, behavior). Together the class explores these works of art in terms of (1) the qualities they share and (2) how those qualities have influenced students' lives or the lives of others. This launch sets students up for their investigation of influential artists and ultimately to presenting a case for the artist whose work they believe has had the most significant impact on the world—and why.
Solving a Real-World Problem	How can professional sports teams allocate their resources to improve their records?	Students are asked to consider the relationship between *spending* and *winning* for professional sports teams. Six stations in the classroom include prompts on poster paper. Each station's prompt corresponds to one of the six Facets of Understanding (see sample prompts in Figure 2.5). Small groups of students rotate through each station and add thoughts to the poster paper. Debrief as a whole class, then preview the task at http://www.mathalicious.com/lessons/win-at-any-cost.
Meeting a Design Challenge	How can we design a memorial to honor our community's veterans from the U.S. wars in Iraq and Afghanistan?	Students examine a feature of their school or community that is designed to serve as a memorial and discuss its effectiveness at achieving that goal. They develop a list of questions for the designer regarding background, purpose, process, and medium used. Students then examine select interviews with veterans in which they discuss their wartime experience and challenges in returning from war. This launch sets up the task's driving question and challenge.
Conducting an Investigation	What factors affect erosion? How does erosion affect ecosystems?	The teacher leads a simulation of soil erosion. Using three planter boxes—one containing sod, one with scattered vegetation, and one with bare topsoil—the teacher simulates rainfall with a watering can. Several trials are run, each with varied slopes of the planter boxes. Independently, students make observations about the soil run-off at the bottom of the planter boxes after each trial. The class then discusses what they observed and the hypotheses they have about implications to the environment in their community and beyond.
Taking a Position on an Issue	Should some books be censored?	Read aloud the children's book *Where the Wild Things Are*, by Maurice Sendak. The class is divided into two teams—one that develops reasons for why the book would be good for children to read and one that develops reasons why people may *not* want children to read it. Teams engage in a minidebate over whether the book should be read in school. At the debate's conclusion, the class makes a list of criteria each team considered when preparing its case. These activities lead to the project's introduction.

No matter what type of question is driving the unit, an effective launch should set both the tone and the groundwork for sustained inquiry, in-depth thinking, and students' application of learning. The unit launch serves as the kick-off (or jump ball, puck drop, whistle blow) to set the game in motion. It also sets the stage for *teaching for transfer* throughout the rest of the unit.

Practice: Rehearsing the Skills of the Game

In every performance-based task or project, certain skills emerge as central to success. In many cases, those skills involve conducting research, evaluating sources, using evidence, and engaging in discussion. Two high-leverage strategies that can help students develop all three skill sets include Socratic seminar and ThinkDots.

Socratic Seminar

Also called a "Paideia seminar," the Socratic seminar puts students at the helm of a discussion. Armed with evidence from reading or research and guided by norms such as *listen actively, ask questions, use classmates' names, share the air[time],* and *reference the text,* students engage in debate and discussion while the teacher chimes in periodically with guiding questions. Socratic seminars can also be conducted in an inside/outside circle formation; the inside circle engages in discussion while the outside circle monitors and evaluates classmates' interactions using a back channel chat—a form of online communication. Inside and outside partners meet to debrief the discussion before switching places (the former outside partner becomes the inside discussant, and the former inside partner becomes the back channel monitor).

Teachers can use this technique with the whole class when launching a unit and at critical checkpoints throughout instruction. Socratic discussions (1) provide the teacher with formative assessment information about students' grasp of content, (2) encourage students to dig deeply and push past obvious answers or solutions, and (3) allow students to practice the skills of respectful discourse. If the teacher notices that students struggle to "share the air," the use of a strategy called Talking Chips may be helpful. Each student receives two to five chips (actual game chips or slips of paper); they must use a chip each time they contribute to the discussion. They are encouraged to use all their chips but to keep in mind that once they run out, they may no longer contribute to the discussion. It's also a good idea to establish the expectation that, if several students begin to speak simultaneously, students should yield to the classmate with the most chips left. This approach sets the tone for speaking and listening and for considering the perspectives of others. For examples of lessons employing Socratic seminars, visit https://www.paideia.org/our-approach/paideia-seminar/sample-paideia-seminar-plans.

ThinkDots

Conceived by educator and author Kay Brimijoin, ThinkDots provides a structure for thinking and talking about a concept, a topic, an idea, or an issue from multiple perspectives. The teacher creates six ThinkDots cards, numbered 1 through 6 to correspond to the dots on a die. Students work in groups of six with one die and one set of ThinkDots cards per group. Each student is responsible for answering one card's prompt or question. Students roll the die to divide the cards according to "chance"; then they silently read and respond to their prompts. In creating their responses, students may need to engage in research and gather and cite evidence to support their answer. After students have had time to prepare, they take turns sharing within their small group in numerical order. ThinkDots is a versatile strategy that may be introduced as a discussion-starter before being used as a research-based activity. It's also possible to "jigsaw" the process and have students collaborate with students from other groups who have rolled the same number. Together, they discuss or research their prompt, jot down answers, and then return to their home groups to share those ideas (Doubet & Hockett, 2015, 2017a).

Consider the sample prompts, based on the Facets of Understanding, shown in Figure 5.3. These prompts help students consider an issue from multiple lenses. Because the lens each student assumes is literally left to chance (i.e., the roll of a die), in all likelihood, students will be asked to examine an idea from a perspective that differs from their personal lens. This stretches students to push beyond their initial assumptions about a topic and to think both critically and creatively, fueling well-rounded discussion and debate. After modeling ThinkDots with a full group, teachers can use the technique in a variety of ways—for example, assigning different prompts to different groups to target varying needs or assigning a single group to complete a ThinkDots activity to get "unstuck."

Formative Assessment: Monitoring Progress

Throughout the course of a performance-based unit, teachers will need to check in with students to discover how they are progressing. Some of the strategies

Figure 5.3
ThinkDot Prompts for Examining a Current Issue

Explain	**Interpret**	**Apply**
Explain your current position on this issue. Include the *why* behind your thinking.	What is this issue *like*? What can it be compared to, or what does it remind you of?	How does this issue affect or relate to your everyday life?
Have Perspective	**Empathize**	**Self-Reflect**
What are the main "pro" and "con" arguments around this issue?	What might someone who sees this issue differently from you have experienced?	How could personal experience affect how you view this issue?

Source: Jessica Hockett, 2013. Used with permission.

that help to build essential collaborative and thinking skills (e.g., Socratic seminars, ThinkDots) can double as whole-class or small-group check-ins, as they provide important insights into how the class is developing. But progress monitoring must also extend to individuals if teachers are to make sure each student succeeds. Using the prompts in Figure 5.4 may help ascertain how individuals are faring in pursuit of their tasks or inquiries.

Formative Assessment at Its Best

Effective formative assessment must reveal each individual student's grasp of learning goals as well as misconceptions they may harbor. At its best, formative assessment serves as assessment *for* learning (Earl, 2003; Stiggins & Chappuis, 2011) rather than assessment *of* learning. It is not used to grade performance, but to inform and guide instruction. Therefore, at its best, formative assessment is aligned with key learning goals and scattered throughout a unit or project with the goal of tracking students' grasp of small chunks of knowledge, understanding, or skills. And, at its best, formative assessment questions require students to apply or use key understanding, knowledge, or skills in some way—in essence, to provide evidence that will "convict" them of learning (Wiggins & McTighe, 2005).

Figure 5.4
Sample Prompts to Monitor Progress and Foster Investment

Where Am I?
1. What did I accomplish today? Explain and attach evidence.

  • Explanation:

  • Attached evidence:

2. What do I still have to do to meet the task goals?

3. What are my next steps? What's my plan of attack for tomorrow? The next day?

Where Were You?
1. Check the learning station(s) you visited today.
   ____ Station 1
   ____ Station 2
   ____ Station 3
   ____ Station 4

2. Did the task at the station help your learning? Why or why not? (Be specific!)

This Just In!
1. Restate the most interesting thing you've learned this week as either a news headline or a billboard sign.

2. What made this interesting to you? Explain.

How Will You Learn Best?
As we continue our lesson, would you rather learn about _____ by
• Watching _____?
• Reading _____?
• Listening to _____?

Source: From *Differentiation in the Elementary Grades: Strategies to Engage and Equip All Learners* (pp. 187–188), by K. J. Doubet and J. A. Hockett, 2017, Alexandria, VA: ASCD. Copyright 2018 by ASCD. Adapted with permission.

Frequency and Types of Formative Assessment

Many teachers ask us how often they should use formative assessment. Should it be every day? Every week? How much is enough? Too much? A good rule of thumb is that formative assessment should be used regularly enough for (1) students to be accustomed to its purpose and classroom use and (2) teachers to be able to use the information to guide their instruction. In other words, if you don't plan to examine and use the results, don't give the formative assessment. Using too much formative assessment can cause teachers to feel buried in piles of exit slips or other evidence, and students may see it as a meaningless exercise without purpose. On the other hand, not using enough creates conditions in which large learning gaps can form without the teacher's (or the student's) knowledge. Used properly, formative assessment provides teachers with the fuel to plan informed, targeted lessons and interventions and gives students a sense of both accountability and support when they see that their responses are being used to help them grow.

Formative assessment may be productively used after a lesson (or minilesson) in the following circumstances:

- To monitor progress with a key skill
- After an important learning experience (interview, guest speaker, field trip)
- After individuals or small groups have worked autonomously for a length of time
- Before moving to a new topic or skill (to make sure students are ready for the transition)

Let's return to the driving questions used for unit launches presented earlier in the chapter (see Figure 5.2) to see where and how formative assessment can be used to gauge student learning and growth. Each of these units should be punctuated by formative assessment to gauge student growth. Figure 5.5 presents sample formative assessment prompts around important learning goals in relationship to the purposes outlined in the bulleted list above.

Each formative assessment prompt featured in Figure 5.5 moves beyond checking for student compliance or memorization. Each requires students to apply what they've learned in context; in other words, each prompt is structured so that students can provide evidence that will let teachers know if they are "getting it" and determine the feedback students will need to grow.

Figure 5.5
Sample Prompts to Gauge Students' Grasp of Learning Goals

Driving Question	Sample Formative Assessment Prompt	Purpose/Use
How can art exert influence?	• Make one claim about why your artist is influential. • Provide two pieces of evidence to support your claim. Be sure to cite sources properly.	Used to check understanding following a minilesson on using evidence to support a claim.
How can professional sports teams allocate their resources to improve their records?	Data have been collected on the number of years NBA players have played and the salaries they have received. Examine the following linear model that presents a summary of the data, where t is the number of years played and d is the salary in dollars. Then answer the following questions: • What is the equation for the model? • What is the slope? • What is the intercept? • Make one prediction based on the graph.	Used as a check for students' grasp of a key unit skill: *Interpret the slope of a linear regression function in context.*
How can we design a memorial to honor our community's veterans from the U.S. wars in Iraq and Afghanistan?	Defend and destroy the following claim using evidence from the primary sources you studied today: "The Iraq War was winnable."(Adapted from Doubet & Hockett, 2015, p. 165)	Used after students have worked in small groups to conduct research on primary sources curated by the Carnegie Council.
What factors affect erosion? How does erosion affect ecosystems?	• List three criteria the World Wildlife Fund (WWF) considers when deciding to intervene in an ecosystem. • Describe two sites that have met these criteria. • List one thing you hope I will clarify tomorrow.	Used following a presentation, via video chat, by a guest from the WWF.
Should some books be censored?	• One misunderstanding someone might have about censorship and free speech is _____. • Here's what I might say to help someone better understand the issue. (Adapted from Doubet & Hockett, 2015, p. 165)	Used as a misconception check to determine student readiness to move on to next lesson.

Assessment Response: Providing Targeted Feedback to Individuals and Groups

In Hattie's (2012) meta-analysis of the effects of instructional interventions, *feedback* was included as one of the practices with the most influence on student learning. The most effective feedback provides guidance for each student that is "'just in time,' 'just for me,' 'just for where I am in my learning process,' and 'just what I need to help me move forward'" (Hattie, 2012, p. 122). Giving instructional feedback, then, is the process by which we use what we know about a student's learning (gleaned from formative assessment) to move that student forward.

Qualities of Effective Feedback

As Wiliam (2011) and Wiggins (2012) point out, feedback is not about value judgments or praise; rather, it focuses on providing targeted information that will help students reach established goals. According to various sources (Fisher & Frey, 2009; Hattie, 2012; Wiggins, 2012; Wiliam, 2012), the most effective feedback has the following characteristics:

- Specific and descriptive
- Goal specific (not personal)
- User friendly (understandable to the receiver)
- Guided by clear criteria
- Timely (based on recent evidence)
- Actionable

As this list implies, feedback is an exchange between the teacher and the learner—or between peers. It can be delivered in written or oral form (e.g., conferencing) and can be directed to individuals or to small groups of students who require the same type of feedback (more about this in Chapter 6). Although the qualities of effective feedback remain the same regardless of grade level or subject matter, the nature of it (e.g., level of vocabulary, number of facets, mode of delivery) may change to suit learner needs. Figure 5.6 provides examples of teacher feedback that adheres to the bulleted list of characteristics.

This kind of feedback, delivered at key points throughout the investigation or unit, will help students stay on track and continue to improve. The practice of frequent monitoring and feedback catches gaps in performance and nips misconceptions in the bud (shown in the math and social studies examples in

Figure 5.6
Examples of Effective Feedback

Content Area	Feedback Example
Math	You have properly distributed the term with the variable and even properly distributed the term with the negative sign, but you made a mistake when distributing the x. What should happen when you multiply $3x$ by $2x$?
Science	You accurately captured the differences between positive and negative feedback in a system. Because this is a confusing concept, please add at least one example of each to make the distinction clear.
English/ Language Arts	Good character descriptions reveal how a character reacts to people and situations *and* how other characters react to her. I see clear examples of your main character reacting to other people and situations. Can you add a few examples of characters reacting to her?
Social Studies	Your blog post is informative. You have clearly described the common characteristics and roles of special interest groups in a democracy. Now, help your readers understand the concerns some people have about how interest groups might undermine democracy. Be sure to highlight examples of important regulations.

Figure 5.6). Further, it provides all students with a next step (as in the science and ELA examples in the same figure), even if they've completed work in a technically correct fashion. This kind of teacher feedback reinforces the growth mindset and propels *all* students forward.

Peer Feedback

When students work as part of a collaborative team, they must be willing and able to provide support and guidance to one another. Students in performance- and project-based classes, then, must become adept as peer reviewers. As students work to fine-tune performance tasks and project presentations, they will need to provide each other with feedback. To do so, they need guidance on how to give—and receive—feedback in ways that lead to improvement. Peer feedback is enhanced when students (1) understand the purpose of constructive feedback; (2) base their feedback on established criteria, through rubrics and models; and (3) follow an established protocol for giving and receiving feedback.

Understanding the purpose of constructive feedback

Practically everything is reviewed online in both formal and informal ways, with valid and invalid claims, and in both respectful and (more commonly) disrespectful fashions. Together, teachers and students can explore and evaluate feedback on a variety of online forums (e.g., YouTube, blog posts, news stories, music/movie sites), gathering a collection of examples and nonexamples of effective reviews. Using these for guidance, students can create their own responses with the goal of emulating constructive responses and eliminating unhelpful or hurtful comments.

Younger students might benefit from a more concrete approach, such as a sorting activity to illustrate the difference between appropriate and inappropriate comments. In one such approach, the teacher distributes small bags containing slips of paper printed with online comments of varying degrees of positivity (e.g., "I'm not sure I agree," "That's a silly thing to say," and "You're a moron"). In small groups, students sort these into categories, name the categories, and share with the class to help them distinguish helpful from unproductive comments (Carbaugh & Doubet, 2016).

Using rubrics and models

As discussed in Chapter 4, a well-designed rubric given to students before an assessment can provide support during both peer and self-evaluation. To be sufficient, however, the meaning of each criterion and descriptor must be clear to students. Phrases on the rubric such as "logically organized," "insightful interpretation," and "sufficient evidence" may have little meaning for inexperienced students. Before asking students to use rubrics to provide peer feedback, share examples of what would constitute a high-quality performance. Supplementing rubrics with models showing a range of products (excellent, good, fair, and poor) helps students better understand the performance levels of a rubric. Teachers can then use modeling or role-play to illustrate how to review draft work against the rubric criteria in order to provide specific, actionable, and constructive feedback.

Following a protocol for giving and receiving feedback

Based on a discussion technique developed by Himmele and Himmele (2011), Debate Team Carousel provides an effective protocol for peer evaluation and requires students to provide both praise and constructive criticism about a draft product in a specific, actionable fashion. Sitting in groups of five or six, each group member receives a full-page, four-square peer review protocol such as the one shown in Figure 5.7.

The students attach the protocol to their draft and pass the work to the classmate on the left to begin the carousel, which proceeds as follows (adapted from Doubet & Hockett, 2015 & 2017a):

1. Students review the rubric criteria associated with the task or project.
2. Students carefully study their peer's draft in relationship to the rubric criteria. In box 1 of the protocol, students respond to the prompt, supporting their assertion with both reasoning *and* evidence from their classmate's work and language from the rubric. They initial their comments in the box they just completed, then pass both their classmate's draft and the protocol (with box 1 completed) to the group member on their left.
3. Students study the new draft they have received, as well as their peer's response on line 1, before answering the prompt in box 2 (again using reasoning and evidence). They then pass the draft and protocol to the group member on their left.
4. Students repeat step 2 for boxes 3 and 4.
5. Students return the papers to their original owners and read their classmates' responses to their work. They ask for clarification if necessary, and they begin revising their drafts according to the feedback they've received.

Figure 5.7
Debate Team Carousel Protocol for Peer Feedback

Box 1	**Box 2**
The biggest strength of this draft is _____ , because _____ .	Other strengths include: _____ _____
Box 3	**Box 4**
Some small changes that could make a big difference include: _____	The change that could make the biggest improvement might be _____ because _____ .

Paired with the discussion frames presented in Chapter 7 (see Figure 7.3, p. 149), this protocol sets the expectation that there are always next steps we can take to make our work stronger.

Minitasks: Incorporating Opportunities for Scrimmage

Used regularly, formative assessment and feedback are keys to student success in any classroom. In a performance-based classroom, however, an additional practice component is necessary to support student success: the scrimmage. Recall our definition of *scrimmage* is "a practice game." If the game is the final performance or presentation, then students must have opportunities to approximate part or all of that performance or presentation. Those approximations should (1) have lower stakes than the game itself, (2) provide opportunities for the "coach" to provide more nuanced feedback, and (3) mirror the authenticity of the game. Students scrimmage when they complete miniversions of the final task, engage in smaller performances that target key skills, and conduct dry runs of the performance or presentation. Let's examine some content-specific examples.

Content-Specific Examples

Athletes may scrimmage for a quarter rather than for an entire game just as actors may concentrate on one scene in a rehearsal. Likewise, as students work toward completing a major performance or project, they can complete several smaller versions of the task as a way to approximate the final performance. These minitasks may consist of short research projects or mini-investigations on topics of high interest to students. Students can engage with all the steps of the design or research process in a timely manner if they are focused on a discreet topic. Here are some examples of mini-investigations and projects:

- To introduce his 4th graders to the design process, Mr. Parker grouped them according to their favorite fast-food restaurant and charged them with designing a new advertisement for one of its products. He introduced the steps of the design process one at a time—*define the problem, collect information, brainstorm and analyze ideas, develop solutions or build a model, present idea and get feedback, improve the design*—and gave students time to work on each. After students presented their ads, Mr. Parker reviewed the design process itself. Students made posters clarifying each step; these were hung around the room to serve as supports as students engaged in their actual (more lengthy, authentic, and rigorous) design challenge around the driving question, "How can we transform the display case in our school into a celebration of civil rights heroes?"

- Students in Ms. Buquoi's 1st grade class were charged with creating a persuasive presentation to deliver to the manager of their local pet store in an effort to convince him to donate an animal to be their class pet. Before creating their presentations for the manager, the students explored the elements of effective persuasion in minilessons and created smaller practice presentations for their friends and family on topics of their choice. These practice presentations allowed students to experiment with persuasive techniques in low-stakes situations before using them in their presentations to the store manager. (See the video at https://www.you tube.com/watch?v=fsJXcaF6vHo.)

- For their 11th grade project around the driving question "Should books be censored?" (see the "Taking a Position on an Issue" component, p. 103, in Figure 5.2), students in Ms. Robertson's class read various books that have been censored and conduct research on censorship laws and court decisions. For the production phase, they were to create infographics summarizing the issue for the public and write letters to the National School Board Association expressing their views (Larmer et al., 2015). To prepare students for the production phase while encouraging text analysis, Ms. Robertson had students practice making mini-infographics using Canva.com, a graphic-design tool website. Students chose a "process" infographic template and used it to chart the evolution of a character from one of the books they were reading. This exercise gave them (1) experience with the software and (2) a chance to demonstrate their understanding of character development.

- High school pre-calculus teachers designed a simulated performance task around the idea of disaster mission relief. In the final performance, teams of three or four students acted as air traffic controllers (housed in classrooms) and pilots (in the gym). Using a video chat application, the air traffic controllers gave pilots the polar coordinates to help them navigate toward a location to save citizens from a disaster. In the final performance, students had to navigate to four different disaster sites, choosing from all available formulas to do so. (See https://www.edutopia.org /video/performance-based-assessment-making-math-relevant.) As a dry run, students worked with a partner to produce and interpret *one* set of written directions for a *single* navigation completed in the hallway. Practicing the skill in a simpler context gave students a preview of the kind of computational and communication skills they would need to perform successfully on the final task.

Targeting Key Skills

In a scrimmage, a coach may focus on running specific plays rather than incorporating all of them. So it is in performance-based classrooms. Sometimes a teacher needs students to exercise key skills in context before they are ready to transfer those skills to the final product or performance. For example, students can have the opportunity to analyze and interpret data sets in groups before they attempt to analyze and interpret the data they have collected on their own. Likewise, full-class validity checks of online sources could precede the research phase of a project. Students could practice investigations of sources (much like those conducted by the website Snopes.com) and debrief their process and findings together to set the expectation—and build the skills—to evaluate the credibility of the sources they employ in their own research projects. Here are some other examples:

- For one of their projects, students in Ms. Dawson's 6th grade class were exploring the driving question "How does rainfall affect soil on slopes?" (See Appendix L for a more thorough description of this project and Figure 5.2 for its launch.) As part of this investigation, students would conduct virtual interviews with members of the World Wildlife Fund about the effects of soil erosion in different parts of the world. Ms. Dawson knew her students needed to become skilled in crafting and posing interview questions, so she required them to conduct several mock interviews—face-to-face interactions with peers and virtually with others in the school—for which they were responsible for writing the interview questions. After each mock interview, the class would debrief about which questions teased out information effectively and which did not. They searched for common patterns and made a list of criteria to drive the creation of questions for the experts they would interview. This targeted rehearsal led to more effective interviews during the performance.
- Students in Mr. Gregory's 10th grade history class were researching the U.S. wars in Iraq and Afghanistan as part of their design challenge to build a community memorial for war veterans (see the list of pre-assessment

questions in Figure 5.1 and the "Meeting a Design Challenge" component in Figure 5.2). Because these two wars could be controversial topics, Mr. Gregory wanted his students to become skilled in the art of civil discourse; so he took several opportunities to engage his students in structured arguments using both claim and counterclaim. He used the Debate Team Carousel protocol similar to the one depicted in Figure 5.7 to evaluate the strength of arguments (rather than drafts) and Structured Academic Controversy to examine all sides of central issues (for more on Structured Academic Controversy, see http://teachinghistory.org /teaching-materials/teaching-guides/21731). Because they practiced the art of diplomatic argument in contained settings, Mr. Gregory's students were able to use it fluidly when engaging in authentic conversations with both peers and experts.

- Ms. Harris's 8th grade students spent the entire school year curating their own personal young adult book collections (with summaries and recommendations) on the website Goodreads.com. They created several digital "bookshelves" for different genres and added texts to those shelves throughout the year. Because this cumulative task required students to write a *review* of each text, Ms. Harris began the year by exploring the hallmarks of effective reviews. She used a strategy originated by Kelly Gallagher (2011) to provide students the opportunity to practice the skills of review in a high-interest/low-stakes setting: Students chose a product that they were excited about *or* a product they were interested in purchasing. They looked up the item on Amazon.com (or another website) and read the product's reviews. After surveying the reviews, students chose the three most "helpful" ones and made notes about why they were helpful. They also chose the worst reviews and made notes about why they were *not* helpful. After this independent portion of the investigation, students shared their findings, and the class made a list of criteria for a helpful review. Each student then wrote a product review, posted it on an online bulletin board using the application Padlet, and partnered up for a peer review using the class-generated list as a set of guidelines. They also received feedback from Ms. Harris (on Padlet) and had to receive her approval before posting the review to the actual product website. The list of review criteria and the models explored through this scrimmage activity supported students throughout the year as they wrote reviews on their young adult book choices. Because students finished their texts at different rates, Ms. Harris needed them to be able to review and post independently; this scrimmage set them up to do so.

Each scrimmage example presented in this chapter reflects a relevant, real-world scenario, designed to give learners a sense of purpose. Engaging in these minitasks exercised both disciplinary and 21st century skills while providing students with practice opportunities. Teachers used these scrimmages to gather formative assessment data and provide targeted feedback to prepare students to effectively tackle the summative task or project. The "Planning for Instruction" portion of the planning tool in Appendix B prompts teachers to proactively consider opportunities for assessment, practice, and scrimmage within their own performance-based units of study.

Shaping Instruction as the Unit Concludes

Returning to our athletic metaphor, good coaches consider the culminating performance—the game or the meet—as a learning opportunity in itself. It is like a summative assessment in that it counts—scores or times are posted on a scoreboard, in the paper, and on websites. Moreover, athletic events embody authentic performance—that is, the players compete against others, and there is usually an audience (spectators) watching the performance. But effective coaches don't simply celebrate victories or lament defeats and move on. They use the game performances, win or lose, as rich learning experiences.

A teacher in a performance-based class can also treat the summative assessment—the final performance or project presentation—as a formative experience. Although a summative assessment most likely results in a grade in the gradebook, lessons learned from it can inform success in future assessments (projects or performances). Using valid, reliable rubrics (as described in Chapter 4) is part of this process. Students should know exactly why they were or were not successful on each aspect of the performance or project. Some teachers approach the evaluation of a final project or performance as a game tape—they allow students to study their feedback, make necessary revisions, and resubmit. Other teachers prefer to address any patterns of weaknesses and shortfalls in student performance through targeted instruction in the future.

Although individual teachers can use authentic tasks and projects to benefit their own students, having a common set of performance tasks or projects opens up the potential for teachers to examine student work together through professional learning communities (PLCs). McTighe (2013) describes the benefits of such a PLC process:

When teachers meet in role-alike professional learning teams (e.g., by grade level and subject areas) to evaluate the results from assessments, they begin to identify general patterns of strengths as well as areas needing improvement. By regularly examining student work, teachers properly focus on the broader learning goals (including understanding, transfer, habits of mind), while avoiding a fixation on standardized test scores only. The regular use of such a professional learning process provides the fuel for continuous improvement while establishing a professionally enriching, results-oriented culture. (p. 5)

Finally, like a good coach, a good teacher is mindful that the game isn't everything. Accordingly, teachers in performance-based classrooms collect and report on *multiple measures* of student learning. Although we are advocates for increased use of authentic assessment tasks and projects, these do not come at the expense of more traditional assessment measures. Certainly, teachers will continue to use tests, quizzes, and skill checks to assess students' learning of basic knowledge and skills. Teachers may use a test to assess knowledge and a performance to assess key skills and understandings (Wiggins & McTighe, 2005).

Conclusion

Teachers in performance-based classrooms function like coaches in athletics. They recognize that their goal is not to simply cover the playbook, page-by-page. Instead, they focus on the game—the authentic performances that are targeted—and plan backward from them so that their learners can develop the necessary knowledge, skills, and strategies to perform successfully. Like coaches, performance-oriented teachers launch their season by setting the tone for success. They assess students at the start to determine the priorities for instruction and practice. Rather than waiting until the final game to see how their students are doing, they use ongoing formative assessments and scrimmages (e.g., minitasks) to determine the feedback students will need to improve.

Just like coaches on the field or on the court, effective teachers are also mindful that their students differ in their prior knowledge, interests, and preferred ways of learning. Accordingly, they will look for opportunities to tailor their teaching and assessment to meet the diverse needs of the students they serve. We'll dive into this topic in Chapter 6 as we explore specific ways of ensuring that every student finds a way to be successful.

6

Tailoring Tasks and Projects
for All Students

Good coaches do not treat all team members as if they were the same athlete. They recognize that each player has unique areas of strength and weakness, and they coach with the purpose of bolstering areas of strength and fortifying areas of weakness. Based on players' strengths, coaches often assign specific roles (e.g., positions in baseball) or grouping configurations (e.g., special teams in football). Based on areas that need improvement, effective coaches provide players with targeted conditioning routines, specialized drills, and even tailored sideline "conferences." Classroom teachers can apply the same approach by tailoring performance tasks and projects to learners' strengths and needs.

In this chapter we will explore various ways that teachers can ensure equity by providing the appropriate degree of challenge and instructional supports suited to the needs and talents of *all* of their students. We will use the framework of *differentiation* as a guide to tailoring performance tasks and projects, practice, scrimmage, and game-time learning experiences.

Differentiation is a systematic approach to setting up the classroom "with the goals of honoring each student's learning needs and maximizing each student's learning capacity while developing a solid community of learners" (Tomlinson, 2017). It involves tailoring instruction and materials for specific students—or groups of students—based on needs revealed by pre- and ongoing formative assessments.

Subsumed within the model of differentiation is the concept of Universal Design for Learning (UDL). Broadly speaking, UDL suggests providing the entire class with multiple ways to engage with, gain access to, and express understanding of content for the benefit of many students (http://www.udlcenter .org/aboutudl/whatisudl). Ideally, performance-based classrooms include ideas from both UDL and differentiation as means of ensuring equity of opportunity and appropriate challenge for all learners.

Tailoring the Classroom Environment

Practically speaking, teachers can efficiently address the varied needs of their students by tailoring the following aspects of the classroom environment: (1) assigning roles and groups and (2) using space strategically. Let's examine each approach.

Assigning Roles and Groups Strategically

In a performance-based classroom, teachers can assign students to groups and roles where their talents will be genuinely needed, used, and appreciated. Generally, this is feasible only after the teacher has had ample time to both formally (through pre- and formative assessment) and informally (through observations, surveys) note areas of student strength.

For example, because some performance tasks and projects involve group work, teachers can build collaborative skills by engaging students in activities that help them rehearse the skills of respectful talk, active listening, and other positive group behaviors. Teachers can tailor and assign these roles strategically so that students are supported and stretched in their various collaborative skills. They may begin by letting students try out different discussion roles or duties (such as those outlined in the next chapter, in Figure 7.1), encouraging students to experiment with each of the roles until they find a few that work best for them.

Some performance tasks and many projects require students to be self-directed. If so, teachers will need to cultivate the skills that students will need to manage the process and the resulting products. See Figure 6.1 for some examples of processing and production skills that contribute to the successful completion of performance tasks and projects.

Teachers can strategically *group* students according to their talents but also allow the students themselves to *choose the roles* that suit them best by discussing what particular strength each member brings to the table. To begin, teachers may provide a general instruction such as the following:

To complete this task, you will need to locate among yourselves one or two students matching the description of each of the following:

- Someone with strong digital skills
- Someone with strong illustrating/graphic skills

- A good organizer of time and resources
- A good communicator (in both oral and written forms)

As students discuss and assign roles, the teacher circulates, redirecting as necessary. Because both the teacher and the students need to be aware of one another's strengths, a great deal of groundwork is necessary, including culture-building strategies such as those we'll describe in Chapter 7.

Using Space Flexibly

Teachers in performance-based classrooms can arrange the physical space strategically to support a variety of student learning needs. For team collaboration, desks can be arranged in "pods" in the middle of the room, with resource centers located around the perimeter, along with quiet spaces where individuals can complete independent work. It's also a good idea to make sure that the pods can be rearranged if students need to regroup for other purposes (such as review, remediation, and expert and interest groups) and desks can be moved back into full-class formation—rows—for direct teaching, quizzing, and certain other activities. Whatever the room arrangement, the placement must fit the purpose. Teachers can set up learning stations to help accomplish that goal.

Figure 6.1
Student Process and Performance Skills

Process Skills
- Managing time
- Locating and accessing resources
- Storing and organizing resources
- Accessing, using, and troubleshooting research technology (digital skills)
- Extracting important ideas; summarizing
- Motivating people
- Resolving conflicts

Performance and Production Skills
- Organizing ideas
- Communicating via writing
- Communicating orally
- Communicating through multimedia
- Accessing, using, and troubleshooting production technology (digital skills)
- Illustrating (graphic skills)
- Designing/building/assembling

Learning stations offer a practical and efficient means of "delivering" differentiation. Teachers can design learning stations dedicated to supporting the various skills required by different aspects of tasks and projects, with stations in designated areas and available for a short time or for the duration of the task or project. Students can move to stations within their project groups or according to academic need (as demonstrated on a formative assessment).

For example, a class working on a project exploring the driving question "How healthy are the 'healthy' menu options offered at fast-food restaurants?" may need stations dedicated to the following skills: locating reliable and pertinent resources, analyzing nutrition reports, constructing effective interview questions, designing effective infographics, and writing various kinds of letters. At each of these stations, students may find research materials, recorded instructional modules, exemplar products, or important devices, sites, and apps. Although students will most likely visit all stations initially, they can revisit any particular station throughout the course of the project as needed—for example, when stuck or to receive additional guidance.

Learning stations also provide a practical approach for delivering differentiated practice and feedback. Once students are accustomed to moving among—and focusing while working in—learning stations, the teacher can specialize the content and materials located at each station to meet specific learning needs. Returning to the "healthy menu" task, assessment or observation may reveal that some students still struggle to articulate open-ended interview questions, whereas others missed important information in the nutrition reports. In response, the teacher could bookmark a YouTube video for students to view before revising their questions (e.g., https://www.youtube.com/watch?v=G pDRj5TgSh8) at one station while providing highlighted nutrition reports and guiding questions at another. Alternately (or additionally), the teacher may choose to run a teacher-led station; although all students may be asked to visit that station, the teacher can differentiate the instruction given to different groups based on needs revealed by assessment, observation, or student questions.

Differentiating Tasks and Projects

Several variables, including some discussed in Chapter 3, provide excellent opportunities to adjust tasks and projects. Student choice is one such variable. Others, related to student readiness, include access to resources, kinds of resources, scaffolding, feedback, and challenge opportunities. Let's examine how each of these can be used to tailor tasks and projects so that they provide appropriate levels of accessibility and challenge for the wide array of learners.

Differentiating According to Student Choice

Few things motivate learners of all ages more than choice, especially when their choices are linked to their interests. To foster investment from the entire class, teachers can construct tasks and projects that allow for student choice, based on two kinds of interests: *personal* and *situational* (Schraw, Flowerday, & Lehman, 2001). Personal interests are those students bring with them to the classroom (we will discuss these in the "Personalizing Choice" section later in this chapter). Situational interests are those that arise from a situation, such as a teacher-designed lesson or task. To facilitate student engagement and connection with tasks and projects, teachers should strive to design tasks around areas known to be of interest to students. For example, video games capture the time, attention, and imagination of many of today's learners. However, although video games may spark the interest of *most* students, they won't necessarily appeal to *all* students. Designing a task so that students can focus on video games *or* team sports *or* individual competitive sports (e.g., running, skating, tennis) gives the teacher a better chance of connecting with all students than does focusing solely on the popular yet narrower topic of video games.

Varying the degree of choice

Larmer and his colleagues (2015) suggest four options when considering various degrees of choice to offer students within a task or project. The options relate to product and content-area focus and are explained in Figure 6.2.

As the number of choice points increases, so does the required level of students' autonomy in directing their own work. We encourage teachers who are just beginning to experiment with providing task options to start by offering one choice point for students per task (as illustrated in Options 2 or 3). As students (and the teacher) become more comfortable with the freedom that accompanies choice, the number of choice points per assignment or task can increase (as illustrated in Option 4), or the complexity of choices can change.

Offering multifaceted choice

By manipulating several variables of task design, teachers can construct tasks and projects that vary in more complex, less predictable ways. The GRASPS format presented in Chapter 2 offers various possibilities for student choices: the *roles*, the *audiences*, the *situation* (context), and the *products* and

Figure 6.2
Providing Students with Choice

The tasks in the first option are standardized and do not offer opportunities for choice.

Option 1—Same product, same focus
- Create a presentation on water quality in our region. Include a comparison to a nearby region.
- Construct a series of social media posts explaining the lessons Greg learns in *Diary of a Wimpy Kid.*
- Compose an editorial on the efficacy of the electoral college in democratically electing the president of the United States. Be sure to include support for your argument.
- Create a budget proposal (using assigned format) for the yearly operating costs of a new teen center in our town.

The tasks in Option 2 and Option 3 provide students with one opportunity for choice—either product or focus.

Option 2—Different product, same focus
- Create a presentation or photo essay on water quality in our region and how it compares to a nearby region.
- Construct a series of social media posts or YouTube video confessionals explaining the lessons Greg learns in *Diary of a Wimpy Kid.*
- Compose an editorial or record a public service announcement on the efficacy of the electoral college in democratically electing the president of the United States. Be sure to include support for your argument.
- Create a budget proposal (choose from several format options) for the yearly operating costs of a new teen center in our town.

Option 3—Same product, different focus
- Create a presentation on water quality in two different parts of our region (your choice). Compare these to the quality of a nearby region.
- Construct a series of social media posts explaining the lessons learned by the protagonist in a story of your choice.
- Compose an editorial—with support—on the efficacy of a specific aspect of federal elections in democratically electing the president of the United States (e.g., electoral college, nominating conventions, primaries and caucuses, campaign finance laws).
- Create a budget proposal (assigned format) for the yearly operating costs of a new teen center or a new community park in our city.

The tasks in the fourth option present two opportunities for students to make choices.

Option 4—Different product, different focus
- Create a presentation or photo essay on water quality in various parts of our region and how it compares to a nearby region.
- Construct a series of social media posts or YouTube video confessionals explaining lessons learned by the protagonist in a story of your choice.
- Compose an editorial or record a public service announcement on the efficacy of a specific aspect of federal elections in democratically electing the president of the United States (e.g., electoral college, nominating conventions, primaries and caucuses, campaign finance laws). Be sure to include support for your argument.
- Create a budget proposal (choose from several format options) for the yearly operating costs of a new teen center or a new community park in our city.

performances. Teachers can use this framework to design—or to help students design—tasks that differ from one another in various ways.

For example, Ms. Keener wanted to provide her high school students with choices in the performance component of her summative assessment on domain and range (see Figure 6.3). She provided several options for roles, audiences, and situations. No matter which options students selected, they were required to complete the same operations and calculations and to produce the same type of product. In addition, she structured the tasks so that student work could be evaluated with the same rubric.

Choices can contain even more facets. In the math example in Figure 6.3, the product was kept consistent. In the secondary ELA example in Figure 6.4, the teacher has constructed three options (shown across the rows in the figure), each featuring a different role, audience, situation, *and* product; still, all three options will lead students to demonstrate the same transfer goal.

Figure 6.3
Math Performance Task Options

Transfer Goal: Interpret data to make decisions regarding efficiency.		
Option 1	**Option 2**	**Option 3**
Role: Entrepreneurs of a private lawn-mowing business, Math Mowers, Inc.	**Role:** Hungry high school students	**Role:** Football team captains
Audience: Customers of Math Mowers, Inc.	**Audience:** Yourself (and your wallet)	**Audience:** Your teammates
Situation: You seek to understand the logistics of the business to better serve your customers.	**Situation:** You are trying to determine which pizza coupon will give you the best price for a two-topping pizza.	**Situation:** You have been tasked with determining which play will gain you the highest number of yards.
Product: Report your findings in a report to your stakeholders. You must include your calculations for the following work: Plot functions P(t) and R(t) on a graph and find the x- and y-intercepts, and the domain and range of both functions. Then interpret what the x- and y-intercepts reveal in relation to the given functions P(t) and R(t). Use that graphical representation to evaluate the best option. Finally, given the graph of a discontinuous floor function, find the x- and y-intercepts, and the domain and range of this function to interpret what the x- and y-intercepts reveal in relation to the given function.		

Source: Adapted from Hannah Keener. Used with permission.

Figure 6.4
Multifaceted Task Options for Secondary English/Language Arts

Transfer Goal: Select and manipulate language to craft powerful messages that bring about changes in readers' impressions, perspectives, beliefs, or actions.			
Role	**Audience**	**Situation**	**Product/Performance**
Storyteller	Listeners of *The Moth*—a podcast featuring amateur storytellers sharing significant life events	You have been selected to share your "pivotal moment" story on *The Moth* podcast.	A podcast (recorded story with script) of a pivotal moment in your life
Author	Members of the Scholastic Art & Writing Awards committee for the new edition of *The Best Teen Writing*	The theme of this year's edition is "The Power of Words."	Story or essay adhering to *The Best Teen Writing's* publishing guidelines
Journalist	Selection committee for new articles at Commonlit.org, which is soliciting student-created informational texts	Commonlit.org has put out a call for the student perspective on what leads to happiness (to add a new theme to those we studied in class).	An original piece—with supporting evidence—on what actually can "buy" or give us happiness

Note: See Scholastic Art & Writing Awards website for more information. An anthology of *The Best Teen Writing* is published each year. See more at www.artandwriting.org/Publications.

When constructing complex task options such as these, teachers must work proactively to ensure both engagement and alignment. In both examples, teachers used authenticity to foster *engagement*. The authenticity in Figure 6.3 stems from the teacher's focus on making sure each option featured situations students might encounter in their everyday lives. The authenticity of the tasks in Figure 6.4 flows from their real-world contexts (although the "journalist" option includes a manufactured scenario, students must still examine a real website and emulate the work of experts). The teachers ensured the *alignment* of the three tasks by designing them to link directly to an identified transfer goal. Alignment is further achieved by using the same rubric to evaluate student work, regardless of the option chosen (see Appendixes J and K for these rubrics as well as more detailed task instructions). Using the same rubric is a good rule of thumb any time choice is built into a task or project. (Chapter 4 provides practical guidance on how to focus evaluation tools on learning goals rather than only on product features so that a single rubric can be used to evaluate student work on several task options.)

Personalizing choice

Although the options in Figures 6.3 and 6.4 offer students many choices, they are still designed by the teacher; thus, they may not necessarily appeal to the personal interests of every student. As stated earlier, *personal interests* are those that students bring with them to the classroom. They are typically unique because students tend to "own" their personal interests and develop them over time (Sousa & Tomlinson, 2018). Examples of personal interests include specific animals, particular video games, certain music groups, or distinct hobbies. We have taught students obsessed with the water strider (a kind of insect), fruit stickers (showing where the fruit originated), puppetry, ham radios, and movie-set design! It's difficult to design tasks that spotlight such divergent interests while including everyone else in the class; however, we can empower students to *create their own* personalized tasks or passion projects.

One way to support such personalization is through task frames, or templates, which provide a basic structure to guide the design of performance tasks around anchor standards and other priority learning goals. (See Chapter 8 for more on task frames.) Although they are designed as tools for *teachers* who are constructing tasks, they can also help *students* design their own avenues of inquiry. For example, the following informational or explanatory task template could be used to help students with unusual interests—along with the rest of the class—develop projects that propel them to further explore the topics that fascinate them already:

> Consider your chosen topic as a system. *How do the parts of your system work together?* After reading _____ (literature or informational texts on your topic), create a/an _____ (essay, article, or website) that defines and explains *how interdependence works in your chosen system.* Support your discussion with evidence from the text(s). What conclusions or implications can you draw?

Such self-directed inquiry tasks harness personal interests in a powerful way. Because of their cocreated nature (teacher-constructed frame with student customization), these tasks can be classified as "personalized learning" (Zmuda & Kallick, 2017). Although the curricular goals remain the same for all learners, students have a say in determining how they will arrive at those learning goals and how they will demonstrate their learning. As they seek the insight of experts and make decisions about how to pursue their goals, they both develop and exercise their voice. Such self-discovery encourages deeper learning, because students' brains engage and stay focused when they are pursuing a challenge with personal relevance (Sousa & Tomlinson, 2018).

Differentiating According to Student Readiness

The more invested students are in their assignments and projects, the more likely they are to persevere in the face of difficulty. Still, there will be times when some students get stuck and need additional help, while others pursue avenues that lead to more questions and thus need additional challenge. When students display differing levels of readiness for completing a task, teachers can respond by providing varying levels of resources, scaffolding, or feedback.

Differentiating access to resources

Some performance tasks and projects involve research, requiring students to locate, critically appraise, and synthesize information from multiple sources. Teachers can intervene in several ways to support students who become stuck in this research process. When the focus is on students *gleaning* important information from sources rather than on *finding* those sources, teachers can streamline the process by gathering pertinent texts and other resources in advance. These readings and reports can be stored in the school's learning management system (LMS) folders, classroom computers, or physical file folders. Students will still need to peruse the gathered texts for those that are most helpful, but they won't have to spend hours sorting through the infinite resources that are available from a simple online search.

Differentiating literacy resources

Most performance tasks and projects require reading, and some involve research as a central component. If students have a reading disability, struggle with attention issues, or are learning English as a second (or third, or fourth) language, they are likely to struggle with reading- and research-based tasks and projects. Fortunately, teachers can use a variety of practical and proven strategies, tools, and resources to support struggling readers, including the following:

- *Simplifying reading levels*—Simply curating a collection of texts will not be enough for many students. To provide additional support, teachers may need to simplify the language of the text so that students are able to process what they are reading. Note that Rewordify.com is a handy tool for this; see the description in Figure 6.5.

- *Highlighting text*—By choosing and highlighting approximately 15 percent of an article, a report, or a book chapter, teachers can help students work through the fluff and focus on the important portions of a text. Highlighted portions can include critical passages, key quotes or statistics, and important graphics. It might take a struggling reader as much time to process the highlighted text as it would take a fluent reader to digest an entire text. The highlighting gives students with reading disorders and students learning English a fighting chance to glean important material, and it helps students with attention issues focus as they read (Tomlinson, 2005).

- *Accessing web-based resources*—Many online resources and apps can support students at varying reading levels. Figure 6.5 features tools that can help make text accessible to a wide range of learners.

- *Adjusting the delivery mode*—Teachers can support students with reading and language difficulties by delivering texts via audio. Teachers can record themselves reading stories, key passages, directions, and other materials. Even more handy are the free apps from Apple, Google, and other providers that translate text to speech. Using the speech function in combination with the text can help students increase their reading fluency.

- *Challenging expert readers*—Students who can quickly and easily comprehend grade-level material are ready for texts that are more complex. Consider pulling and linking or bookmarking expert-level texts from professional organizations, universities, and other sources to expose strong readers to texts that will keep them on their toes.

Differentiating content-based resources

If teachers set the stage for students to access resources through stations or other classroom routines (see "Tailoring the Classroom Environment" earlier in this chapter), then they should be able to use those same structures to seamlessly provide these differentiated resources to students at all readiness levels.

After a formative assessment administered midway through project completion, Mr. Daniels realized that his 4th graders were in different places in their grasp of angles and lines in two-dimensional figures. The next day, he placed students in trios or quads according to readiness and provided them with one of the following tasks:

> Task 1. Students with a solid grasp of the learning goals were asked to visit the following site: https://www.khanacademy.org/math/cc-fourth-grade -math/cc-4th-geometry-topic/4th-decomposing-angles/v/decomposing

Figure 6.5
Websites and Apps for Differentiating Resources

Website/App	Description
Google Translate	Used properly, this tool is not a cheat for students who are learning English; it can serve as a scaffold that actually supports language learning (Ferlazzo, 2017). Students who are learning English can use the translate function as an efficient dictionary to help them quickly understand key terms in their reading; this helps them to process and use that information as they explore meaningful essential or driving questions.
Rewordify.com	This site allows the user to simplify the text of a difficult website, article, or report. Simply paste the text into the highlighted box and hit the "rewordify text" button, and the site simplifies the language (e.g., vocabulary, sentence structure).
Newsela.com	This unique site presents free current events articles on many academic and high-interest topics including science, social studies, arts, and sports. Each article is offered at five different reading levels (and some in Spanish) so that teachers can assign the level that best suits each student. A for-purchase version is also available and offers options including varied levels of primary sources, reference texts, and paired texts with opposing viewpoints.
Booksthatgrow.com	Like Newsela, this site provides varied reading levels of the same text, but it offers additional scaffolding such as read-aloud and highlighting functions. One advantage of this site is that it features well-known texts such as Poe's "The Tell Tale Heart" and James Madison's *Federalist Paper #10*. It offers a wide variety of genre choices (fiction, nonfiction, articles, and essays) but requires a subscription.
Commonlit.org	This free site offers ever-growing collections of text sets united by *common themes*. When teachers or students choose a theme, they are presented with text sets (representing various genres and reading levels) reflecting that theme. This structure allows students to read a text on their level–and even in the genre of their choice–and use insights from that text to contribute unique ideas to shared discussions and explorations of themes (e.g., identity) and/or essential questions (e.g., "What makes you who you are?").

-angles. This video asks students to stretch their thinking by exploring lines and angles to solve for "mystery angles." After watching the video and solving for mystery angles, students were asked to develop a group response to the question "What connections can you make between this video and the work you are completing for your project? How might this change or broaden your thinking?"

Task 2. Students who needed additional support distinguishing between perpendicular, parallel, and intersecting lines were asked to watch the following video: https://www.khanacademy.org/math/basic-geo/basic-geo -angle/angles-between-lines/v/identifying-parallel-and-perpendicular -lines. This video takes a more direct and concrete approach to reviewing the concept. Students took targeted notes while viewing the video, pausing when necessary to ask questions of one another and the teacher. When they finished processing the video, they developed a group response to the question "How does this video clarify what you need to do to complete your projects?" Although Mr. Daniels used this strategy in class on this occasion, he regularly "flipped" instruction and assigned videos for students to watch to review, catch up, or receive additional support/challenge.

After students finished watching their videos and moved back into their collaborative project groups, they shared lessons learned from the two videos, solidified their action plan (checking it with Mr. Daniels first), and moved back into project work.

Ms. Forbes relied heavily on primary sources for her U.S. history investigations. Because of the depth and breadth of the collections at the Library of Congress (https://www.loc.gov), she was able to strategically assign different sources to various students as they examined events from the perspectives of those who had experienced them. For example, she could ask some students to analyze verbally complex newspaper stories from the date of a historical event (https://chroniclingamerica.loc.gov/#tab=tab_newspapers) and ask others to piece together ideas and perspectives from newspapers presenting visual portrayals of the same event (https://www.flickr.com/photos /library_of_congress/sets/72157619452486566/).

Ms. Forbes could also jigsaw perspectives by strategically assigning different primary sources chronicling or commenting on a single event or piece of legislation. When studying the Emancipation Proclamation, for example, she assigned some group members the first draft, others the final draft, others Jefferson Davis's response, and others visual depictions of the Proclamation being read (https://www.loc.gov/rr/program/bib/ourdocs/emanproc.html). Because every one of the examined sources was authentic and important, Ms. Forbes was able to ensure that each student was engaging in significant and respectful work, regardless of readiness to tackle the arcane language in some of the primary-source documents.

Differentiating the degree of scaffolding

In the building industry, *scaffolding* refers to a temporary support system that holds a structure steady while it is under construction. Likewise, in performance-based classrooms, *scaffolding* refers to the support systems we provide students as they work on their tasks or projects. As discussed in Chapter 3, there are varying levels of support that teachers can provide:

- *No scaffolding*—Present the task and provide no extra support (i.e., the students must perform the task autonomously, without teacher guidance).
- *Selected scaffolding*—Present the task and offer some support (e.g., graphic organizers, process guides, checklist of required elements).
- *Comprehensive scaffolding*—Present the task and provide extensive support as needed (e.g., step-by-step process guides, tips, more frequent and extensive feedback).

Here are some of the many available methods for supporting student success:

- *Recording video tutorials.* Using free online tools such as Zoom or Flipgrid, or using apps on tablets or laptops, teachers can record their voices (and screens) to reteach concepts and skills that formative assessment has shown to be problematic for some (or all) students. Students can replay these videos as they work through problems, construct arguments, experiment with artistic techniques, and so on. Teachers can also record directions for tasks or portions of projects so that students can access them as needed. This approach builds a sense of autonomy in students while it frees up the teacher to do other things, such as work with small groups.
- *Allowing students to record rather than write.* Often there is a disconnect between a student's *thinking* and the student's readiness for *writing* those

thoughts. This is especially true for students who are learning English, have dyslexia, or struggle to maintain attention. To capture the ideas gleaned from research (as well as other thoughts running through students' heads) and "save" them for writing, teachers may ask students to first record themselves annotating a text, explaining a process, or proving a point. They can use online tools such as Seesaw or simply use the voice-record function on their tablets. As students listen to their own recorded voices, they can capture—and even refine—their thinking as they type, write, or solve. This process highlights what students *can* do and uses it to help them accomplish what they perceive they *cannot* do. Along the way, it builds both confidence and capacity.

- *Providing graphic organizers or process logs.* Graphic organizers can support students' thinking and progress as they research, plan, solve, and write. Teachers can create their own organizers or choose from the vast selection of ready-made organizers available online (for starters, try https://www.teachervision.com/lesson-planning/graphic-organizer and https://www.greatschoolspartnership.org/wp-content/uploads/2016/11/25QuickFormativeAssessments.pdf). They can also create two different versions of an organizer so that one version, providing a high level of support, *directs* students' progress (e.g., outlines steps, provides guidelines), whereas the other version, providing a relatively low level of support, *captures* student progress (e.g., records steps and reflections). Figure 6.6 (p. 135) provides an example of a graphic organizer in the form of differentiated process logs for a unit in human geography.

- *Varying the specificity of directions.* Some students will be ready to embark upon a task or project with little extra guidance or direction; they relish the freedom and are stretched when asked to embrace it. Other students can become stuck when beginning their work; these students benefit from kick-starts in the form of more detailed directions and tips for success. For example, as described in Figure 4.15 (see p. 91), high school geometry teacher Jenna Guenther gave her students the challenge of constructing ADA-compliant ramps for local businesses. Although some students got to work immediately, others needed more direction, so she provided the prompts and questions shown in Figure 6.7. By providing these extended instructions only to students who needed them, Ms. Guenther was able to provide all students with the appropriate degree of support and challenge.

Figure 6.6
Examples of Differentiated Process Logs

Human Geography—Low Level of Support	
Historical Impact of Growth on • Industry • Economy • Geography • People's lives	**Potential Impact of Future Growth on** • Industry • Economy • Geography • People's lives
Human Geography—High Level of Support	

Use the unit's resources to review the **Historical Impact of Growth on**
• Industry
• Economy
• Geography
• People's lives
	Based on past changes and your calculations, predict **Potential Impact of Future Growth on**
	• Industry (Consider what businesses may benefit from the stadium and consider relocating near it)
	• Economy (Consider the effects of the influx of business on those living in the region, as well as those who engage in trade with them)
	• Geography
	  - (Consider remaining natural landmarks and how they might be affected)
	  - (Consider existing waterways, potential ways to circumvent them, and effects on surrounding area)
	• People's lives (Consider work, religion, transportation, and leisure)

Offering targeted instruction and feedback

Based on formative assessment results, teachers can provide instruction and feedback targeted to particular student needs. For example, after collecting drafts of student e-mail messages to experts on their project topics, ELA teacher Ms. Yob examined the drafts to identify patterns related to areas of strength and areas for growth. She then crafted several stations to address these patterns: one reviewing the proper format, another focusing on striking the proper tone, and another providing examples of grabbing the reader's attention. Each station would feature resources such as video-recorded tutorials, links to examples and nonexamples, and revision protocols. By assigning students to visit the station or stations that corresponded to their needs as revealed by their drafts,

Figure 6.7
Extended Directions for a High School Geometry Performance Task

Prompts and suggestions to use in providing further guidance and support for students (as needed).

Prompting questions for the information gathering phase:
• Is there something wrong with the business's "access" now? If so, what? If not, how could it be made even better?
• What information will you need from the business? What's necessary to know? What's nice to know?

Prompting questions/suggestions during the design phase:
• What's the ideal angle for a ramp? At what point does a ramp become too steep? Choose your angles carefully! If it's too steep, consider designing a two-run ramp.
• Is your design realistic? Could it be successfully implemented?
• Make a general sketch to get grasp of a big idea you have. Then, translate that sketch to graphing software to work on more precise calculations and the blueprint.

Prompting suggestions during the production of the final product:
• Blueprints and designs need to include all labels, calculations, and descriptions of what features are (i.e., label the door, the parking lot)
• Here's a potential outline for your letter: (1) a brief discussion of the importance of ADA; (2) a diagram and explanation of proposed ramps and how they comply with ADA; (3) an argument as to why the proposed ramp designs are better than the business's current access (compliance, ease of use, appearance); and (4) a brief conclusion in which you advocate for your designs and ask for a contract.

Other considerations:
• For more advanced students–Consider what materials could be used, including cost, sustainability, and appearance, and incorporate that information into your letter.
• For students who struggle with language and writing–Consider offering the opportunity to present some or all information and products verbally in an interview setting.

Ms. Yob maximized her use of time while targeting instruction to provide the best fit possible for all students.

Teachers can also use targeted small-group instruction to provide needed support or remediation. For instance, if a formative assessment reveals that only some students are making a key error, reteaching the entire class is unnecessary. Rather, as students continue work on their project or task, the teacher can pull a small group of students for a group huddle and address the error only with those students who need it. Likewise, if only some students are ready for an extension, the teacher can meet with those students and provide a probing question, an anomaly in the data, or a design glitch to stretch their thinking. In this way, all students receive the appropriate support *and* challenge.

Providing additional challenge

Performance-based classrooms offer the ideal setting for making sure all students—including high-performing students—are challenged and operating within the appropriate "zone of proximal development" (Vygotsky, 1978). When providing challenge, the goal is not to simply give students *more* work; rather, the goal is to give them *more appropriate* work. Methods for infusing challenge into a performance or project include the following:

- Moving beyond the familiar
- Considering alternate perspectives
- Increasing the level of expertise
- Including additional factors (Tomlinson, 2017)

Let's return to the task ideas featured in the list of four options in Figure 6.2, p. 125. Using each of the four ideas for infusing challenge, we can ratchet up the intellectual demand of the tasks without simply giving students more work (see Figure 6.8). In each of these instances, students are asked to complete the same basic task but with an additional level of challenge that stretches their minds rather than just their time.

Differentiation in Action—Two Snapshots

So, what does differentiation look like in practice? How can varying degrees of support and challenge be seamlessly woven into performance tasks and projects? To examine these principles in action, we'll take a look at two examples—a kindergarten unit on measurement and a high school course on human geography.

A Kindergarten Unit on Measurement Using Multidisciplinary Performance Tasks

Before revamping her measurement unit to be more performance based, Mrs. Grand thought about the ways in which she used measurement in her own life. This led her to develop the following driving question: "How can measurement help us communicate and make choices?" With that question in place, she found natural ways for students to use measurement to communicate (e.g., measuring the lengths of various animals and conducting a "meeting of scientists" to reveal their findings) and to make decisions (e.g., deciding which treat to choose by weighing several different snack options). Instead of creating one large performance task, she grouped her standards and learning goals into three smaller performance tasks, as this seemed more manageable for young learners (see Figure 6.9). Her highly participatory approach invited the active participation of all of her students, allowed her to simultaneously address math, ELA, and science standards, and presented natural points for differentiation according to both student readiness and student choice (Brighton, Moon, Jarvis, & Hockett, 2007).

For Mrs. Grand, the kind of differentiation she used was driven by the student needs she anticipated as a result of her pre-assessment (e.g., student readiness to use rulers) and through observation of student performance in a previous unit (e.g., tiered resources). In addition, the open-ended nature of the tasks allowed her the flexibility to create small groups for additional support or challenge.

Figure 6.8
Examples of Increasing Challenge

Original Task: Create a presentation on water quality in our region. Include a comparison to the water quality in a nearby region.
Type of Challenge: Moving beyond the familiar
New Task: Create a presentation on water quality in our region. *Include a comparison to a developing country.*

Original Task: Construct a series of social media posts explaining the lessons Greg learns in *Diary of a Wimpy Kid.*
Type of Challenge: Considering alternate perspectives
New Task: Construct a series of social media posts explaining the lessons Greg learns in *Diary of a Wimpy Kid. Half of your posts should feature responses from other characters evaluating whether or not Greg actually learned those lessons.*

Original Task: Compose an editorial on the efficacy of the electoral college in democratically electing the president of the United States. Be sure to include support for your argument.
Type of Challenge: Increasing the level of expertise
New Task: Compose an editorial on the efficacy of the electoral college in democratically electing the president of the United States. *Include statements from current politicians who oppose your argument and offer a logical rebuttal to their position.*

Original Task: Create a budget proposal (using assigned format) for the yearly operating costs of a new "kid center" in our town.
Type of Challenge: Including additional factors
New Task: Create a budget proposal (using assigned format) for the yearly operating costs of a new "kid center" in our town *(Note: The assigned format includes the additional component of cutting 20 percent of total costs if the budget is not approved).*

Figure 6.9
Kindergarten Performance Tasks with Differentiation

Task Focus	Performance Tasks	Differentiation
Length	**Goal:** To use measurement to compare and describe **Role:** A scientist **Audience:** Other scientists in our classroom community **Situation:** You have been studying _____ (animal's teeth, animal's feet, kinds of lizards) and have discovered that these objects are very different in length. You want to share your findings with other scientists at a conference (a meeting of scientists). **Product/Performance:** You will share your findings with all the other scientists in a "grand scientific discussion" at our conference. You will use measurement to describe the length of the items you discovered. You should also compare those lengths to other things we can recognize (e.g., a finger or a marker).	• **Readiness**—Complexity of items measured varies (e.g., collection of teeth contains samples smaller than an inch). • **Readiness**—Complexity of measurement tool varies ("teeth" scientists use actual rulers, "feet" scientists use simplified rulers without half-inch marks; "lizard" scientists use inch-worm unit blocks).
Temperature	**Goal:** To use measurement to communicate **Role:** A weather reporter **Audience:** Television news viewers **Situation:** You are giving a report on the best kind of day (temperature and clouds) to do two activities (your choice) in two different seasons (your choice). **Product/Performance:** We will record a video of you delivering a news report explaining the temperature and kind of weather that works best for two different seasonal activities (e.g., sledding and swimming). You will share pictures and key words in your news report, including the temperature in degrees (F) and as it looks on the thermometer.	• **Readiness**—Students who need extra support are given a menu of activity options for each season and associated leisure activities for that season. Resources for temperature and cloud formations are also tiered (some are more expert-like than others). • **Student Choice**—Students choose their favorite activities and associated temperature, clouds, and seasons.
Weight	**Goal:** To use measurement to make choices **Role:** You! (A hungry shopper) **Audience:** Grocery store owners **Situation:** You have been given permission to shop for your favorite snack! You can only purchase 1.5 ounces of your chosen snack (e.g., goldfish crackers, sweet cereal, gummy worms, or fruit snacks). Choose your favorite snack and draw it on your "receipt." Report to the weigh station to see how much snack you can get for 1.5 ounces. Weigh some of the other snacks to compare how much you can get for 1.5 ounces.	**Student Choice**—Students choose their snack and can choose to change their minds, if desired, or to stick to their original choice (e.g., some students would rather eat a portion of a gummy worm than a bag full of cereal).

(continued)

Figure 6.9
Continued

Task Focus	Performance Tasks	Differentiation
Weight	**Performance/Product**: Draw what you discover at the weigh station on your "receipt." Then, circle your final choice of snack (you can change your mind). Report to the register to purchase it. You will be interviewed by the store owners while you are at the register, so be ready to explain the choice you made and why you made it. They will consider your opinion when deciding how much of each snack they should order.	

Source: Adapted from Brighton, Moon, Jarvis, & Hockett, 2007. Used with permission.

A High School Course on Human Geography

Mr. Torres launched his human geography course with the following driving question: "How does where we live affect how we live, and how does how we live affect where we live"? The investigation began by focusing that question on students' personal lives and experiences but quickly expanded to the civilizations they studied as part of the course's required curriculum. With the question established, Mr. Torres was able to introduce the course's culminating performance task (Figure 6.10) in the first marking period. He encouraged students to keep this lens in mind as they progressed, often pausing for small "scrimmages" in which students examined particular aspects of a culture according to their driving question.

As the students worked, Mr. Torres was able to gauge student needs, which allowed him to provide the appropriate degree of support and challenge. For example, although he required all students to use process logs, some students' process logs contained additional scaffolds and supports, whereas others simply tracked progress (see Figure 6.6). Because he used these logs over the course of a semester, Mr. Torres was able to gradually remove the prompts and scaffolds as students neared completion of the unit. They had indeed acted as scaffolding—guiding the process until they were no longer needed.

Figure 6.10
Human Geography Performance Task with Differentiation

Task

Goal: To analyze patterns from the past in order to make inferences about the future; to demonstrate that where we live affects how we live and how we live affects where we live

Role: Urban planner

Audience: The Urban Planning Commission of _____ (major city located in one of the civilizations we've studied)

Situation: The city you have selected wants to build a multipurpose stadium, the construction of which will affect the geography of the city and surrounding area. You must (1) analyze maps and data from the past that illustrate how growth has affected the community thus far, and (2) make two recommendations about where the stadium should be constructed.

Product/Performance: The analysis and recommendations will be presented to the commission in the form of a multimedia presentation including maps you've researched that demonstrate what's happened thus far and maps you've created that illustrate how placement of this stadium will affect the geography, industry, and economy of the area *and* the lives of the people living in that community. Discuss political, economic, and other ramifications of your recommendations in light of past trends and data. Make sure you explain why the maps you've analyzed are the best indicators of future trends. Be sure to use the list of vocabulary words in an expert manner.

Differentiation

- *Interest*—Students choose the region that most intrigues them and/or students choose a different structure that is comparable in size (e.g., a concert hall).
- *Readiness*—Assign regions (or even areas of regions) according to how disruptive the introduction of the new structure would be (water supplies, mountains, existing landmarks).
- *Readiness*—Tier resources. Pull resources for all students, as conducting research isn't one of the learning goals (but analyzing sources is). Highlight key areas of sources for those who need it. Reword and record particularly dense text for students who require language support.
- *Readiness*—Scaffold the process. Give some students a process log to *plan* and *record* progress; give others a process log that *guides* their process, while calling for *all* students to reflect/revise. (See Figure 6.6.)

Conclusion

One size may not fit all when it comes to constructing performance tasks and projects. The good news is, that does not mean teachers have to design 25 (or 150) different tasks! By fashioning a flexible learning environment and building in routines for providing additional support and challenge, teachers can customize tasks in a manageable fashion so that every learner is engaged and supported. The "Planning for Differentiation" portion of Appendix B helps teachers consider—in advance—when such customization might be necessary and how it can be delivered.

For students to thrive in performance-based classrooms, however, they will need to rehearse the various routines and strategies presented in Chapters 5 and 6. For example, they will need practice moving among stations, using the technology located there, and accessing and following station directions. Such practice is paramount to student success on a performance or project; it may take time at the beginning of task launch, but that time is earned back as students collaborate effectively, access resources readily, and work efficiently. As is true of performance tasks in general, the effort is worth it.

In the next chapter, we will provide project management strategies to help teachers and students navigate the moving parts that drive performance-based classrooms. The last chapter will expand our view beyond the classroom to explore the idea of mapping an entire K–12 curriculum around authentic performance tasks and projects.

7

Collaborating to Manage Projects and Performances: A Teacher-Student Partnership

As discussed in Chapter 1, a performance-based classroom resembles the 21st century workplace, requiring skills that reflect modern learning and authentic work. Compared with students in more traditional classrooms, students in performance-based classrooms take on a more active role of "constructing meaning" and applying their learning to more authentic situations. Accordingly, the teachers' role in performance-based classrooms expands beyond a dispenser of information to a facilitator of meaning making and a coach of performance. Additionally, both teachers and students in these classrooms must take on the role of project managers to navigate the demands of authentic tasks and projects. According to the work management and collaboration platform *Wrike* (https://www.wrike.com/blog/digital-project-manager), essential skills of project managers include the following:

- Creating and communicating a project plan
- Scheduling frequent check-ins
- Assigning tasks and deadlines
- Providing status reports
- Clearing roadblocks
- Assessing and evaluating project success

Skills such as these are critical to success with complex, long-term performance tasks and projects. They are also valuable life skills that contribute to increased student autonomy. This chapter explores project manager skills in terms of the following questions that teachers and students should consider when developing and implementing a project or longer-term performance task:

1. How might a culture of teamwork be built?
2. What roles are needed, and how should these be assigned?
3. What check-in points are included to ensure that students are mastering (or have mastered) the necessary content and skills and that the project work is on track?
4. What channels of communication will be established so that students can voice their needs, both to the teacher and to other students?
5. How will ongoing feedback be provided and how will students make use of it?
6. What opportunities will students have for self-assessment and reflection?
7. What time management tools can teachers and students employ to increase the efficiency of task and project implementation?
8. How will both individuals and groups be held accountable for their performance, progress, and process?

Although teachers and students share the responsibility for addressing these questions, their respective degrees of responsibility will depend upon the type of task or project pursued (see design variable #8 in Chapter 3, p. 43). Regardless of where the task falls on the spectrum of task direction, teachers should consider how they might address these eight questions while arming and empowering students to do the same. Ultimately, project managers are also *risk managers*—the more effectively they can identify and mitigate potential issues before they arise, the more smoothly these tasks and projects are likely to run. In the following sections we offer suggestions and strategies that might "reduce risk" in regard to each of the questions.

Building a Culture of Teamwork and Determining Roles

Question 1: How might a culture of teamwork be built?
Question 2: What roles are needed and how should these be assigned?

The business world recognizes that team building is essential. In fact, Google's two-year study on team performance revealed that the highest-performing teams have one thing in common: psychological safety (Delizonna, 2017). Likewise, successful teachers in performance-based classrooms recognize that team building is necessary for success. Such teachers create an atmosphere in which members of a team know with certainty that (1) their teammates have their backs, (2) "giving your all" is expected, and (3) failure is a stepping-stone to success. They take time to make sure students know and trust one another. They expect excellence but help students understand that making mistakes—and learning from them—facilitates both growth and success (Dweck, 2006). They create a classroom culture in which students are accustomed to—and comfortable with—working together, and they institute routines for helping students do so efficiently.

Larmer and his colleagues (2015) note that teachers can "build this kind of culture in ways both explicit (e.g., slogans on the wall or structured processes for inquiry) and subtle (e.g., how the teacher responds to student questions or how students are taught to speak to each other)" (p. 49). Thankfully, many culture-building strategies, both explicit and subtle, can serve multiple purposes—fostering healthy classroom collaboration, enhancing constructive communications, and supporting students' performance.

Explicit Strategies

In the world outside school, many jobs require collaboration and communication. This is also true in classrooms where students work in teams on authentic tasks and engage in communication and discussions. The use of strategies such as Discussion Duties, Talking Chips (introduced in Chapter 5), and Thinking Hats can facilitate productive classroom discourse among students.

Discussion Duties. One way to focus student attention, foster student connections, and model norms for productive discourse is the use of Discussion Duties (Doubet & Hockett, 2017a). These duties, or roles, can be used with individual or group tasks or in conjunction with other strategies (e.g., Socratic seminars, described in Chapter 5). Discussion Duties give students specific roles to fulfill, prompts to address, and questions to ask. They can be devised inductively by the class as a whole or created by the teacher. Figure 7.1 provides one example of a set of Discussion Duties that could be divided among group members to encourage balanced participation.

Students can choose their own roles, or the teacher can assign them. It's a good idea to begin modeling a few roles at a time. It's also important to debrief the process with students and make adjustments where needed.

Talking Chips. This strategy helps students to monitor their responses during a group discussion. It encourages reluctant sharers to speak while reining in the "over-sharers" in the group. Each student receives two to five Talking Chips (e.g., game chips, scraps of paper, paper clips). They must use *some* of their chips but cannot speak once they have used *all* of them. It's important to establish the expectation that if several students want to speak at once, they "yield" to the classmates who have the most Talking Chips left (Doubet & Hockett, 2015, 2017a).

Figure 7.1
Sample Discussion Duties

Director	Includer
During Discussion: • Begin the discussion. Use the questions that have been posted as a starting point. • Make sure the discussion doesn't get off topic. • Bring the discussion to a close when time is called. **Sound bites:** • "Let's start by _____." • "Can we get back to _____?" • "What about _____?" • "Let's end by _____."	**During Discussion:** Make sure that all group members contribute to the discussion and feel included. **Sound bites:** • "What do you think about that, _____?" • "I agree/disagree with what you said, _____, because _____." • "I want to hear what _____ thinks." • "Wait, _____, I think you might have just interrupted _____."
Prober	Pacer
During Discussion: Make sure that all group members back up their opinions, ideas, feelings, and observations by giving details, examples, and explanations. **Sound bites:** • "Can you give an example?" • "Do you remember where that is/was? Can you show us?" • "How is that related to what we read?" • "That's interesting! How did you figure that out?" • "What part is that from/in?"	**During Discussion:** • Make sure that the discussion moves at a good pace. • "Refresh" the discussion when you feel like it's lagging. **Sound bites:** • "We've talked a lot about _____. Can we also talk about _____?" • "We have __ more minutes, so let's also talk about _____." • "I'm also wondering about _____." • "Here's something else to think about _____." • "It sounds like we agree/disagree about _____."

Source: From *Differentiation in the Elementary Grades: Strategies to Engage and Equip All Learners* (p. 137), by K. J. Doubet and J. A. Hockett, 2018, Alexandria, VA: ASCD. Copyright 2018 by ASCD. Used with permission.

Thinking Hats. This framework was developed originally for the business world (de Bono, 1999) and can help a group move forward when it has reached stalemate. The six hats—each of which is a prompt for addressing an aspect of problem solving—can be distributed using ThinkDots (an instructional strategy described in Chapter 5). Students roll the die to determine which Thinking Hat they will assume. When students metaphorically don a "hat," they know they are to approach or view the issue at hand through one of the lenses depicted in Figure 7.2. The idea is that, by examining an issue through a variety of perspectives, students will discover new pathways through a thorny problem and be able to move forward together.

Deliberately using—and reflecting upon—explicit team-building strategies such as Discussion Duties, Talking Chips, and Thinking Hats increases students' capacity to engage in productive struggle with both content and one another. It encourages them to seek multiple perspectives and to produce nuanced answers, all while weaving an intricate tapestry of collaboration among classmates.

Figure 7.2
Thinking Hats Problem-Solving Prompts

Hat 1	**Hat 2**	**Hat 3**
Share objective data (e.g., facts and figures) related to the topic/issue.	Provide the emotional views or perspectives that surround the topic/issue.	Examine the weaknesses of our proposed approach(es) to the topic/issue.
Hat 4	**Hat 5**	**Hat 6**
Examine the strengths of our proposed approach(es) to the topic/issue.	Generate new or creative ideas about the topic/issue.	Examine the organization of the topic/issue *or* explore the relationships among other hats.

Subtle Strategies

Nothing will unravel the progress made by *explicit* culture building more than *implicit* messages that erode trust. In a performance-based classroom, subtle communication regarding the value of making mistakes, persevering in the face of challenge, conversing respectfully, and collaborating with a variety of peers truly sets the stage for success. Practiced often and well, such subtle constructors of classroom culture can set the stage for significant learning gains (Bransford, Brown, & Cocking, 2000).

Giving growth-centered praise. According to Carol Dweck (2008), the kind of praise we give students in the classroom can, in part, determine how resilient they are as learners and how much they will grow academically. As Dweck points out, teachers should avoid *intelligence praise* (e.g., "You're brilliant!") and focus on *process praise*, or praise for such things as effort, perseverance, strategy, and improvement. Process praise "fosters hardy motivation. It tells students what they've done to be successful and what they need to do to be successful again in the future" (p. 37). When teachers use process praise, they say things like "You kept searching until you found an article that really supported your point. That took time, but it paid off with that amazing quote!" or "I like the way you tried all kinds of strategies in that design challenge until you finally got it." This type of praise also conveys the notion that mistakes are stepping-stones to success, and it encourages students to avoid settling for the most obvious answer or conclusion. In a performance- or project-based classroom, such behaviors are the keys to success.

Modeling and supporting respectful talk. Teachers who use growth-centered praise for themselves often find it rubs off on their students, who also begin to use growth-centered statements to describe their own performance (Dweck, 2008). Likewise, modeling respectful talk in the classroom can help students emulate it in their own speech. Posting and employing stems for respectful discussions between teacher and students can motivate students to use those same practices with one another. See Figure 7.3 for some discussion frames to use when expressing agreement and disagreement, and for both building upon others' ideas and suggesting new ones.

Grouping students flexibly. In a performance-based classroom, students need to know how to work together with a variety of peers for a variety of purposes. There will be times when collaborative groups work together to plan, research, or create. Those same collaborative groups may subdivide to accomplish multiple purposes. There may be times when a teacher pulls a small group of students with like needs to review a certain skill. Yet a different configuration of students may need to work together to employ a new research tool. Still others may gather in interest groups to study issues that enhance particular aspects of a task or project (e.g., an expert lesson on digital design; an app-based video tour of a local business facility). In other words, in a performance-based classroom, students need to be able to transition quickly and seamlessly. Teachers can set the expectation for this behavior early on by using the following warm-ups:

- Day 1/Grouping 1—Students line up according to birth date (month and day), and the teacher divides them into pairs.
- Day 2/Grouping 2—Students receive a playing card and form "same suit" groups. Students use the same playing card from Grouping 2 (or a new one) to form "like number" quads.
- Day 3/Grouping 3—Students use the same playing card from Grouping 2 (or a new one) to form "like number" quads.
- Day 4/Grouping 4—Students form "four corners" groups by reporting to the area of the room that corresponds to their favorite food: pizza, burgers, tacos, or smoothies; they subdivide into trios.
- Day 5/Grouping 5—Students line up in ROY G BIV order according to clothing color. The teacher "folds" the line to give students a partner from the opposite end of the spectrum. (Hockett & Doubet, 2017)

Figure 7.3
Discussion Frames

Validating or Extending	Probing or Challenging	Summarizing or Closing
• You made a point when you said _____. • Am I correct in understanding that _____? • I like that idea because _____. In addition, _____. • I hadn't considered that. It makes me wonder _____.	• I see what you're saying, but I also think or wonder _____. • I understand that _____, on the other hand _____. • What about this idea _____? • How does that mesh with _____? • Some people might say _____.	• It seems like we agree that _____ but that we disagree that _____. • I/we need to better understand _____ before _____. • A next step might be _____. • The bottom line seems to be _____. • Taking all perspectives into consideration, _____.

Adapted from Doubet & Hockett, 2017b, p. 60.

These kinds of warm-ups—along with continued practice—help students move into various new grouping configurations swiftly and without a lot of drama. Such flexibility pays off when students can efficiently settle into new groups to complete the important work necessary for an excellent performance or product.

Creating Check-in Points to Ensure Student Mastery and "On-Track" Work

Question 3: What check-in points are included to ensure that students are mastering (or have mastered) the necessary content and skills and that the project work is on track?

Although performance-based teaching often results in increased student autonomy, it does not mean that students now run the classroom and the teacher will lose control. Nor does it imply that direct instruction is no longer needed. Certainly, full-class instruction still plays an important role, as it allows teachers to provide direction and keep students anchored in standards, core skills, and dispositions. However, one change that is evident in performance-based teaching is a shift from simply "covering" lots of information to engaging in more "just in time" teaching. In supporting student performance, teachers provide important need-to-know information and skill building through traditional methods such as a lab, a minilesson, or a short lecture (Pieratt, 2018).

The goal of the teacher isn't to become *invisible* but—to return to our Chapter 5 metaphor—to become a *coach*. The teacher still leads the class, but as an orchestrator of learning—a facilitator and manager. And, as the classroom's learning expert, the teacher must discern when to direct, when to support, when to partner, when to offer feedback, and when to get out of the way. Doing so will require regular check-in points to determine student progress. Whether this occurs through a morning meeting or at the beginning or ending of the class routine, students need a chance to check status, pose burning questions, and function as a whole.

A *Scrum board* can be a part of this process. Developed by the IT world, *Scrum* is a framework for managing task completion and breaking down large tasks into manageable chunks (also called "sprints"). The Scrum board is a visual depiction of this process; it includes columns tracking tasks to be completed, tasks in progress, or "busy," and completed tasks (Rhodes, 2017). It also keeps success criteria at the forefront of students' attention while they work by featuring the criteria as the "definition of done" (D.O.D.) at the bottom of the board. A Scrum board is best compiled with flexibility in mind (e.g., digitally or via sticky notes), with the understanding that tasks and goals will need to be adjusted as projects progress. Figure 7.4 shows an example of a Scrum board. The Soil Erosion project associated with the board is featured in Appendix L.

Both teacher and students can manage the Scrum board, and it can be further divided to include rows for each team, if groups are working on different tasks. The visual nature of this structure infuses both accountability and motivation into task completion, as all class members (including the teacher) stay on top of what is working and what is not.

Figure 7.4
Sample Scrum Board

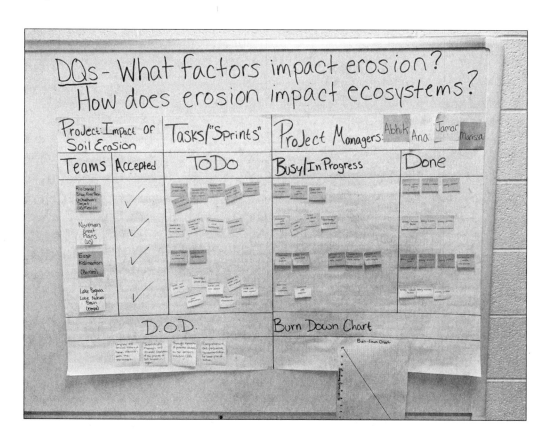

Establishing Channels of Communication

Question 4: What channels of communication will be established so that students can voice their needs, both to the teacher and to other students?

As just discussed, the Scrum board can serve as an overarching system for communicating information about student progress throughout the course of a longer-term task or project. Smaller, lesson-level structures can supplement the Scrum board and give students more immediate channels to seek and receive help. Here are several practical techniques:

Colored Cups and Question Chips. These two systems are efficient ways for students to seek help (Doubet & Hockett, 2015, p. 317). In the Colored Cups system, each group receives a stack of three colored cups (ideally, green, yellow, and red to mimic colors on traffic lights) that are placed upside down on their table or desk arrangement. When the green cup is on top, the group is working fine. When the yellow cup is displayed, students need help, but they can continue working on another step while they wait for assistance. The red cup signals a group's need for immediate attention. When the students complete a task (or a portion of a project), they flip the cups upright to indicate they are ready to move on.

Question Chips help students self-monitor to determine whether their questions about tasks are "must ask" or "could find out myself." Each group—or each student, if they are working independently—receives a limited number of Question Chips (e.g., pennies, paper squares, or game chips). These chips represent the number of times students can call on the teacher for help. If students have only three chips, they are less likely to automatically raise their hands and summon the teacher for easy-to-answer questions. This doesn't mean that the teacher should refuse to answer important content-based questions; rather, Question Chips help students determine whether their queries truly relate to understanding or are simply procedural in nature. If a question is procedural, the teacher can hint, "Do you really want to use a chip on that question?" and even indicate a general area of the directions where students can find the answer.

Clear directions and guidelines. Directions and guidelines can be written or recorded (or both) and, when possible, can include diagrams or examples. These can be posted on walls or boards located at learning stations or in other accessible areas of the classroom. When deciding what topics or procedures might need established directions, teachers should consider the ones they find themselves repeating often. Writing them down or recording them (e.g., via Seesaw, Flipgrid, video tutorials) saves time in the long run.

Routine learning checks. As we discussed in Chapter 5, teachers should collect formative assessment data regularly to check for student progress and understanding. In a performance-based classroom, they should also check in with teams of students to monitor the effectiveness of their relationships and group functioning. Whereas the Scrum board monitors group *progress*, group assessments can monitor group *health*. The following set of questions illustrates one way to collect this information:

- How well did your group stay on task and on time?
- Which role were you assigned for the group work?
- Explain your greatest strength and best accomplishment in playing that role today.
- Describe how you could have done a better job in that role.
- Did your group encounter any conflicts? If so, how did you work around them? (Doubet & Hockett, 2015, p. 187)

When teachers proactively monitor group dynamics, they can attend to any issues that arise in a timely fashion, resulting in stronger group bonds and a more efficiently running classroom.

Providing Ongoing Feedback and Opportunities for Self-Assessment and Reflection

Question 5: How will ongoing feedback be provided, and how will students make use of it?

Question 6: What opportunities will students have for self-assessment and reflection?

Just as group check-ins promote the efficient performance of teams, *self-assessment* facilitates growth for *individuals*. In a performance-based class, success criteria are clearly articulated in the opening phases of the task or project (see Chapter 4). These success criteria should be referenced throughout the unit as skills and content are addressed. Students can review their work in relationship to the criteria as "chunks" of work are completed, as well as when approaching task completion. Success criteria are crucial for both teachers and students to use during formative assessment and peer reviews in order to provide specific, substantive, and actionable feedback. Without clear criteria, feedback will more likely be imprecise (e.g., "I like it" or "Try harder") and not lead to improved performance.

After students receive constructive feedback from their peers or teacher, they can self-assess and reflect on their progress and performance using the prompts in Figure 7.5. This reflection can help students set future goals for improvement.

Students can also keep individual progress logs, recording their self-assessment in terms of evaluation, reflection, goal setting, and planning. They can also discuss their reflections in team or teacher conferences. To fully capitalize on the power of self-assessment, students should revisit their evaluations and reflections periodically, especially before embarking on new tasks or projects. The hope is that students will carry the lessons they learn in one performance into the next, growing with each new task they encounter.

Figure 7.5
Self-Assessment and Reflection Prompts

Evaluating	Reflecting
• What was most effective in _____? • What was least effective in _____? • What are you most proud of? • What are you most disappointed in? • What are your strengths in _____? • What are your deficiencies in _____? • What would you do differently next time? • How could you improve _____? • What follow-up work is needed? • What grade or score do you deserve? Why?	• What do you really understand about _____? • What questions/uncertainties do you still have about _____? • How difficult was _____ for you? • How does your preferred learning style influence _____? • How does what you've learned connect to other learnings? • How has what you've learned changed your thinking? • How does what you've learned relate to the present and future?

Source: Adapted from McTighe & Wiggins, 2004, p. 223. Used with permission.

Using Time Management Tools to Increase Efficiency of Implementation

Question 7: What time management tools can teachers and students employ to increase the efficiency of task and project implementation?

In a performance-based classroom, students must balance the reality of teacher-imposed deadlines with their own personal or group stepping-stones to completion. Whereas the Scrum board can serve as mission control for this purpose, other classroom structures and routines such as teacher- and student-generated schedules can support students as they navigate both self- and teacher-imposed benchmarks.

Teacher-Generated Agendas/Schedules

Posting an agenda or a schedule with dates for students to access (either electronically or physically) will help keep students abreast of key teacher-imposed deadlines and check-ins. Teachers should consistently reference important due dates, particularly because due dates might shift based on the needs of the students. Kristina and Eric both teach performance-based curricula with their college students. Although due dates are highlighted on the class syllabi, they also send out regular announcements to students reminding them of due dates for various readings, assignments, drafts, and tasks. They have found that being explicit with expectations helps students stay on track in a classroom where a linear timeline is seldom the norm.

Student-Generated Schedules

Establishing clear deadlines—along with both short- and long-term goals—is paramount to student success in working with open blocks of work time for projects and longer-term tasks. Whereas teachers may provide the overall due dates, students can take responsibility for setting their own targets for segments of task completion. At the launch of a project or a longer task, individuals or groups can set up their own schedule for completing various benchmarks along the way. The high school world geography example in Figure 7.6 illustrates both teacher- and student-generated deadlines for a seven-day project with both group and individual components.

Even with clear deadlines in place, however, students—or groups of students—may complete their projects at different times. The establishment of anchor activities can help address this inevitable variation.

Anchor activities are stand-alone tasks that are aligned with, or of value to, a particular discipline; ideally, they should supplement the primary focus of a particular project or performance. They can reduce the amount of "ragged time" (when students finish at different rates) that often results from a more student-centered approach to instruction (Tomlinson, 2017). Here are some examples of anchor activities:

- Exploring additional perspectives on a topic or issue
- Communicating with experts in the discipline
- Engaging in creative writing or generating multimodal representations
- Solving challenging or counterintuitive problems
- Conducting personally relevant research
- Interacting with engaging texts or videos
- Exploring computer-based or online programs or apps

Anchor activities work best when

- They enhance or augment the task or project in one or more dimensions.
- Expectations are clear.
- Students are accountable for on-task habits and task completion.
- There is an element of choice.
- Students are drawn to them. (Doubet & Hockett, 2017a, p. 331)

Figure 7.6
**Teacher- and Student-Generated Project Deadlines
for a High School World Geography Class**

Task: Travel Vlogger
Congratulations! Your group has been chosen to participate in the inaugural travel vlog program!

Why: Many of the countries in North Africa and Southwest Asia are misrepresented in the mainstream media. As we will learn throughout this unit, geographic characteristics often lead to regional labels that only tell a small part of the history and culture of a region. We are counting on you to research your region and accurately represent the culture and the people through your travel vlog.

What: Your group has been asked to make a 20-minute travel vlog to highlight the important geographic characteristics of your chosen region in either Southwest Asia or North Africa. The sponsors have set the following guidelines for the content of your video:

- Introduction of your region (1 min)
- Population distribution and lifestyle (3 min)
- Population distribution map and analysis (7 min)
- Major religion(s) and important religious buildings (3 min)
- Cultural spaces (3 min)
- Current events (3 min)

How: Follow the steps listed in the work schedule. It is important that your group work collaboratively during the designated project time each class. I will be rotating from group to group during project time to check progress and assist in any way needed.

Travel Vlog Work Schedule and Due Dates

Day and Topic	Task	Progress Check Due at End of Class
Day 1 Introduction	Review the regional options for this unit's PBL. Rank your choices on your exit ticket.	• Exit Ticket with your preferred region
Day 2 Population Distribution	Complete the introduction segment requirements by starting your video in iMovie. Next, move on to the Population Distribution planner. Make sure to get your maps from a reputable source and use the map analysis skills we have been practicing this year.	• PBL Population Distribution Segment Planner
Days 3, 4, 5 Religions and Religious Buildings	Work at your own pace to complete the following: • Use the Religion Segment Planner to guide you as you analyze religious art and discover important religious buildings. Remember to incorporate multiple images or other video clips of the art/buildings to capture viewers' attention. As you analyze the art, remember that art is a primary source so utilize all you have learned about primary source analysis!	• PBL Religions Segment Planner
Cultural Spaces	• Use the Cultural Spaces Planner to make sure that you incorporate all the requirements. Choose engaging images to help viewers understand why these cultural spaces are so important to the region.	• PBL Cultural Spaces Planner
Current Events	• Use the Current Events Planner to make sure that you incorporate all of the requirements. Choose sources that avoid bias and make sure to get multiple perspectives on your event. Incorporate images or video clips to help explain what is going on in your region.	• PBL Current Events Planner
Day 6 Vlog Editing Day	You are almost done! Today is all about the finishing touches. Use the Conclusion Planning Sheet to make sure that you wrap up your video correctly. Submit your draft bibliography and don't forget to turn in your PBL rubric with your self-assessment. Each group member must turn in a completed self-assessment rubric.	• Draft Bibliography • Rubric with Self-Assessment • Final Travel Vlog
Day 7 Film Screening	Film Screening Day! All of your hard work has paid off and it is now time to premier your travel vlog for your peers. As you watch your classmates' vlogs, complete the film matrix and turn it in at the end of class. Make sure to submit your final bibliography.	• Film Matrix • Final Bibliography

Source: Laura VanDenmark, James Madison University, Harrisonburg, VA. Used with permission.

Consistency is key when using anchor activities. Students should be aware of expectations regarding the use and location of these activities for a more seamless transition upon completion of projects and performance tasks (or segments of the projects and tasks). Used properly, anchor activities can support a more student-centered, flexible approach to the design and management of projects and performances.

Educator Kate Summers uses collaborative digital presentations as the standing anchor activity in her high school biology class (see https://www .edutopia.org/video/collaborative-digital-presentations-enrich-projects-tech2learn-series). If students finish a task or project early, they transition to work on an associated minitask, which is to create a digital presentation for their classmates on a science topic not usually addressed in the standard curriculum. Not only do students stay focused and on task at all times in Kate's class, but they also have the opportunity to explore areas of science they would not otherwise encounter. By pausing periodically to ask students to share their work with their classmates, Kate fosters investment and engagement while making sure students continue to move forward in their learning (rather than simply "tread water" while waiting for their classmates to finish their projects).

Holding Individuals and Groups Accountable

Question 8: How will both individuals and groups be held accountable for their performance, progress, and process?

Although collaboration is a key component of any performance-based classroom, it presents a challenge for assessing and evaluating the work of individuals and groups. Indeed, teachers often struggle with how to grade or assess a performance or project if multiple students have worked together to complete it. Some of the issues surrounding grading group projects include the following:

- Group grades do not accurately reflect an individual student's achievement or mastery regarding key content learning goals or objectives of the assessment. This issue affects the validity of not only that assessment but also the grade assigned for a particular grading period, semester, or year.
- Similarly, individual students might achieve the same level of content mastery but receive different grades or scores on a project because of the work of their group members.

- Group grades or feedback fail to target individual student areas for growth. Some students might view group feedback as worthless because it fails to help them progress forward on their individual learning trajectories.
- Individual group members might feel a need to pick up the slack for others in the group who, for whatever reason, won't or can't do the work. Sometimes the more appealing option for certain students is to pick up the slack and avoid confrontation. (Brookhart, 2013, pp. 2–3)

Research also suggests that when engaging in complex problem solving, the best ideas are developed when student collaboration is intermittent in nature, allowing time for individual work between group sessions (Bernstein, Shore, & Lazer, 2018). The implications for a performance-based classroom are clear: although collaboration is important, students should also be given time to *individually* process and reflect on the ideas generated during collaboration in order to determine the best solutions to the problems they are working to solve.

Thus, both assessment literature and research on collaboration support balancing individual accountability and collaboration—something designers should consider when developing and evaluating projects and tasks. Here we share three suggestions for assessing projects and performances that encourage collaboration but still ensure a measure of individual achievement.

Suggestion #1: Consider what could be assessed versus graded. Teachers often use grades in an attempt to motivate students. The logic behind this practice is that if an assignment is graded (or of "higher stakes"), students are more likely to invest in completing it. Although this strategy works for some students, for many others it does not. Assessment and grading, however, are not synonymous. Often the best assessments are those that provide students with useful feedback to improve their work—referred to as assessment *for* learning (as discussed in Chapter 5). To help address the issue of grading group work, teachers should consider when to assign grades and when assessment for learning is warranted. We advocate that any assignments completed in groups should be assessed for learning, and grades should be reserved for individual assignments. Consider the multidisciplinary example presented in Figure 7.7. This example, featuring a performance task for upper-elementary math and language arts, illustrates how teachers might balance the assessment of group work with the grading of individual content knowledge and skills.

Of course, if one of the learning goals is collaboration, then the performance of the group should also be scored using a rubric for collaboration (see Appendix K for a sample rubric to assess cooperation and teamwork).

Figure 7.7
Mascot Mania Performance Task

Task: Propose a new mascot for our school and facilitate schoolwide support for adopting your animal as the new mascot.

In Groups:
• Develop a campaign for your chosen animal, including a short speech (to be read over the intercom during morning announcements) and posters for display around the school.
• Conduct an election; then collect votes and tally the results on a spreadsheet.

Note: Neither of these activities is formally scored, but group work is formatively assessed and feedback is provided.

Individually:
• Develop an appropriate graphic display of the collected data to use in communicating the results of the mascot vote to the PTO executive board and the school principal.
• Compose a letter to the principal and PTO board recommending which animal should be selected as the school's mascot. You must present your reasons, including your vote data display, to make your case.

Note: Both of these individual activities are assessed with rubrics based on the respective standards: (1) display of data and (2) persuasive writing with evidence.

Suggestion #2: Administer individual pre- and post-assessments. A second strategy to address some of the issues related to grading group work is to use pre- and post-assessments to determine student mastery of content before and after a project. The format of these assessments can vary depending on purpose and need; more traditional, selected-response assessments are limited by what they can assess. For example, a multiple-choice assessment cannot measure student transfer of learning. As such, choose your assessment method purposefully, based on desired learning goals.

Suggestion #3: Consider the "Three Ps" of grading and report them separately. In an ideal grading system, teachers would assess students on three separate areas:

- *Performance* against grade-level standards or teacher-identified content or process outcomes
- *Progress* or growth over the course of a grading period
- *Process* or the habits of mind that help students achieve success (e.g., active engagement in group work, responding to feedback, asking for assistance when needed) (Adapted from Tomlinson & McTighe, 2006, p. 135)

Collaboration, most likely, would fall under the third *P*—did students actively contribute to the success of a group or team? The method of communicating such information to students would vary depending on the grading system used, but it could be as simple as holding brief conferences with students to discuss their roles and how effectively they contributed to the success of the group. E-mails, criterion performance lists, rubrics, and other methods can all be used to help students understand that the process of effective collaboration is valuable and leads to learning. Such methods would provide important feedback on students' *process* without muddying their individual *performance* grades with assessments of their collaborative skills. Figure 7.8 illustrates how the "three *P*s" can be practically applied to a Spanish I performance task. The task was assessed as follows:

- *Performance:* Students were individually graded on their proper use of the verbs *ser* and *estar* in the formal letter written to Señora Perez as well as their ability to translate the "travel buddy" interviews into Spanish.
- *Progress:* Before and after completing the performance task, students were given a pre- and post-assessment on their use of *ser* and *estar* in a variety of situations similar to those they were expected to use in their letters to Señora Perez. Although improvement from the pre-assessment wouldn't be included in their performance task score, growth would be factored in to students' participation grades kept throughout the grading period.
- *Process:* Students met with the teacher individually to discuss their roles and contributions during the partner-interview portion of the assignment. The teacher used a general "effective interview" participation rubric (Figure 7.9) to evaluate students. These ratings were given to students along with specific feedback to help them work more effectively with partners on future assignments or to encourage their continued use of desired actions and behaviors.

Strategically using one or more of the suggestions offered in this chapter can help teachers achieve balance in their assessment system while fostering both individual and group accountability. Regardless of the approach chosen, the goal is to foster a *growth-centered* classroom (as discussed earlier in this chapter)—one that honors the contribution each individual brings to the success of the team.

Figure 7.8
Performance Task: Using *Ser* and *Estar*

Goal: Describe customs and traditions of Spanish-speaking cultures related to the role of family members by correctly using *ser* and *estar*.

Role: Tourist traveling to _____ . (Choose one of the three Spanish-speaking countries that we have studied throughout the unit.)

Audience: Travel agent, Señora Perez

Situation: You are going on a seven-day vacation to _____ (Spanish-speaking country) with two members of your family and your best friend. You have hired a travel agent, Señora Perez, to help you plan the trip. To suggest activities that everyone will enjoy, Señora Perez needs some information about you and your travel group. Your task is to write a letter to the travel agent describing yourself and each of your travel companions. Do not assume that Señora Perez knows anything about any of you. You *must* be specific in describing yourself, your family members, and your friend, as well as the activities you each prefer.

Product: You will write a formal letter to Señora Perez, providing information about you and your travel companions that will help her suggest the best places to visit and activities to partake in during your vacation. You will also need to conduct an interview with one of your travel companions discussing that person's interests. This interview can be conducted in English but should be translated to Spanish. Please include both versions when you turn in the final product.

Source: Jessica Roy, James Madison University, Harrisonburg, VA. Used with permission.

Conclusion

In the wider world outside school, effective project management "involves planning, delegating, tracking, reviewing, and measuring results.... The goal of every project is different, but the overarching objective is to *grow*" (Lowe, 2018). The same premise holds true in a performance-based classroom. Strategic approaches to team building, check-ins, communication, time management, self-assessment, and evaluation can help the classroom run like a well-oiled machine. When such strategies are in place, both teachers and students can dedicate their time and energy to pursuing the ultimate goal of *growth* in academic, intellectual, personal, and social realms. The "Crafting the Environment" section of the *Task and Project Planning Tool* (Appendix B) provides prompts to help teachers make strategic, proactive decisions about how to support growth.

In our final chapter, we will expand beyond the classroom to consider how authentic performance tasks and projects can be used to map an entire preK–12 curriculum and assessment system.

Figure 7.9
Rubric for an Effective Interview

	Home Run	On Base	Foul Ball— Give It Another Swing
Content	I answered each interview question to the best of my ability, providing enough detail so that my partner could accurately represent me and my interests when completing the assigned task.	I answered each interview question, but I could have provided some additional details to help my partner develop a richer description of me and my interests.	I gave answers that were insufficient (or I didn't provide answers) and/or wasn't cooperative. I need to do a better job remembering that we are all part of a learning community and can help each other be successful. Honestly, it just wasn't my day, and I'd like to try again.
Professionalism	I interacted with my partner in a completely professional, cooperative manner. My partner would definitely want to work with me again on future assignments.	I interacted with my partner in a mostly professional, cooperative manner. There were one or two times when I became frustrated or annoyed when I shouldn't have. Next time I hope to show my partner that I can be more professional.	I interacted with my partner in a mostly unprofessional and/or uncooperative manner. On more than two occasions, I became frustrated or annoyed. I understand why my partner wouldn't want to work with me again and will do my best to learn from this before the next assignment.

8

Creating a
Performance-Based Curriculum

In the previous chapters we have presented ideas for designing authentic performance tasks and projects and their associated evaluation tools. We have examined the nature and practices of performance-based teaching and considered ways of differentiating instruction to support the success of all students. We have addressed practical challenges in both the design and implementation of performance- and project-based learning. Individual teachers and teams can apply all these ideas when they design units or plan for PBL in their classrooms. In this concluding chapter, we zoom out and ask readers to consider the larger (macro) use of performance tasks and projects at the school, program, or district levels to organize the curriculum. More specifically, we will outline the role of recurring tasks and projects in establishing a more coherent, vertically aligned curriculum that concurrently contributes to more focused teaching, more reliable evaluation, and more meaningful learning.

Throughout this book, we have described the potential benefits of authentic tasks and projects. Such tasks and projects can serve as worthy teaching targets because they reflect what we want students *to be able to do* with their learning. Due to their authentic nature, they help learners see relevance in their learning. Preparing students for successful performance leads to effective and differentiated instruction that contributes to deep and lasting learning. Finally, authentic tasks and projects provide robust assessment evidence of students' understanding and ability to transfer their learning. But what exactly does it mean to organize the curriculum around authentic tasks and projects?

To explore this idea, let's begin with an analogy suggested by McTighe and Wiggins (2011):

If builders were going to construct a high-rise building, they would not start by dropping off building materials in piles and say to the workers, "Here are the materials for the third floor. You third-floor builders start building. And over there is a pile for you eighth-floor builders. And the twelfth-floor materials are around the corner. Get to it." Unfortunately, we often see school curricula that reflect a "piles" approach; i.e., the curriculum is presented in terms of scope-and-sequence lists of content to be covered in accordance with a pacing calendar. Such a curriculum structure may unwittingly convey to teachers that their job is to march through long lists of grade-level standards, teaching and testing them in isolation. At its worst, this kind of curriculum can lead to superficial and fragmented learning of discrete knowledge and skills, unmoored from longer-term outcomes. In other words, one could easily become lost in the trees and miss the forest. (p. 2)

A Performance-Based Curriculum Blueprint

Let's use the building analogy to consider an alternative approach to avoid this potential problem. Architects and builders always begin a construction job with a blueprint. The blueprint provides an overall vision of the desired building while serving as a guide to its construction. Moreover, the blueprint is meant to ensure structural integrity and aesthetic cohesion. We would not want to see a staircase ending at a ceiling, or one floor reflecting a modern architectural design and others displaying classical styles. We believe that the blueprint analogy can be effectively applied to the development of a coherent K–12 curriculum. Just as builders are directed by a blueprint, curriculum teams and teachers are guided by a curriculum blueprint as they design learning experiences and assessments.

McTighe and Wiggins (2013b) offer a conception of a performance-based curriculum as an alternative to the conventional scope-and-sequence approach:

> [O]ur conception is that curriculum should be framed and developed in terms of worthy *outputs*; i.e., desired performances by the learner, not simply as a listing of content *inputs*. (p. 10)

Rather than asking, "What will we teach in the curriculum?" (indicating a focus on content inputs), the fundamental curriculum question becomes "What do we want students *to be able to do* with their learning? (indicating a focus on student outputs). In other words, we can structure the curriculum around authentic tasks and projects. Here is how.

Cornerstone Tasks and Projects

Recall that in the first chapter we discussed long-term transfer goals as important outcomes of a modern education. Here we recommend that a set of long-term transfer goals, both within and across the disciplines, become the destination points of a contemporary K–12 curriculum. Then, with those ends in mind, we can plan the curriculum backward by identifying the *performances* that reflect transfer and provide evidence of deep learning. (See Appendix M for a set of transfer goals and associated cornerstone tasks developed by a K–12 social studies curriculum team with these principles in mind.)

Continuing the analogy with architecture and construction, we propose that a K–12 curriculum be organized around a coherent set of performance tasks and projects that are intended to engage students in applying their knowledge and skills in an authentic context. Just as a cornerstone anchors a building, these tasks are meant to anchor the curriculum around the most important performances that we want learners to be able to do with their learning. They honor the intent of academic standards in the disciplines while also addressing important transdisciplinary outcomes, such as creative problem solving, collaboration, argumentation, research, design thinking, and habits of mind.

McTighe (2017b) further characterizes cornerstone tasks and projects by saying that they

- Are embedded in the curriculum;
- Recur across the grades, becoming increasingly sophisticated over time;
- Establish authentic contexts for performance;
- Call for understanding and transfer via genuine performance;
- May be used as rich learning activities or assessments;
- Integrate 21st century skills (e.g., critical thinking, technology use, teamwork) with subject area content;
- Evaluate performance with established rubrics;
- Engage students in meaningful learning while encouraging the best teaching; and
- Provide content for student portfolios.

One of the key characteristics of cornerstone tasks and projects is that they *recur* across the grades. When learning a sport or a musical instrument, we improve as a result of multiple opportunities to practice and perform. Similarly, students will achieve proficiency on sophisticated skills such as writing, research, problem solving, argumentation, and oral communication only through ongoing opportunities to learn to apply these skills to increasingly complex situations across the grades. In the following section, we offer ideas for designing sets of recurring tasks and projects over the course of a year and across the grades.

We can illustrate this idea with a sample K–12 map (Figure 8.1) that targets specific writing tasks by genre and grade level based on the following long-term transfer goals: Students will be able to

1. **Write to communicate effectively** in various genres for a variety of audiences and purposes (e.g., explain, entertain, guide, argue, and challenge).

2. **Produce high-quality writing** in which the genre, conventions, organization, and style are appropriate for various purposes, audiences, and contexts.

Notice that this task map identifies the kinds of writing performances that we want students to be able to do at the various grade levels. Teachers can then plan backward from those writing tasks to help students develop the requisite knowledge, skills, and understandings. In other words, the content to be taught is derived from the demands of authentic performances, in the same ways that athletic coaches focus their practices to prepare players for the demands of the game.

Before proceeding, we offer the following notes about the writing map example:

- This map is simply intended to illustrate possibilities, *not* recommend specific writing tasks. Schools and districts will decide on the types of writing appropriate for each grade level.

- Once cornerstone tasks and projects are established, they become part of the curriculum; that is, all 2nd graders write a personal narrative and all 10th graders prepare a news article. However, the identification of three writing tasks per year in no way limits teachers and students from additional amounts and types of writing. Indeed, we would expect students to have multiple writing opportunities every year, including low-stakes, high-interest writing tasks.

- Some of these writing tasks can be naturally linked with other subject areas. For example, in 8th grade, a social-issue essay can be written around issues from science or social studies, and a historical fiction narrative would appropriately reference historical events and characters.

- Although the types of writing in the curriculum may be standard, there are many opportunities for student "voice and choice." For example, the 1st grade task for a narrative involving an imaginary character will allow choice of character, setting, and storyline; the 5th grade research project can allow students to choose a specific topic within a general area of study; and the 12th grade position paper would be constructed around an issue chosen by the students.

Figure 8.1

Sample K–12 Performance Task Map for Writing

Grade	Informative/Explanatory	Narrative	Opinion/Persuasion/Argumentative
K	Science observation picture book	"All About Me" picture book	—
1	"My Favorite Animal" book	Imaginary-character story	—
2	How-to book (illustrated)	Personal narrative	—
3	Friendly letter	Modern-day fairy tale	Opinion letter
4	Feature article	Poetry collection	Issue analysis
5	Research project	Descriptive narrative	Argumentation essay
6	How-to guide	Autobiography	Editorial
7	Cause-and-effect essay	Myth, fable, fairy tale, folktale, or legend	Position paper
8	Research project	Narrative/historical fiction	Social-issue essay
9	Problem-solution essay	Poetry, song/lyrics	Editorial
10	News article	Memoir	Project that includes a policy evaluation
11	Technical manual	Dramatic script/one-act play	Argumentation essay
12	Independent research project with a written product and presentation	Parody, satire, irony	Position paper on issue chosen by student

To continue with the building analogy, a blueprint provides a vision of, and a plan for, a desired building. Then the construction begins. If you have ever watched a house or an apartment building being constructed, you know that carpenters frame out the individual rooms to outline the walls, doors, windows, closets, and ceiling based on the dimensions specified in a blueprint. This framing guides the installation of sheetrock (drywall) on the walls and ceiling. Then, the finishing touches are applied—installing windows and doors; laying carpeting or tile on the floors; painting, wallpapering, or paneling the walls. The idea of framing applies to the construction of performance tasks and projects as well. In the next sections we describe three methods to use in building coordinated sets of recurring tasks and projects: matrices, templates, and starters.

Design Method #1: Design Matrices

We'll begin by examining a set of matrices that can be applied to developing performance tasks and projects for literacy, mathematics, science, social studies, and other subjects. The essence of this technique involves setting up a matrix with content standards and topics on one axis and processes and practices on the other. Then, the intersection of the cells suggests possible performance tasks and projects involving the application of content through one or more processes. Let's examine three such matrices and illustrative task examples.

A Matrix for Mathematics

The Common Core State Standards (CCSS) for mathematics call for students to apply mathematical content through the use of one or more practices. This CCSS framework has influenced state standards throughout the United States, and it naturally suggests a matrix in which mathematical practices are intersected with math concepts. A matrix, such as the one shown in Figure 8.2, lends itself to both curriculum planning and to the design of performance tasks and projects.

Designers can link math content standards with one or more of the practice standards to generate ideas for performance tasks and projects. Here is an example of a 3rd grade task that merges several CCSS Practice Standards (represented on the horizontal axis in Figure 8.2) with specific CCSS Content Standards (found along the vertical axis in Figure 8.2).

Sample Performance Task

Part 1—The PTSA of your school wants to hold a fund-raiser for a new playground and they have asked for your ideas. You decide to open a lemonade

Figure 8.2
Planning Matrix for Mathematics (CCSS)

				Practice Standards				
2nd Grade Content Standards	1. Make sense of problems & persevere in solving them	2. Reason abstractly and quantitatively	3. Construct viable arguments & critique the reasoning of others	4. Model with mathematics	5. Use appropriate tools strategically	6. Attend to precision	7. Look for and make use of structure	8. Look for and express regularity in repeated reasoning
2.OA.A.1—Represent and solve problems involving addition and subtraction								
2.OA.B.2—Add and subtract within 20								
2.OA.C.3-4—Work with equal groups of objects to gain foundations for multiplication								
2.NBT.A.1—Represent and solve problems involving addition and subtraction								
2.NBT.A.1-4—Understand place value								

2.NBT.B.5-9—Use place value understanding and properties of operations to add and subtract						
2.MD.A.1-4—Measure and estimate lengths in standard units						
2.MD.B.5-6—Relate addition and subtraction to length						
2.MD.C.7-8—Work with time and money						
2.MD.D.9-10—Represent and interpret data						
2.G.A.1-3—Reason with shapes and their attributes						

Source: Adapted from © 2017b Jay McTighe. Used with permission.

stand to raise money, but you need to ask for money to buy the supplies you will need. You learn that lemonade mix costs $3.19 and will make enough lemonade for 48 cups. You can buy 50 plastic cups for $3.87. A 10-pound bag of ice costs $2.13 and you will need 2 bags. How much money will you need from the PTSA Board to set up your lemonade stand? You will need to show your calculations to the PTSA Board to get the money you need to buy the supplies.

Part 2—Decide how much you will charge for each cup of lemonade. If you sell all of the lemonade, how much profit will you make after your expenses? Show your work and explain your reasoning so that the PTSA Board can understand your plan. (Adapted from Maryland Assessment Consortium, 1994)

This performance task addresses the *Mathematics Content Standard,* "Solve problems involving the four operations," and the *Mathematical Practice Standards*, "Make sense of problems and persevere in solving them" and "Reason abstractly and quantitatively."

This matrix can be used throughout 3rd grade to help task designers make sure they address all content and practice standards over the course of the year. Further, the framework can grow from grade level to grade level by creating matrices that keep the practice standards constant and adjust the content standards to reflect grade-level expectations.

A Matrix for Science

A similar matrix can be constructed for science using the Next Generation Science Standards (NGSS). Similar to the mathematics matrix, the practices can be listed on the horizontal axis, and the key content topics, core ideas, or cross-cutting concepts can be recorded on the vertical axis. Figure 8.3 provides an example, showing practices for science and engineering along the horizontal axis and the seven cross-cutting concepts along the vertical axis. The matrix can be used to design tasks at every grade level and in all science discipline areas by simply varying the content, concept, or practice focus of each task.

Performance tasks can be designed by examining the intersection of key practices and cross-cutting concepts. For example, here is a performance task for high school based on the intersection of Practice 3 (Planning and Carrying Out Investigations) and Cross-Cutting Concept E (Energy and Matter):

Sample Performance Task: Design an investigation to answer the following question: *How much does it cost to take a shower?* Identify the variables that must be considered, and then develop a plan for conducting the investigation. Your plan should be specific enough so that other investigators could follow it and answer the question.

Figure 8.3
Planning Matrix for Science Standards (NGSS)

Content Topics (Core Ideas)	Cross-Cutting Concepts	1. Asking questions and defining problems	2. Developing and using models	3. Planning and carrying out investigations	4. Analyzing and interpreting data	5. Using math and information technology	6. Constructing explanations; designing solutions	7. Engaging in argument from evidence	8. Obtaining, evaluating, and communicating information
	A. Patterns								
	B. Cause and Effect								
	C. Scale, Proportion, and Quantity								
	D. Systems and System Models								
	E. Energy and Matter								
	F. Structure and Function								
	G. Stability and Change								

Practice Standards

Source: © 2017 Jay McTighe. Used with permission.

A Matrix for Social Studies

The new College, Career, and Civic Life (C3) Framework for the Social Studies State Standards is also well suited to the use of a matrix because of the four identified processes or dimensions of informed inquiry: (1) developing questions and planning inquiries; (2) applying disciplinary concepts and tools; (3) evaluating sources and using evidence; and (4) communicating conclusions and taking informed action. In the sample matrix shown in Figure 8.4, the four inquiry processes are further divided into seven practices that are listed on the horizontal axis, with the key social studies concepts on the vertical axis.

The following sample performance task illustrates the intersection of Concept E (Society and Identity) with Practices 2, 3, and 4 (Analyze and Interpret Data from Multiple Sources and Perspectives; Critically Evaluate Sources; and Construct Reasoned Arguments Based on Evidence).

> **Sample Performance Task:** Studying international relations helps you understand how the world outside our borders affects your life and community. Your task is to analyze the impact of international relations on your local or state economy. In a cohesive paper or presentation,
>
> 1. State a position on the effects of international relations on your community.
> 2. Provide background on the position by
>   • Describing two or more stakeholders involved in an international agreement or policy related to a local product, service, or natural resource; and
>   • Analyzing how they are affected by this involvement.
>
> 3. Provide reason(s) for your position that include
>   • An analysis of how a specific international agreement or policy has affected the buying, selling, or use of the local product, service, or natural resource selected with one or more examples; and
>   • An explanation of how the forces of supply and demand influenced the buying, selling, or use of the product, service, or natural resource selected.
>
> 4. Make explicit references within the paper or presentation to three or more credible sources that provide relevant information, and cite sources within the paper, presentation, or bibliography.

This task has been adapted from a classroom-based assessment task developed through the Washington State Office of the Superintendent of Public Instruction (n.d.). A set of similar social studies tasks for elementary, middle, and high school levels is available at http://www.k12.wa.us/SocialStudies/Assessments /default.aspx.

Figure 8.4
Planning Matrix for Social Studies

Topics	Concepts	1. Develop questions and plan inquiries	2. Analyze and interpret data from multiple sources and perspectives	3. Critically evaluate sources	4. Construct reasoned arguments based on evidence	5. Critique arguments of others based on reasoning and evidence	6. Communicate conclusions using appropriate media	7. Take informed action
						Practices		
	A. Time, Continuity, and Change							
	B. Connections and Conflict							
	C. Geography							
	D. Culture							
	E. Society and Identity							
	F. Government							
	G. Production, Distribution, Consumption							
	H. Science, Technology, Society							

Designers can also create a transdisciplinary matrix for long-term transfer goals that transcend individual disciplines. For example, they can list 21st century skills (e.g., critical thinking, creativity, communication, collaboration, citizenship) across the horizontal axis and content standards or topics on the vertical axis. Then, looking for natural intersections when one or more of the transdisciplinary skills could be coupled with content, they can generate a task or project.

Such matrices can be useful to individual teachers not only for planning a variety of performance tasks throughout the year, but also for program-level mapping of tasks and projects across the grades at the school and district levels. Such mapping leads to greater coherence of the curriculum and associated assessments by helping to ensure that desired performances are methodically targeted, that evidence of student proficiency is systematically collected, and that important standards and other learning goals (such as 21st century skills and habits of mind) do not fall through the cracks because they are never assessed.

Design Method #2: Task/Project Templates

Task frames, or templates, provide a basic structure to guide the design of performance tasks around anchor standards and other priority learning goals. The Literacy Design Collaborative (LDC, n.d.) has developed a wonderful collection of such templates to support the integration of the Common Core Standards (6–12) in English language arts with core content in science, social studies, and technical areas. The LDC templates are fill-in-the-blank shells into which teachers can insert the content to design customized tasks. The resulting performance tasks require students to read, analyze, and comprehend written materials and then write cogent arguments, explanations, or narratives in the subjects they are studying. Here are several examples of generic LDC templates that were used to create tasks:

Informational or Explanatory Task Template

[Insert general question here (see next example)] After reading _____ (literature or informational texts), write a/an _____ (essay, report, article, or substitute) that defines and explains (term or concept). Support your discussion with evidence from the text(s). What _____ (conclusions or implications) can you draw?

Social Studies Example: What did the authors of the U.S. Constitution mean by "rights"? After reading *the Bill of Rights,* write an *essay* that defines *"rights"* and explains *"rights" as the authors use it in this foundational document.* Support your discussion with evidence from the text. What implications can you draw?

Science Example: How can energy be changed from one form into another? After reading *scientific sources on energy transformation,* write a *report* that examines the *causes of energy transformation* and explains *the effects when energy is transformed.* Support your discussion with evidence from the texts. What conclusions or implications can you draw?

Argumentation Task Template

After researching _____ (informational texts) on _____ (content topic or issue), write a/an _____ (essay or other form of writing) that argues your position on _____ (topic, issue, essential question). Support your position with evidence from research. Be sure to acknowledge competing views. Give examples from past or current events issues to illustrate and clarify your position.

Social Studies Example: After researching *academic articles* on *censorship,* write a *blog* or an editorial that argues your position on the *use of internet filters by schools.* Support your position with evidence from research. Be sure to acknowledge competing views.

English/Language Arts Example: What makes something funny? After reading *selections from Mark Twain and Dave Barry,* write a *review* that *compares their humor and argues which type of humor works best for a contemporary audience and explains why.* Be sure to support your position with evidence from the texts.

The LDC also offers accompanying instructional modules, which include a description of the skills students need in order to be successful, a set of mini-tasks to guide instruction, and a scoring rubric. Each module is designed for approximately two to three weeks and uses an instructional ladder to organize instruction. You can access the many LDC templates, task examples, and related resources at http://www.literacydesigncollaborative.org.

Design Method #3: Task/Project Starters

Similar to task frames, task/project starters offer general ideas for jump-starting task and project design (McTighe, 2017b). The sets of starters shown in Figures 8.5–8.8 are based on long-term transfer goals, derived from two sources: (1) key processes contained in disciplinary standards and (2) ways in which content knowledge is applied in the wider world. In other words, the starters reflect what it means to *do* the subjects; thus, they reflect authentic performance. Organized by discipline areas, we have found these starters to be especially valuable in creating sets of recurring cornerstone tasks and projects, with the application of increasingly sophisticated content as the grade levels progress.

These three methods—matrices, templates, and starters—can be used to construct a K–12 set of recurring cornerstone tasks and projects. Invariably, a practical question arises when districts and schools consider our recommendation: How many cornerstone tasks and projects should we have? Although there is no hard-and-fast number, we suggest four to six per year across the major subject areas (see Appendix N for a sample map of cornerstone tasks). As we have noted, when performance tasks and projects are developed around an authentic context, they are likely to involve more than one subject area and to include one or more of the 21st century skills. Accordingly, a single task or project can often provide evidence of several important outcomes within and across subjects.

Benefits of a System of Cornerstone Tasks and Projects

Once identified, cornerstone tasks and projects become an expected part of the curriculum for all students. In other words, all 4th graders and all 9th graders will work on their designated tasks, regardless of which school they attend or which teacher they have. Having a coordinated set of authentic tasks and projects identified for each grade and course offers four noteworthy benefits: (1) curriculum focus, (2) student engagement, (3) evidence collection, and (4) a culture of continuous improvement.

1. *Curriculum focus.* Having students apply their learning in authentic situations properly focuses the curriculum around achieving important performance outcomes—what we want learners to be able to do with their learning—rather than simply trying to cover large numbers of discrete knowledge and skill objectives. Without a coordinated plan for teaching and assessing valued outcomes, such as research, argumentation, oral discourse, or media literacy, such outcomes can easily fall through the cracks of conventional teaching and assessment. In other words, all important learning outcomes need to be developed and assessed—by design. Further, a curricular focus on performance encourages teaching that prepares students to apply their learning across new and varied situations and contexts, as outlined in Chapter 5.

Figure 8.5
Task Starters for Social Studies

Task/Project Starter	Elementary Example	Secondary Example
Gather information from primary and secondary sources to construct a "history" or to evaluate historical claims or interpretations.	Interview long-time residents of your community to learn about how things have changed over the years. Construct and display your community history through an illustrated story booklet for the community library.	Research various historical claims/interpretations regarding the rationale for the United States entering into the Vietnam War or the 2nd Iraq war. Use at least two primary and two secondary sources, including at least two interviews with veterans or citizens. Prepare to communicate your findings and your evaluation of the various claims/interpretations.
Critically analyze current events/issues to reach a decision or a solution to a problem.	Identify an issue in your class or school (e.g., sharing the playground equipment, preventing bullying). Identify the causes and effects; then propose a resolution.	Analyze current debates over national immigration policy. Compare the different points of view on the issue. Analyze various factors, including "push-pull" and cause-and-effect. Propose a policy that you favor and provide reasons and evidence for your position.
Make predictions for _____ [current or future events or issues] based on an understanding of historical patterns.	Examine the class plaques left by previous 4th grade classes. What values were important to them? How do you know? How might your class plaque communicate similar and different values at the end of this year? Why do you say so?	Compare the Arab Spring with previous cases of popular uprising, revolution, insurrection, and civil conflict. Make a prediction: Will governments in Middle Eastern countries become more or less democratic within the next five years?
Act as a responsible citizen by _____ (e.g., staying informed, studying issues, participating in community events, expressing opinions respectfully, voting).	You have an idea that you believe will make your school better, and you want to convince school leaders that they should act on your idea. Identify your audience (e.g., principal, PTO board, students) and 1. Describe your idea. 2. Explain why and how it will improve the school. 3. Develop a plan for acting on your idea. Your idea and plan can be communicated to your target audience in a letter, an e-mail, or a presentation.	Develop a position (for or against) a proposal affecting students (e.g., mandatory school uniforms, allowing cell phones to be kept on during class). Select information from articles and interviews with teachers, parents, and students to prepare your argument. Be sure to consider and address predictable objections to your position. Prepare to present your argument and support to the PTSA Council or School Board via a 90-second oral presentation.

(continued)

Figure 8.5
Continued

Task/Project Starter	Elementary Example	Secondary Example
Whose story is this? Identify and explain differing points of view about _____.	Write a story in which two characters have very different points of view about the same event that they both experienced.	Identify and explain differing points of view about the display of the Confederate flag on government buildings and in public places.
Other: _____		

2. *Student engagement.* A curriculum and assessment system built around authentic tasks and projects can contribute to student motivation and engagement in two ways: (1) students are more likely to see purpose and relevance in learning content and working to develop skills that they recognize as relevant to the world beyond the classroom, and (2) learners are more engaged in schoolwork that allows them some choice and connects to their interests and talents (Dabrowski & Marshall, 2018). As noted, cornerstone tasks and projects are set in genuine, real-world contexts, and they allow for students' voice and choice within task and project frames.

3. *Evidence collection.* A system of cornerstone tasks and projects, choreographed across the K–12 spectrum, enables a district, school, or program to gather evidence of growth of important outcomes. It's one thing to declare in a mission statement a commitment to developing 21st century skills and quite another to have a curriculum and assessment system for systematically developing—and compiling evidence to track students' growth on—these important outcomes. Without a coordinated approach for assessing *all* valued outcomes, schools are likely to fixate on the results of a once-a-year snapshot assessment (e.g., state tests) as the primary measure to gauge the performance of their students and the successes of their programs. Educational organizations need more robust data to affirm their collective efforts. As an added benefit, a system of cornerstone tasks and projects supports the development of digital portfolios that students, parents, and educators can use to trace the growth of important skills and to capture evidence of genuine accomplishments.

Figure 8.6
Task Starters for Science

Task/Project Starter	Elementary Example	Secondary Example
Design and conduct an investigation or experiment to • *Answer a question.* • *Explain a phenomenon.*	Design and conduct an investigation to determine which of three different brands of paper towels are most absorbent. Create a data table to record your observations and document your procedure so that others can follow it to replicate your investigation.	Design an investigation to determine how much it costs to take a shower.
Effectively use scientific tools to • *Observe _____.* • *Collect data on _____.* • *Measure _____.* • *Record data about _____.* • *Classify _____.* • *Draw conclusions about _____.*	Observe a variety of objects to determine which will sink or float in water. What characteristics do the "floaters" have in common?	Use pH strips to test water samples from three different sources (e.g., water fountain, local stream or pond, collected rainwater, bottled carbonated water). Conduct at least two tests for each sample. Record and analyze your data. Draw a conclusion from the results and be prepared to explain it.
Create a representation or model to • *Illustrate a scientific concept or principle.* • *Symbolize a phenomenon.* • *Other: _____.*	Develop a visual representation to show the relationship (if any) between school lunch menus and the percentage of students who bring their lunch versus buying lunch at school.	Using a basketball as the sun, create a scale model of our solar system for display in the school gymnasium. Use other spherical objects to represent the planets.
Evaluate a claim involving science.	Cyril says that an apple falling from a tree will hit the ground faster than an acorn falling from the same height at the same time because it is bigger and heavier. What do you think? How could you test his claim?	Evaluate the following claim: Following a strict high-protein diet is a safe way to lose weight. Do you believe this claim? What does the evidence suggest?

(continued)

Figure 8.6
Continued

Task/Project Starter	Elementary Example	Secondary Example
Analyze current issues involving science or technology to reach a decision or pose a solution to a problem.	Which areas of our community do and do not have internet access? Why? Conduct interviews to discover the answers to these questions. Then, come up with a plan to convince community leaders to bring internet access to everyone in the community.	Is hydraulic fracturing (fracking) an environmentally safe way to extract oil and natural gas from bedrock? Research the question and consider various points of view. Then, develop a position paper or blog post to convince voters to support your position.
Critique experimental design or conclusions.	Chris wants to decide which of two spot removers is best. First, he tried Spot Remover A on a T-shirt that had fruit stains and chocolate stains. Next, he tried Spot Remover B on jeans that had grass stains and rust stains. Then he compared the results. Explain what Chris did wrong that will make it hard for him to know which spot remover is best, and redesign his investigation so that he will be able to answer the question.	Carefully review students' science fair projects involving experimental design. Was the investigation sound? For example, were • Procedures consistently applied? • Variables isolated? • Sufficient samples taken? • Data accurately recorded? • Logical conclusions drawn from data?
Other: _____		

4. *A culture of continuous improvement.* Common tasks and projects afford the opportunity for teachers in a grade level or course to meet together to examine the resulting student work. Many schools and districts have formal structures for such teacher collaboration, known as professional learning communities, or PLCs (DuFour, 2004), and some have enacted schedules that enable PLC teams to meet periodically across schools (e.g., through an early-release day four times a year). When teachers meet in role-alike professional learning teams (e.g., by grade level and subject areas) to evaluate the results from the common tasks and projects, they begin to identify general patterns of strengths

Figure 8.7
Task Starters for Mathematics

Task/Project Starter	Elementary Example	Secondary Example
Create a mathematical representation/model of _____ (e.g., quantity, size, rate, motion, change).	Create a mathematical model to show: • the average daily temperatures for a given month. • Growth in height of 3rd grade students during the school year.	Create a mathematical model to use in evaluating international stock funds using data from the past five years. Which funds would you recommend to an investor?
Make and justify predictions or decisions based on pattern analysis.	Based on an analysis of the growth in height of 3rd grade students during the school year, make a prediction for current 2nd graders about their rate of growth next year.	Predict the winning time of the women's marathon event in the next two Olympic games based on the pattern of the winning times in previous games. Explain your reasoning. Compare the women's marathon times to the men's times since 1984. Given the results, will the women ever run faster? If so, in what year? Explain your answer.
Design a physical structure.	Design the tallest self-supporting straw structure using 16 paper straws and 2 feet of masking tape. What geometric shapes do you think will allow you to achieve the greatest height? Why?	Design a three-dimensional shipping container to maximize volume and safety for shipping glass marbles. What shape and size container do you propose? Explain your reasoning.
Evaluate a mathematical or statistical claim.	Maria says her dad told her that when you add an even and an odd number, you will always get an odd number as the result. Is he right?	Claim: Fifty percent of all Americans eat at least one meal at a fast-food restaurant every week. How would you go about evaluating this claim?
Correct flawed mathematical reasoning.	Ricardo said, "Four plus three times two is 14." Angela replied, "No, it's 10." Did someone make a mistake? Explain the reasons that they came up with the different solutions. Then, tell which one is correct and explain why.	The winner of a state lottery was given a choice to receive one million dollars or a penny doubled every day for 30 days. The winner chose the million-dollar payout. Was this a wise choice (assuming the winner was interested in maximizing the amount)? Explain your reasoning.
Other: _____		

in student performance as well as those areas needing improvement. Then they pool their best instructional ideas for addressing the weak areas. This collaborative approach is familiar to coaches of team sports and sponsors of extracurricular activities such as band and drama. As an example, football coaches often meet at someone's home to review game film from Saturday's game and then plan next week's practices based on their collective analysis of the team's weaknesses. A system of cornerstone tasks and projects enables teachers in academic subject areas to participate in the proven performance-enhancing methods historically applied in the arts and athletics. Additionally, the regular use of teacher teams to review student work on authentic tasks and projects offers an antidote to the isolation of the classroom, fosters a collaborative culture of continuous improvement, and establishes a professionally enriching, results-oriented environment (McTighe, 2008).

Figure 8.8
Task Starters for Health

Task/Project Starter	Elementary Example	Secondary Example
Be an advocate for wellness: Encourage others to engage in healthful activities and behaviors that promote wellness throughout a lifetime.	Develop a comic book for younger students to illustrate (1) the importance of good nutrition, (2) examples of balanced meals that can taste good, and (3) potential health problems that can result from poor nutrition.	Develop a multimedia public relations campaign to encourage people to make healthful choices and decisions regarding _____ (e.g., diet, exercise, sleep, stress management, alcohol and drug use).
Set a goal and develop and implement a plan to improve some aspect of your health or fitness. Record and track data on your performance and periodically set new goals.	Set a personal performance goal (e.g., time for a 50-yard dash, percentage of made free-throws, minutes of jump roping). Collect data on your performance (and improvements) over time.	Develop a personal fitness plan to improve your • Strength. • Endurance. • Flexibility. • Skills in a selected sport.
Other: _____		

Source: © 2017b Jay McTighe. Used with permission.

Conclusion

The development and implementation of a curriculum and assessment system around cornerstone tasks and projects will enable districts and schools to realize the "guaranteed and viable" curriculum that Robert Marzano's research recommends (Marzano, 2003). Such a system focuses instruction and assessment around learning outcomes that matter most—long-term transfer goals, within and across disciplines. Moreover, the cornerstones infuse authenticity, relevance, engagement, and student choice into the educational process.

Constructing a system of cornerstone tasks and projects needs to be recognized—and undertaken—as long-term work. It is reasonable to consider phasing in such a K–12 system over the course of two to five years. With that in mind, we recommend that district and school leaders follow a four-part aphorism: *think big, start small, work smart, and go for an early win* (Wiggins & McTighe, 2007). *Think big* calls for leaders to develop a comprehensive action plan and schedule for developing and implementing the cornerstones over time, beginning with a plan for communicating the intent and building understanding and support from various constituents. *Start small* bids leaders to begin with one or two discipline areas that are ready, willing, and able to get started. Once they have a successful beginning, it will be easier to incorporate other disciplines into the system. *Work smart* reminds us that we do not have to reinvent wheels and develop cornerstone tasks and projects from scratch. Instead, start with well-developed and validated tasks and projects from established organizations, such as Stanford's SCALE Performance Task Database (https://performanceassessment.stanford.edu) and the PBLWorks library of projects (https://my.pblworks.org/projects). *Go for an early win* suggests building on those areas (e.g., writing, STEM) where teachers are already comfortable using performance tasks and projects. Savvy leaders recognize that it is easier to build on early successes than it is to recover from moving too fast with too many groups at the start!

We offer an important cautionary implementation note when rolling out cornerstone tasks and projects, especially at the middle and high school levels: be careful not to overload students or teachers by having multiple tasks and projects with similar due dates. This potential problem can be averted by mapping the cornerstones on a schoolwide calendar to coordinate schedules and minimize conflicts and overloads.

Grant Wiggins opined that "students should graduate with a résumé of demonstrated accomplishments rather than simply a transcript of courses taken and a GPA." We can act on his idea by developing and implementing the kind of curriculum and assessment system described in this chapter. So, think big, start small, work smart, and go for early wins. Your students will be the beneficiaries.

Appendixes

Appendix A
Glossary

analytical rubric—An evaluation tool for student products and performances on selected traits. Each trait is evaluated independently and receives a separate rating or score. For example, a piece of writing may be evaluated according to organization, use of details, attention to audience, and language usage/mechanics. Trait scores may be weighted and totaled.

assessment—A process for making inferences about student learning based on evidence.

authentic—A term that refers to performance tasks and projects that elicit the application of knowledge and skills in a real-world manner and context. An authentic task presents students with a realistic challenge that calls for genuine products and performances. Another connotation of the term refers to tasks that establish a context that connects to the experiences and interests of learners.

bias—Factors that interfere with a valid inference regarding a student's knowledge and skill. For example, an English language learner may know the science content but not be able to read the test items in English.

content standard—A goal statement specifying desired knowledge, skills, and understandings to be learned.

criteria—The guidelines, rules, or norms by which student responses, products, or performances are evaluated. Criteria identify the attributes of a successful performance.

criterion performance list—An evaluation tool consisting of designated criteria, but without descriptive details. Unlike a rubric, a performance list merely provides a set of features without defining the terms or describing varying degrees of quality or proficiency. These are sometimes referred to as "single-point rubrics."

evaluation—A process for judging the quality, proficiency, or depth of learning. Sound evaluation is based on multiple sources of information.

holistic rubric—An evaluation tool for arriving at an overall judgment of a product or performance. Holistic evaluation yields a single rating or score.

performance task—Any learning activity or assessment that asks students to construct a multifaceted response, create a product, or produce a demonstration.

project—An individual or collaborative enterprise that is carefully planned and designed to achieve a particular aim.

project-based learning (PBL)—A pedagogical approach in which learning develops as students pursue answers to complex (driving) questions through work on extended learner-directed projects.

reliability—The degree to which the results of an assessment are dependable and yield consistent results across raters, over time, or across different versions of the same assessment.

rubric—A set of general criteria used to evaluate a student's performance in a given outcome area. Rubrics consist of a fixed measurement scale (e.g., four-point) and a list of criteria that describe the characteristics of products or performances for each score point.

transfer—The ability to apply one's learning to a new situation beyond the context in which it was learned.

transfer goals—Long-term goals that specify particular transfer abilities; that is, what students are able to do when they confront new information, issues, challenges, and opportunities. Transfer goals can be discipline based as well as transdisciplinary (e.g., 21st century skills or habits of mind).

validity—An indication of how well an assessment measures what it was intended to measure; specifically, validity refers to the extent to which the results of an assessment can be used to make inferences about targeted learning.

Appendix B
A Planning Tool for Tasks and Projects

This tool includes a variety of prompts to consider during task or project planning. Not all prompts require consideration, so focus on those that most closely align with the purpose of the task or project, student needs, and available resources (including time). See Chapter 3 for a more detailed overview of the design variables. We've noted alignment to the chapters for ease of reference.

Content Area(s):   Topic:

Grade Level: Time allotted:

Planning Task/Project Elements
1. What key learning goals will be targeted (including transfer goals)? (*Chapters 1 and 3*)
2. What are the Driving Questions? (*Chapter 3*)
3. How will authenticity be achieved? Select as many as are applicable. (*Chapters 2 and 3*): ☐ Context ☐ Impact ☐ Processes ☐ Product ☐ Audience ☐ Personal Connection
4. Individual Element (*Chapters 2 and 3*):
5. Collaborative Element (*Chapters 2 and 3*):
6. What are the success criteria (i.e., rubric categories)? (*Chapters 4 and 7*)
   a. Individual Element(s):
   b. Collaborative Element(s):
7. Task/Project Vignette (brief description) (*Chapters 2 and 3*):

Planning Instruction
1. What kind of research–if any–will students complete? (*Chapters 5 and 6*)
   a. What *digital* resources may you need (e.g., websites, tools [see Appendix C])?
   b. What *physical* resources will you need (e.g., supplies, equipment)?
   c. What *personnel* resources will you seek (e.g., experts, audience)?

2. What authentic models or examples of previous student work might you present as exemplars? (*Chapter 4*)
3. What information do you want to gather/pre-assess before you launch the task/project? (*Chapter 5*)
4. How will you launch the task/project? (*Chapter 5*)
5. What topics/skills may require full-class instruction? Small-group instruction? (*Chapter 5*)
6. What topics/skills may require iterations of practice? (*Chapter 5*)
7. What "scrimmage" opportunities will you provide? (Chapter 5)
8. When and how will you monitor progress and provide feedback throughout the unit? (*Chapter 5*)
9. What additional assessments may be needed to supplement the evidence gained from the task or project (e.g., tests, quizzes, skill checks)? (*Chapter 5*)

Planning for Differentiation
1. What additional scaffolds might be needed? (*Chapter 6*)
   a. For students who need support with time management:
   b. For students who are learning English:
   c. For students who need reading support:
   d. For students who need writing support/alternative modes of delivery:
2. When might you need to provide targeted tasks to different groups of students (e.g., through stations)? (*Chapter 6*)
3. What opportunities might you provide for student choice? (*Chapter 6*)
   a. Personalizing or generating the driving questions:
   b. Providing options for project focus:
   c. Providing product, performance, or audience options:
4. How might you provide additional challenge to students needing more advanced work? (*Chapter 6*)
   a. Providing more complex readings and resources:
   b. Introducing alternative perspectives:
   c. Increasing the level of expertise:

Crafting the Environment
1. How might you structure the physical arrangement of your classroom for different parts of the task/project? (*Chapter 7*)
2. How might you build a culture of teamwork? (*Chapter 7*)
3. What roles are needed and how should they be assigned? (*Chapter 7*)
4. What channels of communication will you establish so that students can voice their needs, both to you and to other students? (*Chapter 7*)
5. What time management tools might you and your students employ to increase the efficiency of task and project implementation? (*Chapter 7*)

Appendix C
Technology Tools for
Tasks and Projects

Category/Use	Technology Tool
Book report	Book Hooks—http://www.bookhooks.com GoodReads—https://www.goodreads.com iMovie—create a book trailer; see sample trailers at https://www.youtube.com/user/mhmediaspec Voicethread (iPad app)—http://voicethread.com/
Bulletin board	Canva—https://www.canva.com/create/photo-collages/ Educlipper—http://www.educlipper.net Padlet—http://www.padlet.com Pinterest—https://www.pinterest.com/
Cartoon/comic	Animaker—https://www.animaker.com/ Pixton—http://www.pixton.com/ Storyboard That—https://www.storyboardthat.com/storyboard-creator Strip Designer—https://itunes.apple.com/us/app/strip-designer/id314780738?mt=8 ToonDoo—http://www.toondoo.com/ Toontastic—https://itunes.apple.com/us/app/toontastic-3d/id1145104532?mt=8
Coding	Code—https://code.org Hour of Code—https://hourofcode.com/us/learn Microsoft MakeCode—https://www.microsoft.com/en-us/makecode?rtc=1 Scratch—https://scratch.mit.edu/ ScratchJr (K–2 app)—https://www.scratchjr.org/

Category/Use	Technology Tool
Creative thinking/ brainstorming	Bubbl.us—https://bubbl.us/ Inspiration—http://www.inspiration.com/ Popplet—http://popplet.com/ SmartDraw—https://www.smartdraw.com/
Digital storytelling	Book Creator—https://bookcreator.com/ Pic-Lits—https://www.piclits.com/compose_dragdrop.aspx Slidestory—https://slidestory.com Storybird—https://storybird.com/ Storyboarder—https://wonderunit.com/storyboarder/
Explanation (written, verbal)	Educreations—http://www.educreations.com/ Explain Everything—https://itunes.apple.com/us/app/ explain-everything/id431493086?mt=8
Formative Assessment	Flipgrid—https://flipgrid.com Goformative—https://goformative.com Google Forms—https://www.google.com/forms/about/ Kahoot—https://create.kahoot.it/login Mentimeter—https://www.mentimeter.com/ Kahoot—https://create.kahoot.it/login Pear Deck—https://www.peardeck.com/ Quizizz—https://quizizz.com/ Quizlet—https://quizlet.com/
How-to guide	Create an App—https://www.yapp.us/ Educreations—http://www.educreations.com/ Snagit (screencasting tool)—https://www.techsmith.com /screen-capture.html Zoom—https://zoom.us/
Multimedia product	Animoto—http://animoto.com/ Animoto (app)—https://itunes.apple.com/us/app /animoto-videos/id459248037?mt=8 Biteable—https://biteable.com/infographic/ Edmodo—http://www.edmodo.com HyperDocs—https://hyperdocs.co iMovie—http://www.apple.com/ilife/imovie/ Photostory—http://microsoft-photo-story.en.softonic.com/ Prezi—http://prezi.com/ SlideShare—http://www.slideshare.net/

Category/Use	Technology Tool

Oral presentation/ podcast	Anchor (podcasting app)—https://anchor.fm/
	Audacity (podcasting software)—
	    https://www.audacityteam.org/
	Audioboom—http://audioboom.com/
	Sway (Office 365)—https://sway.office.com/
	Vodcast (video podcast)—https://itunes.apple.com/us/app
	    /sdpbc-vodcast/id598313309?ls=1&mt=8
	Voicethread (iPad app)—http://voicethread.com/

Pen pal/student connection	Empatico—https://empatico.org/ Skype chat—http://skype.com Zoom chat—https://zoom.us
Poster, infographic	Adobe Spark—https://spark.adobe.com/ Canva—https://www.canva.com/create/infographics Glogster—http://www.glogster.com/ Google drawing—https://docs.google.com/drawings/ Padlet—http://www.padlet.com Piktochart—http://piktochart.com/ Smore—https://www.smore.com/app Visme—https://www.visme.co/make-infographics/ Venngage—https://venngage.com/
Proposal	Canva—https://www.canva.com/create/proposals/ Proposify—https://www.proposify.com/proposal-templates

Research	History Channel—https://www.history.com/speeches
	Library of Congress—https://www.loc.gov/
	Library Spot—http://libraryspot.com/
	National Geographic Kids—
	    https://kids.nationalgeographic.com/
	National Science Foundation (for math)—https://
	    www.nsf.gov/news/overviews/mathematics/overview.jsp
	NewseumED—http://www.newseum.org/about/
	U.S. Bureau of Labor Statistics—
	    https://www.bls.gov/k12/students.htm

Research report	Doodlekit—http://kids-website-builder.com/ Nearpod—http://nearpod.com/ Sutori—https://www.sutori.com/story/student-tutorial

Category/Use	Technology Tool
Science project/ design	AutoCAD—https://www.autodesk.com/education /free-software/autocad CAST Science Writer—http://sciencewriter.cast.org /welcome;jsessionid=64D53C43AD80D6FAB1A0F95 ABCFCA054
Summary	Emojis—https://chrome.google.com/webstore/detail /emoji-keyboard-by-emojion /ipdjnhgkpapgippgcgkfcbpdpcgifncb?hl=en *Note: This is an emoji download for Chrome so students can create summaries with emojis.* Twitter—https://twitter.com/
Time line	myHistro—http://www.myhistro.com/?utm_campaign =elearningindustry.com&utm_source=%2Ftop-10-free -timeline-creation-tools-for-teachers&utm_medium=link ReadWriteThink—http://www.readwritethink.org/files /resources/interactives/timeline_2/ Time Graphics—https://time.graphics/ Timetoast—http://www.timetoast.com/
Vocabulary notebook	Google Keep (app)—https://play.google.com/store/apps /details?id=com.google.android.keep&hl=en_US OneNote (app)—https://www.onenote.com/?404&public=1 Visual Thesaurus—http://www.visualthesaurus.com/j
Written product	Blogger—https://www.blogger.com/about/ Book Creator—bookcreator.com Edublogs—http://edublogs.org/ Flipsnack—http://www.flipsnack.com/ Issuu—http://issuu.com/ LiveJournal—https://www.livejournal.com/ Meograph—http://www.meograph.com/

Appendix D
Driving Questions Template

Directions

Use these directions to guide you in using the template on the next page to create driving questions.

1. Articulate your key understanding, knowledge, and skill goals. See Chapter 3 for guidance in formatting these goals.

2. Examine the description and examples of each of the five types of driving questions to determine which type best fits the selected learning goals.

3. Use the description and examples of that type of question to develop a driving question for your project.

4. Use the criteria listed in the box "All Driving Questions Should Be"—along with peer and student feedback—to evaluate your work.

Key Learning Goals		
Understanding Goals	**Knowledge Goals**	**Skill Goals**
All Driving Questions Should Be	***Solving a Real-World Problem***	***Meeting a Design Challenge***
☐ **Engaging** (intriguing, age-appropriate, contextual; not a typical "school" question)	*This may be a school-level, local, or global issue.*	*May refer to a product, event, or campaign.*
☐ **Open-Ended** (complex, multiple "right" answers, researchable but no single answer from a search)	✓ How can we help others develop empathy toward diverse peoples?	✓ How can we design a memorial to honor our community's veterans from the wars and conflicts in Iraq and Afghanistan?
☐ **Aligned with Key Learning Goals** (use the goals listed and ensure they encompass standards)	✓ What is the best approach to securing financial aid for college? For whom?	✓ How can we better control afternoon bus traffic?
	✓ How can we support residents who are pursuing U.S. citizenship?	✓ How can we best illustrate sound?
	✓ How can we increase the number and selection of children's books in our local library?	✓ How might we convince a famous author to visit our school?

Key Learning Goals		
Understanding Goals	**Knowledge Goals**	**Skill Goals**
Exploring an Abstract Question	***Conducting an Investigation***	***Taking a Stand on an Issue***
✓ *These are similar to UbD essential questions.* ✓ How is geography "destiny"? ✓ What makes a law "just?" ✓ Who is a hero? ✓ How can art influence people? ✓ How can conflict be both productive and destructive? ✓ How does perspective shape research?	✓ *Usually involves a scientific or historical question.* ✓ What is the optimal price for school yearbooks? ✓ What is the best pet for our class, given the available resources? ✓ What factors cause and deter erosion? How does erosion affect ecosystems? ✓ How has increased access to technology shaped our grasp of spelling and grammar rules?	✓ *Should be arguable with evidence on both sides.* ✓ Should the U.S. government regulate bitcoin? ✓ Should we be required to recycle? ✓ Should some books be censored? ✓ Should public schools continue to teach cursive writing?

Choose the kind of driving question that would work best with your project or unit focus and your key learning goals. Using the description and examples above, craft a driving question.

Driving Question:

Appendix E
Performance Task for 2nd Grade Math

Lunch Specials

Transfer Goal:
- Deconstruct numbers to discover various ways to problem solve

Essential Question:
- How can we use knowledge of place value to deconstruct numbers and gain a better understanding of what is happening in addition when large numbers are combined?

Knowledge:
- Place value and basic addition/subtraction facts
- Multiple ways to approach addition and subtraction problems

Skills:
- Show numerous ways to express addition and subtraction
- Relate manipulatives and images to numbers and algorithms
- Analyze patterns in numbers
- Solve single- and multiple-step addition and subtraction problems

Performance Task:

Goal: Deconstruct menu prices to discover various ways to provide $5.00 lunch specials

Role: Restaurant manager

Audience: The dining public (consumers)

Situation: You are in charge of a restaurant that features individually priced entrées, sides, and drinks. Your job is to go over the menu and find out which items add up to a total of $6.00. If the combined items equal $6.00, you can offer the meal for a discounted price of $5.00.

Performance/Product: Design a menu featuring the combinations. The menu will be presented with proof that the consumer is saving money.

Success Criteria: You will be evaluated on the accuracy of your work, how clearly you communicate your mathematical thinking and problem solving, and the professional quality of your work.

Directions:

- You are about to open a restaurant. To get people into your restaurant, you've decided to have some lunch specials. To make a lunch special, you have to find menu items that go together and add up to $6.00, and then you can sell the lunch special at a discount price of $5.00.
- Remember that in science terms, a "consumer" is something that eats to get its energy. In social studies, a "consumer" is someone who buys goods and services. You are trying to get both of these things to your restaurant—people who will come to spend money on food to eat.
- Your big grand opening is coming soon, and you want to make sure your consumers are happy. You need to get the menu together early. Your menu will have five parts:
  - The main food people would eat—for example: hamburgers, hotdogs, tacos, pizza, sandwiches, and things like that. You must have five entrées. They must cost $2.25, $2.00, $1.75, $1.50, and $1.25.
  - Healthy sides—This can be any fruit or vegetable side that you'd like, such as apples, oranges, bananas, strawberries, broccoli, plantains, and spinach. You must have at least five of these. They must cost $1.65, $1.25, $1.10, $0.95, and $0.40.
  - Unhealthy sides—These will be side dishes such as French fries, cheese sticks, potato chips, tortilla chips, and peanuts. You must have five of these. They must cost $1.25, $1.10, $0.95, $0.65, and $0.40.
  - Drinks—These will be whatever you'd like to serve to drink. You can use any sodas, juices, flavored water, and milk. You must have five of these. They must cost $1.50, $1.00, $0.90, $0.75 and $0.50.
  - Desserts—You can serve whatever desserts you'd like. Maybe you can sell cookies, cakes, pies, or ice cream. You must have five of these. They must cost $1.95, $1.40, $1.30, $1.20, and $0.50.

You don't have to use the foods listed, but you have to use the prices. You can combine the foods listed with the prices listed, or you can make up your own foods and use the prices listed.

- To make a special deal, you have to have an entrée, a healthy side, an unhealthy side, a drink, and a dessert. When you choose these five things, you need to add up their prices. If you add up the five prices and they total $6.00, you can sell the lunch special for a discounted price of $5.00. Here is an example:

Entrée—Pizza =	$1.60
Healthy side—Green beans =	$0.80
Unhealthy side—French fries =	$1.40
Drink—Soda =	$0.75
Dessert—Pie =	$1.45
	$6.00

You could make this combination of foods a special because these items cost $6.00 and you can sell this for $5.00.

- You must come up with five different "Lunch Specials."
- Once you've figured out the specials for your restaurant, you must make a menu. You should name your restaurant and decorate the cover of your menu. On the inside you must show all your menu items and how much they cost. You may use the spreadsheet provided and glue it inside your menu if you'd like, or you may design the inside however you'd like.
- You must also have a place on the menu that shows your special deals, including the combination of food items and how much money your consumer will save. For example, if we use the numbers listed above, you could show something like this:

SPECIAL #1: PIZZA, GREEN BEANS, FRENCH FRIES, SODA, AND PIE.
NORMAL COST: $6.00. YOU PAY: $5.00! YOU SAVE: $1.00!

This is just one example. You may do this however you'd like.

- Take time to make your menu look good. You may use real pictures of food and glue them in, or you may draw pictures. Try your best to make your menu awesome!
- Once your menu is complete, you will share it with the class and explain how you made it, and what you chose to do. You will also meet with your teacher, who will act as a consumer and ask you questions about the menu.

Rubric:

	Open for Business	**Almost Ready to Open**	**Under Construction**
Math (Content) ____/15	• You showed all your work and correctly used and added the numbers that equaled $6.00. • Work is clear, accurate, and makes sense.	• You showed some work and came up with the correct answers. • Work is accurate.	• You did not show your work, or your work was unclear or incorrect.
Mathematical Reasoning (Process) ____/10	• Specials are clearly labeled for categories and pricing. • The menu clearly and convincingly explains why the specials are great deals for consumers.	• Specials include information on categories and pricing. • Menu explains why the specials are good deals.	• Some information on categories and pricing is missing. • Menu does not make it clear why the specials are good deals.
Interview (Process) ____/10	• Was able to explain the menu and answer questions about the menu specials and their costs.	• Understood some aspects of the menu and specials but could not clearly explain them.	• Could not explain the menu or answer questions about it or the specials.
Professional Quality (Impact) ____/5	• Menu is restaurant ready! Name of restaurant and appearance of menu make consumers want to come back over and over again. • The menu is neat and has no major language mistakes.	• The name of your restaurant and the appearance of your menu let consumers know what your restaurant is all about. • Menu is complete but has some language mistakes.	• Name of restaurant or appearance of menu might be missing or confuse consumers. • Menu is hard to follow and has major language mistakes.

Source: Eric Imbrescia. Used with permission.

Appendix F
PBL for 3rd and 4th Grade
ELA and Math

Children's Book Challenge

Transfer Goal:
- Research a need and plan strategically to address it

Driving Question:
- How can we enhance the number and selection of children's books in our local library?

Knowledge:
- Characteristics and examples of various literary genres/purposes: *realistic fiction, historical fiction, traditional literature, science fiction, fantasy, mystery, informational text, biography, autobiography, poetry*
- How to analyze data
- How to create picture graphs, scaled bar graphs, and line plots to display data sets
- Organizational structures and tools for writing

Skills:
- Analyze texts for purpose/genre, topic, and intended audience
- Create and administer surveys to determine favorite topics and genres of the student body
- Conduct research to evaluate text selection for variety in terms of purpose, topic, and intended audience
- Collect and organize facts, details, and reasons to support a main point
- Convey research findings through text and images
- Convey research findings through charts and graphs
- Craft informative and opinion pieces to encourage community action

Project Description:
- We know our school library has a wonderful collection of books for students of all ages. It also offers many choices to students with many different interests in topics and genres, so that—during the school year—we all can be reading something we like.
- We also know that it's important for students to continue reading even when school is closed for winter, spring, and summer breaks. Our local library can help us find books we like even when school is closed. But does it have as wide a selection of book levels, topics, and genres as our school library? Does it have enough books to allow many kids to check out books they like at the same time?
- We will investigate the book topics and genres available in our school library. We will also conduct research to figure out the favorite topics and genres of the students at our school (each group will survey a different grade), as well as how many books they read during school breaks.
- Next, we will investigate the selection of children's books at our local library and decide what kinds of books it might need to add to its collection to meet all students' reading needs.
- We will analyze our research findings and create a list of recommendations for our local library. We will present our findings and recommendations through persuasive presentations that convey facts, reasons, and personal stories through words, images, charts, and graphs.
- Members of the local library staff, city council, and local community groups will attend our presentations, so we must be professional and persuasive if we want to enlist their help!
- Our school librarian and the local librarian will serve as experts for us as we work on this project, so we will need to prepare and ask them good questions.

	Ready to Present	**Minor Revisions Needed**	**Major Revisions Needed**
Research on the number and kind of books in the school library (ELA Content and Process)	• Your explanations of each genre's purpose and characteristics are expertly captured in your descriptions and examples. Students would know exactly how to find books they like. • Your examples reflect a wide variety of topics and grade levels. There is something every reader would relate to.	• Your explanations of each genre's purpose and characteristics are captured in your descriptions and examples. Students would have some idea how to find books they like, but more detail would be helpful. • Your examples reflect a variety of topics and grade levels. There is something most readers would relate to, but more examples would help.	• Your explanations of each genre's purpose and characteristics are incomplete or unclear. Students would need more detail and more examples to find books they like. • Your examples need more variety in topics and grade levels, or more examples are needed for readers to be able to find something they like.
Survey Research (ELA Process)	• Your survey is expertly worded to specifically address students in your target grade level. • Your survey is designed so that it targets only one "data point" per question. • Your survey questions are so clear that students will know exactly how to answer them.	• Your survey is worded so that it would make sense to the students in your targeted grade level. • Your survey is designed so that students might give more than one "data point" per question. • Your survey questions are clear, but students may be confused about how to answer a few questions.	• Your survey needs to be reworded to make sense to the students in your targeted grade level. • Your survey is designed so that most students would give more than one "data point" per question. • Students will be confused about how to answer almost all of your questions.

	Ready to Present	**Minor Revisions Needed**	**Major Revisions Needed**
Research on the number and kind of books in the public library (ELA Content and Process)	• You conducted such a thorough examination of library books that we understand exactly what kinds of books are and are not available to readers in your grade level. • You provide such crystal-clear examples of books that are "plentiful" and books that are "scarce" that the library will know exactly what kinds of books are needed.	• You conducted a thorough examination of library books. We have a good idea of what kinds of books are and are not available to readers in your grade level, but we might need to investigate a bit more. • Your examples of books that are "plentiful" and books that are "scarce" are clear but lack detail. The library may need to do some more research to figure out exactly what kinds of books are needed.	• Your examination of library books needed a closer eye for detail. We have a fuzzy idea of what kinds of books are and are not available to readers in your grade level. • The library staff will need to do more research to figure out what kinds of books are well-stocked and what kind of books they need to add to their collection.
Picture Graph, Scaled Bar Graph, and Line Plot (Math Content and Process)	• You accurately capture and display all important data from your survey research and your library research. • You include at least one of each type of graph (picture, bar, and line); you make wise decisions about which graph to use when so that your data are clearly and expertly communicated.	• You capture and display important data from your survey and your library research with a few missing or inaccurate points. • You include at least one of each type of graph (picture, bar, and line), but your decisions about which graph to use in each situation makes it difficult to understand your findings.	• Your data from your survey and your library research are incompletely or inaccurately captured and displayed. • You are missing at least one type of graph (picture, bar, and line), or you have chosen graphs that are not suited for the kind of data you are trying to display.

	Ready to Present	**Minor Revisions Needed**	**Major Revisions Needed**
Picture Graph, Scaled Bar Graph, and Line Plot (Math Content and Process) —(*continued*)	• Each graph is constructed accurately in both scale and data display.	• There are minor errors in the scale and/or the display of your data.	• There are major errors in the scale or the display of your data.
Presentation (ELA Process)	• Your persuasive argument is expertly supported by important facts, convincing reasons, and moving personal stories. • You used a balanced combination of words, images, charts, and graphs to present your case. • Ideas are compellingly presented, engagingly organized, and easy to follow.	• Your persuasive argument is supported by clear facts, logical reasons, and personal stories. • You used a combination of words, images, charts, and graphs, but one mode was used much more than the others. • Ideas are clearly presented, logically organized, and—for the most part—easy to follow.	• Your argument would be more persuasive if you included more or clearer facts, reasons, and stories. • More images, charts, graphs, or words are needed to make your presentation clear. • Ideas are difficult to follow at times.
Professional Quality and Impact	• Writing style, choice and presentation of visuals, proofreading, and presentation style enhance the credibility of your argument. You make the audience pay attention and motivate them to help the library get more books.	• Writing style, choice, and presentation of visuals, proofreading, and presentation style do not detract from the credibility of your argument. You make the audience pay attention to your whole presentation.	• Writing style, choice and presentation of visuals, errors, and presentation style detract from the credibility of your argument. Your audience pays attention to most but not all of your presentation.

Appendix G
Performance Task for High School History

You Dropped the Bomb (Or Did You?)

Transfer Goals:
- Evaluate the impact of key historical decisions on society
- Develop a persuasive argument based on accurate historical evidence

Essential Question:
- What are the greatest influences on decision making in times of crisis?

Knowledge:
- Key historical events surrounding the decision to drop the two atomic bombs on Hiroshima and Nagasaki

Skills:
- Analyze primary and secondary sources for central ideas and information
- Use evidence and reasoning to inform and defend a decision

Performance Task:

Goal: Your goal is to evaluate whether the United States should drop two atomic bombs on the cities of Hiroshima and Nagasaki, taking into consideration the potential impacts of your decision on the war in the Pacific theater and the people who inhabit these areas.

Role: You are President Truman's Secretary of War.

Audience: Your audience is President Truman and the rest of his cabinet.

Situation: World War II is coming closer to an end. Germany and the European Axis powers have surrendered, leaving Japan as the only remaining area of conflict. A new bomb, the most powerful in the world, has been developed, and President Truman is considering using it to force Japan to surrender and end the war. President Truman has asked you to evaluate the use of the bomb and explain potential effects of such a devastating weapon. To share your findings, you are tasked with creating a presentation or video explaining why the bomb should or should not be used against Japan, and the effects your decision will have on society.

Performance/Product: Your decision will be presented to President Truman (Mr. Reed, your teacher) and his cabinet (your classmates) in the form of a digital presentation (e.g., PowerPoint presentation) or a prerecorded video. You must explain your reasoning using evidence from both primary and secondary sources. Discuss the human, political, economic, environmental, and other effects your decision will have on the war and society as a whole. This should be a polished presentation, which means you are expected to proofread and use professional language (you are preparing this for the president of the United States, after all!).

Success Criteria: Your presentation or video will be evaluated on historical accuracy, analysis of primary and secondary sources, the effectiveness of your persuasive argument, and professional quality.

Directions:
- Your presentation or video should be **between 7 and 10 minutes.**
- You **must** consult **at least three primary sources and three secondary sources** to back up your argument.
  - Examples of primary sources you could use include newspapers, letters, quotes, and declassified government documents.
  - Examples of secondary sources you could use include books on the topic, magazine articles, and pictures.
  - If you need any assistance in finding these documents, ask Mr. Reed or the librarian.
  - Any source you consult *must* be properly cited in a bibliography.
- Your main goal is to explain why the atomic bombs should or should not be dropped on Hiroshima and Nagasaki and the effects (positive and negative) your decision will have on society.
- Last, you are making an argument in this presentation: attempt to convince President Truman (Mr. Reed) as to why he should take your advice.

Schedule:
- May 20—Conduct research in library and begin putting presentation together.
- May 21—Continue researching in library and putting presentation together.
- May 22—Final presentation should be completed and turned in to Mr. Reed.
- May 23—Presentations begin!

	Exceptional (3)	Satisfactory (2)	Revise and Resubmit (1)
Content	• Historical facts are completely accurate and support the argument. • The presentation exhibits a complete and nuanced understanding of the events surrounding the decision.	• Historical facts are mostly accurate; there are minor inaccuracies that do not affect the argument. • The presentation exhibits a partial understanding of the events surrounding the decision.	• Historical facts are inaccurate; there are numerous errors that detract from the argument. • The presentation fails to exhibit an understanding of the events surrounding the decision.
Support (Process)	• The student uses ample evidence from multiple perspectives to present a convincing argument. • The student uses three appropriate primary sources and three appropriate secondary sources that complement the overall presentation. • The overall argument made is logical and sound.	• The student uses evidence from multiple perspectives; however, the argument could be strengthened with the inclusion of additional evidence. • The student uses the required number of primary and secondary sources (three each), but some of these sources are not appropriate and do not complement the overall presentation. • The overall argument made is generally logical and sound.	• The student uses evidence from only one perspective, leading to a weaker argument. • The student does not use the required number of primary and secondary sources (three each), and some of the sources are not appropriate and do not complement the overall presentation. • The overall argument is largely not logical or sound.

	Exceptional (3)	Satisfactory (2)	Revise and Resubmit (1)
Impact	• The presentation/video is highly persuasive; it fully discusses the impact the recommendation would have on society. • The presentation/video is extremely engaging for the intended audience. Viewers hang on every word.	• The presentation/video is moderately persuasive; it somewhat discusses the impact the recommendation would have on society. • The presentation/video is somewhat engaging for the intended audience, although they may take a popcorn break or two.	• The presentation/video is minimally persuasive; it fails to effectively discuss the impact the recommendation would have on society. • The presentation/video is not engaging enough to hold the attention of the intended audience.
Quality	• The presentation/video is polished and professional and fits within the required time frame. • The presentation/video is easy to follow and understand.	• The presentation/video exhibits minor issues with professionalism or polish. It mostly fits within the required time frame (1–2 minutes over or under). • The presentation/video is generally easy to follow and understand.	• The presentation/video exhibits major issues with professionalism or polish and fails to fit within the required time frame (more than 2 minutes over or under). • The presentation/video is difficult to follow and understand.

Source: Ty Reed, East Rockingham High School, Elkton, VA.

Appendix H
PBL for Middle School Science and ELA

Climate Change, Adaptation, and Extinction

Transfer Goals:
- Science—Evaluate the impact of environmental factors on the survival of species
- ELA—Produce effective writing for an appropriate purpose and audience

Driving Question:
- How might climate change affect the survival of various species?

Knowledge:
- Definitions and examples of the following terms: *limiting factors, adaptation, extinction, ancestral traits,* and *derived traits*
- How populations change, and that populations change rather than individual organisms
- Various effects of climate change
- How to format in-text citations and references

Skills:
- Describe the effect of climate change on a species' survival
- Identify trustworthy sources for accurate scientific information
- Translate information expressed visually and graphically into words
- Develop a hypothesis based on scientific research

Project Description:
- Climate change, a limiting factor, is already affecting the survival of some species (https://news.nationalgeographic.com/news/2014/03/140331-global-warming -climate-change-ipcc-animals-science-environment/). The science community is

concerned that there are many other species that will soon be in danger of survival because of Earth's rising temperatures. Scientists are also aware that some species are quicker to adapt to the changes than others.

- To help educate the general community on the effects of climate change and adaptation, you are being asked to develop a series of blog posts discussing **four different species**. In your blog posts, you will describe which two of these species you believe to be in the greatest danger of extinction and which two of these species you believe can adapt most easily to the rising temperatures (one blog post per species, four posts total).
- In each of your blog posts you'll need to describe the specific ancestral and/or derived traits each species possesses and how these are—or are not—affected by climate change based on your research into these species.
- Because your blogs might be read by scientists, you'll need to cite research to support your hypotheses. In addition, you'll be expected to interpret key visuals and graphs from this research and integrate these into your blog posts.
- Consult other scientific blogs for guidance on style of writing, use of visuals and graphics, citation of sources, and effectiveness of communication.

Rubric

	Meets with Excellence	Meets Proficiency	Approaching Proficiency	Below Proficiency
Content Mastery	• Blog posts demonstrate a deep and comprehensive understanding of the impact adaptations and limiting factors have on a species. A scientist would struggle to find any key findings that have been omitted. • All scientific vocabulary is used expertly and in proper context. • All information from visuals and graphs is precisely translated into scientific language.	• Blog posts show a clear understanding of the impact of adaptations and limiting factors on a species. One or two key findings are omitted. • Most scientific vocabulary is used correctly. • Most information from visuals and graphs is precisely translated into scientific language.	• Blog posts show an accurate but incomplete understanding of the impact of adaptations and limiting factors on a species. Several key findings are omitted. • Some scientific vocabulary is used correctly. • Some information from visuals and graphs is precisely translated into scientific language.	• Blog posts show a weak understanding of the impact of adaptations and limiting factors on a species. A significant number of key findings are omitted. • Little to no scientific vocabulary is used correctly. • Little to no information from visuals and graphs is precisely translated into scientific language.
Independent Research (Process)	• All sources are considered trustworthy within the scientific community.	• Most sources are considered trustworthy within the scientific community.	• Few sources are considered trustworthy within the scientific community.	• No sources are considered trustworthy within the scientific community.

	Meets with Excellence	Meets Proficiency	Approaching Proficiency	Below Proficiency
Reasoning and Justification (Content)	• Hypotheses on adaptation and extinction are all aligned with prior scientific research and reflect an accurate interpretation of these previous findings.	• Most (three out of four) hypotheses on adaptation and extinction are aligned with prior scientific research and reflect an accurate interpretation of these previous findings.	• Half (two out of four) hypotheses on adaptation and extinction are aligned with prior scientific research and accurate interpretation of these previous findings.	• Only one (or no) hypotheses on adaptation and extinction are aligned with prior scientific research and accurate interpretation of these previous findings.
Professional Quality	• Ideas are compellingly presented, engagingly organized, and easy to follow for the intended audience. No grammatical/mechanical errors are present. • Writing style, choice and presentation of visuals, and formatting enhance the credibility of your assertions. • The blogs add significant value to the scientific community. • All citations and references are correctly formatted.	• Ideas are clearly presented, logically organized, and—for the most part—easy to follow for the intended audience. Very few grammatical/mechanical errors are present. • Writing style, choice and presentation of visuals, and formatting do not detract from the credibility of your assertions. • The blogs add some value to the scientific community. • Most citations and references are correctly formatted.	• Presentation and organization of ideas are difficult to follow at times for the intended audience. Grammatical/mechanical errors interfere with the posts' readability. • Writing style, choice and presentation of visuals, and formatting somewhat detract from the credibility of your assertions. • The blogs add little value to the scientific community. • Some citations and references are correctly formatted.	• Presentation and organization of ideas are often difficult to follow for the intended audience. Significant grammatical/mechanical errors interfere with the posts' readability. • Writing style, choice and presentation of visuals, and formatting significantly detract from the credibility of your assertions. • The blogs add no value to the scientific community. • Little to no citations and references are formatted correctly.

Appendix I
Algebra Performance Task Options

Functions

Transfer Goal:
- Interpret data to make decisions regarding efficiency

Essential Question:
- How can functions help us make decisions?

Knowledge:
- Characteristics of a function
- Vertical and horizontal line test
- Zeros, and x- and y-intercepts of a function
- Function output and input; domain and range
- Graphical and algebraic representations of functions

Skills:
- Identify the characteristics of an algebraic equation that makes that equation a function
- Interpret the domain and range of continuous and noncontinuous functions
- Solve for the function outputs given an equation and its input
- Calculate the zeros of a function and the x- and y-intercepts (Applying)
- Compare/contrast algebraic and graphical representations of function

Performance Task Options

Option 1	Option 2	Option 3
Role: Entrepreneurs of a private lawn-mowing business, Math Mowers, Inc.	**Role:** Hungry high school students	**Role:** Football team captains
Audience: Customers of Math Mowers, Inc.	**Audience:** Yourself (and your wallet)	**Audience:** Your teammates
Situation: You seek to understand the logistics of the business to better serve your customers.	**Situation:** You are trying to determine which pizza coupon will give you the best price for a two-topping pizza.	**Situation:** You have been tasked with determining which play will gain you the highest number of yards.

Product: Report your findings in a report to your stakeholders. You must include your calculations for the following work: Plot functions P(t) and R(t) on a graph and find the x- and y-intercepts, and the domain and range of both functions. Then interpret what the x- and y-intercepts reveal in relation to the given functions P(t) and R(t). Use that graphical representation to evaluate the best option. Finally, given the graph of a discontinuous floor function, find the x- and y-intercepts and the domain and range of this function to interpret what the x- and y-intercepts reveal in relation to the given function (see graphs below).

Rubric

Skills	2	1	0
Skill 1: Interpret the domain and range of continuous and noncontinuous functions.	The group identified the correct domain and range of the continuous and noncontinuous functions.	The group correctly identified the domain and range of the continuous function but not the noncontinuous functions, or vice versa.	The group incorrectly identified the domain and range of the continuous and noncontinuous functions, or the group did not attempt this skill.
Skill 2: Calculate the zeros and intercepts of the functions.	The group correctly calculated all of the zeros and intercepts of the functions.	The group correctly identified some of the intercepts and zeros of the functions (continuous and noncontinuous).	The group incorrectly identified the zeros and intercepts of the functions, or the group did not attempt this skill.

Skills	2	1	0
Skill 3: Interpret what the *x*- and *y*-intercepts are telling us in relation to the given function/situation.	The group correctly interpreted what the *x*- and *y*-intercepts are telling us in relation to the given function/situation.	The group correctly interpreted what some of the *x*- and *y*-intercepts are telling us in relation to the given function/situation.	The group incorrectly interpreted what the *x*- and *y*-intercepts are telling us in relation to the given function/situation, or the group did not attempt this skill.
Skill 4: Solve for the function's outputs given an equation and its input.	The group correctly solved for all of the function's outputs given an equation and its input.	The group correctly solved for some of the function's outputs given an equation and its input.	The group incorrectly solved for the function's outputs given an equation and its input, or the group did not attempt this skill.

Graphs

Given the graph of a discontinuous floor function, find the *x*- and *y*-intercepts and the domain and range of this function to interpret what the *x*- and *y*-intercepts reveal in relation to the given function.

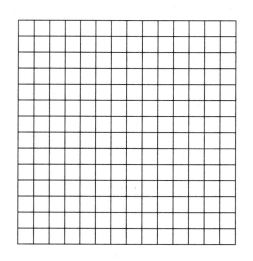

Math Mowers

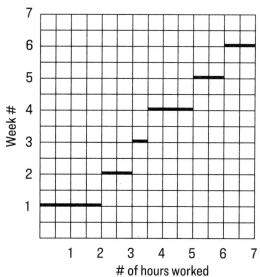

Hungry Students

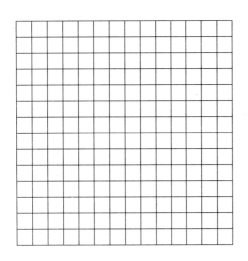

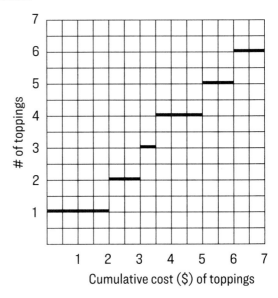

Football Captains

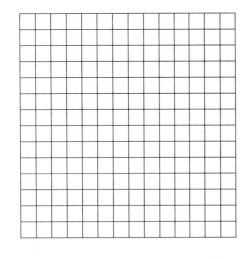

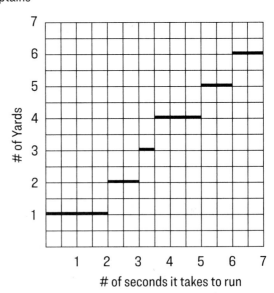

Source: Hannah Keener, Osbourn Park High School, Manassas Park, VA. Used with permission.

Appendix J
ELA Performance Task Options

Powerful Writing

Transfer Goal:

- Select and manipulate language to craft powerful messages that bring about changes in readers' impressions, perspectives, beliefs, or actions

Essential Questions:

- Where does power come from? Who has it? Why?
- What makes writing powerful?
- To what extent does a writer have the power to shape thoughts, beliefs, and actions?

Knowledge:

- Definitions and examples of writing techniques, including imagery, simile, metaphor, analogies, idioms, allusions, and irony.
- Definition and descriptors of voice
- Strategies for finding just the right word or phrase
- Definitions and examples of argumentative techniques and fallacies
- Definitions and examples of claim/counterclaim, logos, ethos, pathos

Skills:

- Determine the meaning of words and phrases as they are used in a text, including figurative and connotative meanings. (RL.8.4/RI.8.4)
- Analyze the impact of word choice on meaning/tone. (RL.8.4)
- Analyze how a text makes connections among and distinctions between individuals, ideas, or events. (RI.8.3)
- Use precise words and phrases, relevant descriptive details, and sensory language to capture the action and convey experiences and events. (W.8.2D)
- Develop a topic with relevant, well-chosen facts, definitions, concrete details, quotations, or other information and examples. (W.8.2B). (from Common Core State Standards)

Performance Task Options:

Choose and follow one of the following rows across to complete your task. You will also write a review of your work in which you recommend it to future listeners and readers by using pathos, ethos, and logos (including claim/counterclaim and supporting evidence from your piece).

Role	Audience	Product/Performance	Situation
Storyteller	Listeners of *The Moth*—a podcast featuring amateur storytellers sharing significant life events	A podcast (recorded story with script) of a pivotal moment in your life	You have been selected to share your "pivotal moment" story on *The Moth* podcast.
Author	Members of the Scholastic Art and Writing Award committee for the new edition of *The Best Teen Writing*	Story or essay adhering to *The Best Teen Writing*'s publishing guidelines	The theme of this year's edition is "The Power of Words."
Journalist	Selection committee for new articles at www.Commonlit.org, which is soliciting student-created informational texts	An original piece— with supporting evidence—on what actually can "buy" or give us happiness	Commonlit has put out a call for the student perspective on what leads to happiness (to add a new theme to those we studied in class)

Note: See Scholastic Art & Writing awards website for more information. An anthology of *The Best Teen Writing* is published each year. See more at www.artandwriting.org/Publications

Task Directions:

The Moth Podcaster:

The Moth podcast (https://themoth.org/podcast) is producing a student series of podcasts for an upcoming episode. Their series title is "A Pivotal Moment." Write a story for this podcast submission. You can use your Memory Poem as the seed, or choose another important moment to describe. The story should be four to six minutes in length when read aloud and should feature imagery and figurative language that has the power to paint pictures of your experience in the minds of the podcast's listeners. Return to the work of Gary Soto and Ray Bradbury for more inspiration on how to do this. Remember—according to the site's description, "Moth stories are true as remembered by the storyteller." So, stay true to your memories and impressions and let your voice shine through so that your audience can picture your moment vividly.

The Best Teen Writer:

You have decided to submit an original piece to be considered for inclusion in the upcoming edition of *The Best Teen Writing of 2018*. The theme of the 2018 edition is "The Power of Words." Write an account—true or fictitious—that illustrates how peoples' words have the power to build up others—or to tear them down. This piece should follow the Scholastic Award Committee's writing guidelines (www.artandwriting.org) and exhibit their criteria for excellence (*Originality, Technical Skill,* and *Emergence of Personal Vision or Voice*). Return to the work of the student authors we studied in class as well as to experts such as Ray Bradbury for demonstration of *Technical Skill*, but make sure your piece is *Original* and compelling in its presentation of how words can affect the trajectory of people's lives. To get your piece noticed among the thousands of entries the committee receives, make sure your *Voice*—or your narrator's *Voice*—leaps off the page and grabs the reader immediately.

The Pursuit of Happiness:

The website Commonlit.org wishes to add the student perspective on "Happiness" to its theme of "Power and Greed." In class, we read and discussed several informational texts presenting varied views about whether or not money has the power to buy happiness (https://www.commonlit.org/themes/power-greed/questions/does-money-buy-happiness). Now Commonlit would like to hear what *you* believe *does* have the power to "buy" happiness. Your first step is to search your heart, your mind, and your values to determine your belief about the true source of happiness. Whatever you choose (such as comfort, friendship, family, faith, sacrifice), you must support your assertion with evidence from other sources, including other articles as well as interviews or surveys you conduct yourself. You will use this evidence—along with strong word choice and a definitive voice—to inform student readers about what you have discovered in your research about the source of true happiness. Be sure to adhere to the length and format of the Commonlit pieces we studied in class.

Rubric

	Accepted for Publication	**Accepted with Minor Revisions**	**Resubmit with Significant Revisions**
Published Piece			
Clarity of Ideas	*Text is clear and focused; captures reader's attention.* • Topic is narrow and manageable. • Details are relevant, interesting, vivid, accurate. • Point is clear; tells whole story; no trivia. • Details support the writing's main idea. • Ideas engage, inspire, or intrigue reader.	*Text's ideas are focused but general, obvious.* • Topic is broad but understandable. • Details are loosely related, obvious, or flat. • Point gives general idea; may be vague or incomplete. • Details provide some support for main idea. • Ideas may leave reader guessing; not specific.	*Text lacks clear idea, purpose, and details.* • Topic is hazy; no evident focus/purpose. • Details are missing, incorrect, or unclear. • Main idea is difficult to identify. • Details seem disconnected from main idea; random. • Ideas may confuse the reader.
Compelling Organization	*Order compels, enhances, and moves ideas.* • Introduction intrigues, invites; conclusion resolves. • Sequencing is logical and effective. • Pacing is well controlled and purposeful. • Organization flows smoothly; matches purpose.	*Order moves reader through with some confusion.* • Introduction and conclusion are evident but weak. • Sequencing makes sense in most parts. • Pacing is inconsistent but fairly well controlled. • Organization offers limited support.	*Order appears random; no identifiable structure.* • Introduction and conclusion are ineffective. • Sequencing seems random. • Pacing is awkward or frustrating. • Organization makes it hard to identify main idea.

	Accepted for Publication	**Accepted with Minor Revisions**	**Resubmit with Significant Revisions**
Powerful Word Choice	*Words are precise, interesting, engaging, powerful.* • Words are specific, accurate; meaning is clear. • Imagery and figurative language paint vivid pictures in the reader's mind. • Words and phrases are striking and memorable. • Language is natural, effective, and appropriate. • Every word counts—any repetition or omission is purposeful.	*Words are common and obvious; they lack energy.* • Features functional, clear language that is used correctly. • Attempts at imagery and figurative language paint hazy pictures. • Words and phrases convey meaning but aren't memorable. • Language may be stilted or reflect thesaurus overload. • Choices may need pruning—or expansion.	*Words are simple, vague, or limited.* • Words are nonspecific, distracting, or vague. • Imagery and figurative language are missing. • Words and phrases detract from meaning. • Language reflects wordiness or unnecessary repetition. • Word choice feels random—not a real "choice."
Clarity of Voice	*Writing is compelling, engaging; aware of audience.* • Writer's voice is as individual as fingerprints. • Writer *and* reader love sharing this aloud. • Writer's presence is powerfully projected on the page. • Expository writing is committed, persuasive. • Narrative writing is honest, engaging, personal.	*Writing seems sincere but unaware of audience.* • Writer's voice emerges in portions of the piece. • There are share-aloud moments in the piece. • Writer's presence stands out from many others. • Expository writing shows some commitment. • Narrative writing is reasonably sincere but plain.	*Writer seems indifferent, distanced from topic/audience.* • There is no sense of person behind the words—yet. • Writer is not ready to share this piece. • Writer's thoughts/feelings do not come through. • Expository writing lacks any commitment. • Narrative writing shows no attempt at voice.

Review			
Use of Pathos and Ethos	• Pathos—Reviewer firmly establishes authority through clear and technically correct writing. • Ethos—Reviewer deliberately and clearly appeals to reader's emotions, imagination, or sense of sympathy.	• Pathos—Reviewer establishes some authority through writing that is some- what clear and mostly technically correct. • Ethos—Reviewer vaguely appeals to reader's emotions, imagination, or sense of sympathy.	• Pathos—Unclear or technically incorrect writing detracts from credibility. • Ethos—Reviewer vaguely appeals to reader's emotions, imaginations, or sense of sympathy.
Logos—Use of Claim/ Counterclaim	• Reviewer poses credible claims. • Reviewer antici- pates several argu- ments that may be posed by critics and logically refutes them.	• Reviewer's claims seem credible but cast reasonable doubt. • Reviewer antici- pates a single argu- ment that may be posed by critics and logically refutes it.	• Reviewer's claim lacks credibility. • Reviewer's attempts at refuting crit- ics' arguments—if present—are pre- sented illogically or incompletely.
Logos—Use of Evidence	• Reviewer refutes arguments and defends stance using specific details from the text and other sources.	• Reviewer uses vague details from the text and/or other sources to refute argument potentially posed by critics.	• Reviewer uses sparse, vague, or incorrect details from the text or other sources in an attempt to refute critics' potential arguments.

Source: Adapted from materials created by Jim Burke. Available: https://www.sayvilleschools.org/site/handlers /filedownload.ashx?moduleinstanceid=581&dataid=2327&FileName=Six%20Traits%20for%20Effective%20 Writing%20Rubric.pdf. Used with permission. Idea based on Vicki Spandel's Six Traits Model in *Creating Writers Through 6-Trait Writing Assessment and Instruction* (6th ed.), by V. Spandel, 2012, Boston, MA: Allyn & Bacon.

Appendix K
Rubric for Cooperation and Teamwork

Score	Criteria		
	Contributes to Group Goals	**Adheres to Agreements and Norms**	**Demonstrates Productive Interpersonal Skills**
4	Actively helps identify group goals and works hard to meet them. Takes initiative to address group's needs and shifts roles when necessary to support the group.	Always adheres to group agreements and norms. Takes the lead in modeling and reinforcing group norms. Reminds others of the importance of following agreements and norms.	Actively and consistently demonstrates productive interpersonal skills. Models effective and supportive interactions for others. Provides respectful feedback to help others improve their interactions within the group.
3	Displays a commitment to group goals and works to meet them. Carries out assigned role independently.	Consistently acts in ways that follow established agreements and norms but may have occasional lapses.	Generally demonstrates productive interpersonal skills. Interacts with others without prompting. Expresses ideas and opinions in a way that is sensitive to the knowledge base and feelings of others.

Score	Criteria		
	Contributes to Group Goals	**Adheres to Agreements and Norms**	**Demonstrates Productive Interpersonal Skills**
2	Puts forth some effort, but sometimes lets others shoulder the work. Needs reminders to stay on task or perform assigned role.	Inconsistently follows established agreements and norms. Needs behavioral reminders to follow the norms.	Use of productive interpersonal skills is inconsistent. Sometimes interactions with others are less than positive. May need reminders; e.g., to listen actively, wait one's turn, avoid put downs, be flexible.
1	Does not actively work toward group goals, *or* is passive and does not contribute to the group, *or* acts in ways that undermine the ability of the group to achieve its goal.	Regularly violates the established agreements and norms. Behaves in ways that disrupt the effective functioning of the group.	Poor interpersonal skills interfere with effective group performance; e.g., does not listen, dominates, interrupts, is insensitive, is inflexible, puts down others.

Source: © 2017b Jay McTighe. Used with permission.

Appendix L
PBL for Middle School
Earth Science and Human Geography

Soil Erosion

Driving Questions:
- What factors affect soil erosion? How does soil erosion affect ecosystems?
- How does human behavior affect Earth? How does Earth affect human behavior?

Transfer Goals:
- Investigate the interaction between humans and their environment.
- Investigate the effects of natural phenomenon on the balance of an ecosystem.
- Design a method for monitoring and minimizing damaging effects on the environment.

Project Description:
- Recall our simulation of soil erosion and the discussion that followed. That discussion led to the formation of several hypotheses about the causes and implications of soil erosion in our community and beyond (see Figure 5.2, p. 103).
- We will now extend those hypotheses to a variety of geographical regions in different parts of the world. You will work in a group with those who select the same geographic area as you do. Your choices include the following:
  — Rio Grande/Rio Bravo River Basin, Chihuahuan Desert (U.S./Mexico)
  — Northern Great Plains (U.S.)
  — East Kalimantan (Borneo)
  — Lake Bogoria/Lake Nakuru Basin (Kenya)
- As a class we will continue to investigate the factors that affect erosion in our own and neighboring communities. Our class findings will inform your group investigations of your chosen environment. You will extend your research to discover the following for your ecosystem/community:
  — What natural factors have affected erosion?

229

— What human factors have affected erosion?
— How has erosion affected the surrounding ecosystem?
— How has erosion affected the human community?
— How might we design a method for monitoring and minimizing damaging effects of erosion?

- You will consult electronic resources (e.g., Google Earth, online research) and human resources (e.g., experts from the World Wildlife Fund, citizens from the community) via face-to-face and virtual forums to complete the tasks or sprints described. You are responsible for monitoring your progress and adjusting pace as necessary.
- Your teachers will hold training workshops for new and required skills as they arise. In some cases, you will attend workshops by choice; in some cases, you will attend workshops by invitation only. You can request a special topic for a workshop at any time.
- Your final product will be a multimedia presentation (text, images, interviews, data, simulations), communicating the options you explored and your final recommended plan of action to reduce soil erosion in the geographic area studied. You will present your findings to local experts (in person) as well as to some of the experts you interviewed who are working in your geographic area (virtually).
- Remember: Your goal is to bring about positive change in your geographic area of focus.

Tasks or Sprints: Please track your progress through these sprints using a class Scrum board, similar to the one shown in Figure 7.4, p. 151.
- History (political, economic, natural factors)
- Interview with residents
- Interview with experts
- Analysis of research for causes
- Cause-and-effect chain
- Terminology/process check
- Potential solution 1: action, cost, time, impact
- Potential solution 2: action, cost, time, impact
- Potential solution 3: action, cost, time, impact
- Recommendation and justification
- Multimedia presentation

Success Criteria/"Definition of Done":
- Complete and detailed history of human interaction with environment
- Scientifically thorough and accurate description of the process of soil erosion in chosen region
- Thorough explanation of potential solutions to soil erosion, including a cost-benefit analysis
- Comprehensive and persuasive recommendation for best plan of action

Appendix M

Transfer Goals and Performance Tasks for K–12 Social Studies

Authors' note: This set of transfer goals was developed for use across grade levels and subject areas by a K–12 curriculum team in the North West Hendricks School Corporation in Lizton, Indiana. The tasks that follow are potential social studies performance tasks that are aligned with (1) Dimension 2 of the C3 Framework and (2) one or more of the district's transfer goals. Notice that the tasks follow the GRASPS framework discussed in Chapter 2.

K–12 Transfer Goals

Students will be able to independently use their learning to
1. Fluently read, comprehend, and analyze complex, grade-level text and media for various purposes.
2. Write effectively to address various audiences and purposes.
3. Utilize strategic thinking and demonstrate reasoning skills to persevere through complex problem solving.
4. Develop and implement logical reasoning to effectively communicate viable arguments and constructively critique the reasoning of others.
5. Engage in the inquiry and research process to analyze, integrate, and present information for the purpose of investigating and solving problems.

Scope and Sequence for C3 Social Studies Framework Dimension 2 concept, "Civics and Political Institutions"

- **K–3:** Create rules, responsibilities, codes of conduct for school-based situations/contexts.
- **4–5:** Examine the legislative process in local, state, and national contexts.
- **Middle School:** Analyze rights of citizens of countries (U.S. and abroad) to discuss the impact of government on the lives of its citizens.
- **High School:** Analyze the impact of decisions made by the U.S. government (current events/policy) on the local, national, and international community.

Performance Tasks at Each Grade Level

Kindergarten Performance Task: Rules for our classroom

Transfer Goals addressed: 2, 4

- **Goal:** Apply concepts of civics (rules) to analyze how rules promote community.
- **Role:** Yourself (student at the beginning of the year)
- **Audience:** Classmates and teacher
- **Situation:** We will develop our classroom rules as a family. You will work in a small group of 3–4 students. You and your groupmates will create "your" list of the three most important rules and guidelines for safety, order, and cooperation in our class.
- **Performance:** You will create a poster using pictures and labels to depict the rules and classroom conduct necessary for a productive learning environment. Your group will present your ideas to the class. You can act out some examples of students following (and not following) your rules. We will use your ideas to develop our set of classroom rules.

1st Grade Performance Task: Rules for a field trip (with reasons)

Transfer Goals addressed: 2, 4

- **Goal:** Apply concepts of civics (rules) to analyze how rules promote citizenship.
- **Role:** Yourself (student preparing for a class field trip)
- **Audience:** 1st grade students, teachers, and parents
- **Situation:** Our class is taking a field trip to the zoo. Before we go, we need to create a list of rules (with reasons) that we will follow. These rules will be included in the permission slips we send home to parents and guardians.
- **Performance:** Working in small groups, you will need to (1) determine the three most important rules needed for a field trip to the zoo, and (2) present these to the class along with reasons to support your choices. Use your personal experiences to inform your decision as you create your list of rules. After each group has presented their rules and supporting reasons to the class, we will choose the five most important rules and include them in a "contract" we send home to parents and guardians. We will also record a video of you explaining to your parent/guardian which rule you think is most important and why.

2nd Grade: Code of conduct for new playground equipment (with reasons and consequences)
Transfer Goals addressed: 2, 3, 4

- **G**oal: Apply concepts of civics (rules) to analyze how codes of conduct promote citizenship.
- **R**ole: Yourself
- **A**udience: School board
- **S**ituation: We want a new piece of playground equipment! We will decide which piece(s) of new equipment we want and then make a case to the school board about why they should provide the funds for this new equipment. In order to convince them, we need to demonstrate that we have thought about what good citizenship is, how the playground equipment will help us become better citizens, how good citizens must behave on the equipment, why these behaviors are important, and what should happen if students do not follow the agreed-upon rules.
- **P**erformance: Working with classmates who have chosen the same piece of equipment as you, create a persuasive presentation that (1) justifies your choice of equipment and explains how having it would help us be better citizens; (2) outlines a code of conduct for using the equipment, explaining why these rules are important for both safety and citizenship, and (3) explains what should happen if a student breaks the code of conduct once . . . and more than once. Be ready to present to the school board.Each member of your group will be responsible for speaking during the presentation. You should divide your speaking time evenly among your group members. Each group member should make notes for his/her share of the presentation. (Note: This simulated "board" will consist of other teachers, administrators, and/or community volunteers.)

3rd Grade: School constitution modeled after the U.S. Constitution
Transfer Goals addressed: 1, 2, 3, 4

- **G**oal: Apply concepts of civics (rules/laws) to analyze how a constitution works as a "citizens' contract."
- **R**ole: Yourself
- **A**udience: Principal
- **S**ituation: We have been discussing how a constitution is built upon shared values. You will use what you know about our school values, the "parts" of the U.S. Constitution, and what "citizenship" is to develop a constitution for our school.
- **P**erformance: You will create written and visual displays of your constitution for the principal. Make sure your constitution contains all necessary parts and acts like a "citizen's contract." Be sure to explain how your school constitution reflects our school values.

4th Grade: Propose a local law and follow it through the local governing process
Transfer Goals addressed: 1, 2, 3, 4

- **G**oal: Apply concepts of civics (laws) to analyze how the local government works to represent its citizens.
- **R**ole: Yourself—a concerned citizen
- **A**udience—City Council
- **S**ituation—You are concerned about the fairness of a current local law (or you think there should be a local law that does not yet exist). You have decided it is time to take an active role in advocating for this change. Using what you have learned about civics and government, advocate for yourself and the local community to seek change for the betterment of the community, or for certain individuals in the community.
- **P**erformance: First we will track a current proposal to see what happens to it and to figure out why it gets passed or why not. Individually, you will record your reactions and what you are learning in your journal/blog. Next, you will create and submit your own proposal for the City Council seeking a change that you feel will benefit certain community members or the community as a whole. We will follow your proposal through the local governing process, reflecting regularly on its progress throughout the year.

5th Grade: Propose a bill and trace its potential path through the legislative process
Transfer Goals addressed: 1, 2, 3, 4

- **G**oal: Apply concepts of civics (laws) to analyze how a bill becomes a law.
- **R**ole: Concerned citizen
- **A**udience: State or national legislator
- **S**ituation: You are concerned about the fairness of a current state/national law (or you think there should be a law that does not yet exist). You have decided it is time to take an active role in advocating for this change. Using what you have learned about civics and government, advocate for yourself and members of your state/nation to seek change for the betterment of the community, or for certain individuals in the community.
- **P**erformance: You will create a bill addressing an area of reform or change that you feel will benefit members or the state or nation. You will write a letter to accompany the bill and send both to the appropriate congress person and/or senator. After you have submitted your letter and bill, you will simulate what might happen from there if the bill were to become a law, tracing it through the legislative process. Present your simulation in a multimedia presentation. Be sure to keep in touch with your legislator to monitor progress.

Middle School
Transfer Goals addressed: 1, 2, 3, 4, 5

- **G**oal: Apply concepts of civics and political institutions to analyze the rights of citizens of countries (U.S. and abroad) and to discuss the impact of government on the lives of its citizens.
- **R**ole: Middle school student
- **A**udience: Parent or guardian
- **S**ituation: Your parent/guardian received a promotion and is planning to move your family within the upcoming year. The promotion allows your parent/guardian to choose between a location in the U.S. and a location in _____. Salary and benefits will be the same no matter which location is chosen. You want to determine which location would be a better fit for you and your family based on the freedoms/restrictions provided to citizens of each location.
- **P**erformance: Prepare a report that details the pros and cons of living in each area. Highlight the laws and policies in place, and explain how they would affect your freedom, rights, and financial security.

High School
Transfer Goals addressed: 1, 2, 3, 4, 5

- **G**oal: Analyze the impact of decisions made by the U.S. government (current events/policy) on the local, national, and international community.
- **R**ole: Journalist who works for a national news network
- **A**udience: Television news viewers
- **S**ituation: As one of the leading journalists in your field, you have been assigned to cover the global impact of one U.S. policy or law that was enacted in the previous year. You have the freedom to choose the policy/law that you want to explore. Regardless of your choice, your producer expects you to explore how that policy/law affects the U.S. and at least two other nations in terms of citizens' rights and lifestyles, economy, geography, and international relations.
- **P**erformance: You will deliver raw footage of a video to your producer. You may use iMovie or a similar app of your choice. Your video should feature your own narration/reporting, interviews with citizens of the U.S. and the two other nations, charts, graphs, and any other visuals that will help you tell your story. The viewing public is counting on you to showcase all sides of the issue in a fair and unbiased nature, so be sure to vary your resources during the research process.

Source: Developed in collaboration with North West Hendricks School Corporation, Lizton, IN.

Appendix N
Sample Map of K–12 Cornerstone Tasks

Grade	Subject Area			
	ELA	**Mathematics**	**Science**	**Social Studies**
12	**Independent Study Project** Linked to Science and Social Studies [Critical Thinking, Communication]	**Mathematical Modeling Project** [Critical Thinking, Communication]	**Independent Study Project** Linked to ELA and Social Studies [Critical Thinking, Communication]	**Independent Study Project** Linked to ELA and Science [Critical Thinking, Communication]
11	**Parody/Satire Skit** Linked to Science and Social Studies [Creativity, Collaboration, Communication]	**Amusement Park Physics** Linked to Science [Critical Thinking, Collaboration, Communication]	**Chemistry Crime Scene** [Critical Thinking, Collaboration, Communication]	**Problem-Solution Campaign** [Critical Thinking, Collaboration, Communication]
9	**Research Project with A-V Presentation** [Critical Thinking, Communication]	**Mathematical Modeling with Linear Equations** [Critical Thinking, Communication]	**Earthquake Science** [Critical Thinking, Collaboration, Communication]	**Contemporary Issues Debate** [Critical Thinking, Communication]

8	**Causes of Conflict Research Project** Linked to Social Studies [Critical Thinking, Communication]	**Design Your Dream Bedroom** [Critical Thinking, Communication]	**Consumer Scientist** [Critical Thinking, Collaboration, Communication]	**Causes of Conflict Research Project** Linked to ELA [Critical Thinking, Communication]
7	**Autobiography** [Communication]	**Evaluate a Contractor's Proposal** [Critical Thinking, Communication]	**Water Quality Testing** [Critical Thinking, Communication]	**History: Whose Story? Examining Perspectives** [Critical Thinking]
6	**Personal Narrative** [Communication]	**Exercise Studies** Linked to Science and Health/PE [Critical Thinking, Creativity, Collaboration]	**Prove It!** [Critical Thinking, Communication]	**Humans and the Environment** [Critical Thinking, Communication]
5	**People on the Move Research Project** Linked to Social Studies [Critical Thinking, Communication]	**Fund-Raiser Project** [Critical Thinking, Creativity, Collaboration, Communication]	**Conduct Your Own Experiment** [Problem Solving, Communication]	**People on the Move Research Project** Linked to ELA [Critical Thinking, Communication]
4	**Authors' Party Presentations** [Collaboration, Communication]	**Geometry Town** [Critical Thinking, Creativity, Collaboration]	**Seed-to-Plant Project** [Critical Thinking, Collaboration, Communication]	**Where We Live and How We Live** [Critical Thinking, Communication]
3	**Personal Narrative** [Creativity, Communication]	**Measure This!** [Critical Thinking Creativity, Collaboration]	**Prove It!** [Critical Thinking, Communication]	**Alike and Different: Community and Culture** [Critical Thinking, Collaboration]

2	**Show and Tell** [Communication]	**Animal Zoo (Habitats) STEAM Project** Linked to Science [Creativity, Critical Thinking, Collaboration]	**Animal Zoo (Habitats) STEAM Project** Linked to Math [Creativity, Critical Thinking, Collaboration]	**Wants and Needs** [Critical Thinking, Communication]
1	**Kinder Kid Advice** [Creativity, Communication]	**Party Time** [Creativity, Collaboration]	**Will It Float?** [Critical Thinking, Collaboration]	**Me and My Family** [Creativity, Communication]
K	**Letter Songs** [Creativity]	**Number Maze** [Creativity, Collaboration, Communication]	**Observing Carefully with All Senses** [Critical Thinking]	**All About Me** [Creativity, Communication]

References

Achieve, Inc. (2013). *Next generation science standards*. Washington, DC: Author.

Barshay, J. (2018, August). A study finds promise in project-based learning for young low-income children. *The Hechinger Report*. Retrieved from https://hechingerreport.org/a-study-finds-promise-in-project-based-learning-for-young-low-income-children/

Bernstein, E., Shore, J., & Lazer, D. (2018). How intermittent breaks in interaction improve collective intelligence. *Proceedings of the National Academy of Sciences, 115*(35), 8734–8739.

Black, P., & Wiliam, D. (1998). Inside the black box: Raising standards through classroom assessment. *Phi Delta Kappan, 80*(2), 139–148.

Bransford, J., Brown, A., & Cocking, R. (Eds.). (2000). *How people learn: Brain, mind, experience, and school* (Expanded ed.). Washington, DC: National Academy Press.

Brighton, C. M., Moon, T. R., Jarvis, J. M., & Hockett, J. A. (2007). *Primary grades teachers' conceptions of giftedness and talent: A case-based investigation* (Technical Report). Storrs, CT: National Research Center on the Gifted and Talented.

Brookhart, S. M. (2013). *Grading and group work: How do I assess individual learning when students work together?* (ASCD Arias). Alexandria, VA: ASCD.

Buck Institute for Education. (n.d.). Why project-based learning (PBL)? Retrieved from http://www.bie.org/about/why_pbl

Carbaugh, E. M., & Doubet, K. J. (2016, August). Setting the tone for technology use. *ASCD Express, 11*(24).

Chappuis, S., & Chappuis, J. (2007, December/2008, January). The best value in formative assessment. *Educational Leadership, 65*(4), 14–19.

Costa, A., & Kallick, B. (2009). *Habits of mind across the curriculum: Practical and creative strategies for teachers*. Alexandria, VA: ASCD.

Dabrowski, J., & Marshall, T. (2018). *Motivation and engagement in student assignments: The role of choice and relevancy*. Washington, DC: The Education Trust.

De Bono, E. (1999). *Six thinking hats*. New York: Back Bay Books.

Delizonna, L. (2017, August 24). High-performing teams need psychological safety. Here's how to provide it. *Harvard Business Review*. Retrieved from https://hbr.org/2017/08/high-performing-teams-need-psychological-safety-heres-how-to-create-it

Doubet, K. J., & Hockett, J. A. (2015). *Differentiation in middle and high school: Strategies to engage all learners*. Alexandria, VA: ASCD.

Doubet, K. J., & Hockett, J. A. (2017a, November). Classroom discourse as civil discourse. *Educational Leadership, 75*(3), 56-60.

Doubet, K. J., & Hockett, J. A. (2017b). *Differentiation in the elementary grades: Strategies to engage and equip all learners.* Alexandria, VA: ASCD.

DuFour, R. (2004). What is a professional learning community? *Educational Leadership, 61*(8), 6–11.

Dweck, C. S. (2006). *Mindset: The new psychology of success.* New York: Ballantine Books.

Dweck, C. S. (2008, October). The perils and promises of praise. *Educational Leadership, 65*(2), 34–39.

Earl, L. M. (2003). *Assessment as learning: Using classroom assessment to maximize student learning.* Thousand Oaks, CA: Corwin.

Ferlazzo, L. (2017, February 28). The promise and peril of using Google Translate in the ELL classroom. Retrieved from https://larryferlazzo.edublogs.org/2017/02/28/the-promise-peril-of-using-google-translate-in-the-ell-classroom-share-your-ideas/

Fisher, D., & Frey, N. (2009, November). Feed up, back, forward. *Educational Leadership, 67*(3), 20–25.

Gallagher, K. (2011). *Write like this: Teaching real-world writing through modeling and mentor texts.* Portland, ME: Stenhouse.

Gambrell, L. B., Hughes, E. M., Calvert, L., Malloy, J. A., & Igo, B. (2011). Authentic reading, writing, and discussion: An exploratory study of a pen pal project. *Elementary School Journal 112*(2), 234–258.

Guha, R., Wagner, T., Darling-Hammond, L., Taylor, T., & Curtis, D. (2018). *The promise of performance assessments: Innovations in high school learning and college admission.* Palo Alto, CA: Learning Policy Institute.

Hattie, J. (2012). *Visible learning for teachers: Maximizing impact on learning.* New York: Routledge.

Hattie, J., & Clarke, S. (2019). *Visible learning feedback.* New York: Routledge.

Hibbard, K. M., Van Wagenen, L., Lewbel, S., Waterbury-Wyatt, S., Shaw, S., Pelletier, K., . . . Wislocki, J. A. (1996). *A teacher's guide to performance-based learning and assessment.* Alexandria, VA: ASCD.

Himmele, P., & Himmele, W. (2011). *Total participation techniques: Making every student an active learner.* Alexandria, VA: ASCD.

Hockett, J. A., & Doubet, K. J. (December 2013/January 2014). Turning on the lights; What preassessment can do. *Educational Leadership, 71*(4), 50–54.

Hockett, J. A., & Doubet, K. J. (2017, July 12). How to use flexible grouping in the classroom. *TeachThought.* Retrieved from https://www.teachthought.com/pedagogy/use-flexible-grouping-classroom/

Kansas State Department of Education. (2011). A cautionary note about unpacking, unwrapping, and/or deconstructing the Kansas Common Core Standards. Available at www.ksde.org/kscommoncore

Larmer, J. (2015). *Gold standard PBL: Essential project design elements.* Novato, CA: Author.

Larmer, J., Mergendoller, J. R., & Boss, S. (2015). *Setting the standard for project based learning: A proven approach to rigorous classroom instruction.* Alexandria, VA: ASCD.

Literacy Design Collaborative. (n.d.). Task template collection. Retrieved from https://ldc.org/ldc-curricula

Lowe, M. (2018, September 18). What it means to be a project manager. Wrike.com. Available: https://www.wrike.com/blog/digital-project-manager/

Marzano, R. J. (2003). *What works in schools: Translating research into action.* Alexandria, VA: ASCD.

Maryland Assessment Consortium. (1994). Lemonade stand. *Performance assessment tasks—elementary level* (pp. 143–144). Frederick, MD: Author.

McTighe, J. (2008). Making the most of professional learning communities. *The Learning Principal, 3*(8), 4–7.

McTighe, J. (2013). *Core learning: Assessing what matters most.* Midvale, UT: School Improvement Network.

McTighe, J. (2017a, March 13). Beware of the test prep trap [blog post]. Retrieved from Newsela at https://blog.newsela.com/blog/2017/7/25/u2tlzoasa0gur7ua7uij7ihtop6dkp

McTighe, J. (2017b). Developing authentic performance tasks to promote meaningful learning and measure what matters [workshop handout]. Columbia, MD: McTighe and Associates.

McTighe, J. (2018a, February). Three key questions on measuring learning. *Educational Leadership, 75*(5), 14–20.

McTighe, J., & Curtis, G. (2019). *Leading modern learning: A blueprint for vision-driven schools* (2nd ed.). Bloomington, IN: Solution Tree.

McTighe, J., & Wiggins, G. (2004). *The Understanding by Design professional development workbook.* Alexandria, VA: ASCD.

McTighe, J., & Wiggins, G. (2013a). *Essential questions: Opening doors to student understanding.* Alexandria, VA: ASCD.

McTighe, J., & Wiggins, G. (2013b). From common core standards to curriculum: Five big ideas. *Wisconsin ASCD Highlighter,* 6–15.

McTighe, J., & Willis, J. (2019). *Upgrade your teaching: Understanding by Design meets neuroscience.* Alexandria, VA: ASCD.

Miller, A. (2015, August 20). How to write effective driving questions for project-based learning [blog post]. Retrieved from Edutopia at https://www.edutopia.org/blog/pbl-how-to-write-driving-questions-andrew-miller

National Association of Colleges and Employers. (2015). *Job outlook 2016.* Bethlehem, PA: Author.

National Coalition for Core Arts Standards. (n.d.). *National core arts standards: A conceptual framework for arts learning.* Retrieved from https://www.nationalartsstandards.org/sites/default/files/NCCAS%20%20Conceptual%20Framework_4.pdf

National Council for the Social Studies. (2013). *College, career, and civic life (C3) framework for social studies state standards.* Washington, DC: Author.

National Governors Association Center for Best Practices, Council of Chief State School Officers. (2010). *Common Core State Standards.* Washington DC: Author.

Partnership for 21st Century Skills. (2009). *P21 framework definitions.* Retrieved from https://files.eric.ed.gov/fulltext/ED519462.pdf

Pieratt, J. (2018, August). God save the routine. *Education Update, 60*(8). Retrieved from http://www.ascd.org/publications/newsletters/education-update/aug18/vol60/num08/God-Save-the-Routine.aspx

Rhodes, S. (2017, November 9). Using scrum boards to organize small-group projects. *Education Update, 13*(5). Retrieved from http://www.ascd.org/ascd-express/vol13/1305-rhodes.aspx

Schraw, G., Flowerday, T., & Lehman, S. (2001). Increasing situational interest in the classroom. *Educational Psychology Review, 13*(3), 211–224.

Sizer, T. (1984). *Horace's compromise.* Boston: Houghton Mifflin.

Sousa, D., & Tomlinson, C. A. (2018). *Differentiation and the brain: How neuroscience supports the learner-friendly classroom* (2nd ed.). Bloomington, IN: Solution Tree.

Spandel, V. (2012). *Creating writers through 6-trait writing assessment and instruction* (6th ed.). Boston: Allyn & Bacon.

Stiggins, R., & Chappuis, J. (2011). *An introduction to student-involved assessment for learning* (6th ed.). Upper Saddle River, NJ: Pearson/Prentice Hall.

Tomlinson, C. A. (2005, July). Differentiating instruction to meet the needs of all learners. Keynote presented at the Institutes on Academic Diversity: Summer Institute on Academic Diversity, Charlottesville, VA.

Tomlinson, C. A. (2017). *How to differentiate instruction in academically diverse classrooms* (3rd ed.). Alexandria, VA: ASCD.

Tomlinson, C. A., & McTighe, J. (2006). *Differentiated instruction and Understanding by Design: Connecting content and kids.* Alexandria, VA: ASCD.

Tomlinson, C. A., & Moon, T. R. (2013). *Assessment and student success in a differentiated classroom.* Alexandria, VA: ASCD.

Virginia Department of Education. (2016). Performance-based and local alternative assessments. Retrieved from http://www.doe.virginia.gov/testing/local_assessments/index.shtml

Vygotsky, L. S. (1978). *Mind and society: The development of higher mental processes.* Cambridge, MA: Harvard University Press.

Washington State Office of the Superintendent of Public Instruction. (n.d.). OSPI-developed assessments for social studies. Retrieved from http://www.k12.wa.us/SocialStudies/Assessments/default.aspx

Webb, N. (2002). Depth-of-knowledge levels for four content areas. Retrieved from http://www.hed.state.nm.us/uploads/files/ABE/Policies/depth_of_knowledge_guide_for_all_subject_areas.pdf

Webb, N. (2006, January). Mathematics DOK levels. Retrieved from https://education.ohio.gov/getattachment/Topics/Learning-in-Ohio/Mathematics/Resources-for-Mathematics/Curriculum-and-Instruction-Resources-for-Mathemati/Mathematics-DOK-Levels-by-Norman-Webb.pdf.aspx

Wentzel, K. R., & Brophy, J. E. (2014). *Motivating students to learn.* New York: Routledge.

Wiggins, G. (2012, September). Seven keys to effective feedback. *Educational Leadership, 70*(1), 10–16.

Wiggins, G., & McTighe, J. (2005). *Understanding by Design* (2nd ed.). Alexandria, VA: ASCD.

Wiggins, G., & McTighe, J. (2007). *Schooling by design: Mission, action, achievement.* Alexandria, VA: ASCD.

Wiggins, G., & McTighe, J. (2011). *The Understanding by Design guide to creating high-quality units.* Alexandria, VA: ASCD.

Wiggins, G., & McTighe, J. (2012). *The Understanding by Design guide to advanced concepts in creating and reviewing units.* Alexandria, VA: ASCD.

Wiliam, D. (2011). *Embedded formative assessment.* Bloomington, IN: Solution Tree.

Wiliam, D. (2012, September). Feedback: Part of a system. *Educational Leadership, 70*(1), 30–34.

Willis, J. (2010). *Learning to love math: Teaching strategies that change student attitudes and get results.* Alexandria, VA: ASCD.

Wise, M., & McTighe, J. (2017, October). Middle schoolers go global: Unleashing problem solvers. *Educational Leadership, 75*(2), 12–18.

Zmuda, A., & Kallick, B. (2017). *Personalizing learning in your classroom* (Quick Reference Guide). Alexandria, VA: ASCD.

Index

Note: The letter *d* following a page locater denotes a definition, the letter *f* denotes a figure.

About the Authors

JAY McTIGHE

KRISTINA J.
DOUBET

ERIC M.
CARBAUGH

Jay McTighe brings a wealth of experience from a rich and varied career in education. He served as director of the Maryland Assessment Consortium, a collaboration of school districts working together to develop and share formative performance assessments. Previously he was involved with school improvement projects at the Maryland State Department of Education, where he helped lead standards-based reforms, including development of performance-based statewide assessments. He directed development of the Instructional Framework, a multimedia database on teaching. Well known for his work with thinking skills, Jay coordinated statewide efforts to develop instructional strategies, curriculum models, and assessment procedures for improving the quality of student thinking. In addition to his work at the state level, Jay has experience at the district level in Prince George's County, Maryland, as a classroom teacher, resource specialist, and program coordinator. He also directed a state residential enrichment program for gifted and talented students.

Jay is an accomplished author, having coauthored more than a dozen books, including the award-winning and best-selling *Understanding by Design* series with Grant Wiggins. His books have been translated into six languages. Jay has also written more than 35 articles and book chapters, and has been published in leading journals, including *Educational Leadership* and *Education Week*.

With an extensive background in professional development, Jay is a regular speaker at national, state, and district conferences and workshops. He has made presentations in 47 states within the United States, in 7 Canadian provinces, and internationally to educators in 37 countries on six continents.

Jay received his undergraduate degree from the College of William and Mary, earned his master's degree from the University of Maryland, and completed postgraduate studies at the Johns Hopkins University. He was selected to participate in the Educational Policy Fellowship Program through the Institute for Educational Leadership in Washington, D.C., and served as a member of the National Assessment Forum, a coalition of education and civil rights organizations advocating reforms in national, state, and local assessment policies and practices. Jay may be reached via e-mail at jay@mctighe-associates.com and on Twitter @jaymctighe.

Kristina J. Doubet is a professor in the College of Education at James Madison University in Harrisonburg, Virginia, where she has received the Distinguished Teacher Award, the Madison Scholar Award, and the Sarah Miller Luck Endowed Professorship for Excellence in Education. As an independent consultant and ASCD faculty member, Kristina has partnered with hundreds of schools, districts, and organizations around initiatives related to differentiated instruction, the Understanding by Design framework, classroom assessment, digital learning, and classroom management and grouping. In addition to authoring numerous articles in journals including *Kappan* and *Educational Leadership,* she is the coauthor (with Jessica Hockett) of *Differentiation in Middle and High School: Strategies to Engage All Learners* and *Differentiation in the Elementary Grades: Strategies to Engage and Equip All Learners.* She also coauthored *The Differentiated Flipped Classroom: A Practical Guide to Digital Learning* (with Eric Carbaugh) and *Smart in the Middle Grades: Classrooms That Work for Bright Middle Schoolers* (with Carol Ann Tomlinson). Kristina's current research focuses on adolescent literacy and innovative school structures for adolescent students who are learning English. She taught middle and high school language arts for 10 years and has also served as an instructional coach and a curriculum developer in elementary and middle school classrooms. Kristina resides in Harrisonburg, Virginia, and can be reached at doubetkj@jmu.edu, www.KristinaDoubet.com, and on Twitter @kjdoubet.

Eric M. Carbaugh is a professor in the Department of Middle, Secondary, and Mathematics Education at James Madison University, where he has received the College of Education's Distinguished Service Award, Madison Scholar Award, and been twice nominated for the college's Distinguished Teacher Award. Eric has worked with more than 80 schools and districts on performance-based assessment, differentiated instruction, the Understanding by Design curriculum framework, effective use of instructional technology, and other various educational best practices. In addition to numerous articles and book chapters, Eric is coauthor, with Kristina Doubet, of *The Differentiated Flipped Classroom: A Practical Guide to Digital Learning*. He is the journal editor and board member for the Virginia ASCD chapter. Eric taught secondary school social studies as well as elementary language arts and history. He lives near Charlottesville, Virginia, and can be reached at carbauem@jmu.edu and on Twitter @emc7x.

Related ASCD Resources:
Authentic & Project-Based Assessment and Learning

At the time of publication, the following resources were available (ASCD stock numbers in parentheses).

Print Products

Authentic Learning in the Digital Age: Engaging Students Through Inquiry, by Larissa Pahomov (# 115009)

Cultivating Curiosity in K–12 Classrooms: How to Promote and Sustain Deep Learning, by Wendy L. Ostroff (#116001)

Everyday Problem-Based Learning: Quick Projects to Build Problem-Solving Fluency, by Brian Pete and Robin Fogarty (#117057)

Learning in the Making: How to Plan, Execute, and Assess Powerful Makerspace Lessons, by Jackie Gerstein (#119025)

Project Based Teaching: How to Create Rigorous and Engaging Learning Experiences, by Suzie Boss and John Larmer (#118047)

Real-World Projects: How do I design relevant and engaging learning experiences? (ASCD Arias), by Suzie Boss (#SF115043)

The Relevant Classroom: 6 Steps to Foster Real-World Learning, by Eric Hardie (#120003)

What If? Building Students' Problem-Solving Skills Through Complex Challenges, by Ronald A. Beghetto (#118009)

ASCD myTeachSource®

Download resources from a professional learning platform with hundreds of research-based best practices and tools at http://myteachsource.ascd.org.

For more information, send an e-mail to member@ascd.org; call 1-800-933-2723 or 703-578-9600; send a fax to 703-575-5400; or write to Information Services, ASCD, 1703 N. Beauregard St., Alexandria, VA 22311-1714 USA.

WHOLE CHILD
TENETS

The ASCD Whole Child approach is an effort to transition from a focus on narrowly defined academic achievement to one that promotes the long-term development and success of all children. Through this approach, ASCD supports educators, families, community members, and policymakers as they move from a vision about educating the whole child to sustainable, collaborative actions.

Designing Authentic Performance Tasks and Projects relates to the **safe, engaged, supported,** and **challenged** tenets. *For more about the ASCD Whole Child approach, visit* **www.ascd.org/wholechild**.

1 **HEALTHY**
Each student enters school healthy and learns about and practices a healthy lifestyle.

2 **SAFE**
Each student learns in an environment that is physically and emotionally safe for students and adults.

3 **ENGAGED**
Each student is actively engaged in learning and is connected to the school and broader community.

4 **SUPPORTED**
Each student has access to personalized learning and is supported by qualified, caring adults.

5 **CHALLENGED**
Each student is challenged academically and prepared for success in college or further study and for employment and participation in a global environment.